North Carolina

North

PHOTOGRAPHS BY

ANN CARY SIMPSON, SCOTT TAYLOR,

AND TOM EARNHARDT

THE UNIVERSITY OF NORTH CAROLINA PRESS

Chapel Hill

BLAND SIMPSON

Carolina

Land of Water, Land of Sky

*This book was published with the assistance of the
William R. Kenan Jr. Fund of the University of North Carolina Press.*

Text © 2021 Bland Simpson
Photographs © 2021 as indicated on page 211
All rights reserved
Manufactured in Canada
Designed by Richard Hendel
Set in Miller, Sentinel, and Walbaum types
by Tseng Information Systems, Inc.

The University of North Carolina Press has been a
member of the Green Press Initiative since 2003.

Cover photographs: front, Ann Cary Simpson; back, Scott Taylor

Library of Congress Cataloging-in-Publication Data
Names: Simpson, Bland, author. | Simpson, Ann Cary, photographer. |
Taylor, Scott, 1956– photographer. | Earnhardt, Tom, photographer.
Title: North Carolina : land of water, land of sky / Bland Simpson ; photographs by
Ann Cary Simpson, Scott Taylor, and Tom Earnhardt.
Description: Chapel Hill : The University of North Carolina Press, [2021] |
Includes bibliographical references and index.
Identifiers: LCCN 2021015362 | ISBN 9781469665832 (cloth) | ISBN 9781469665849 (ebook)
Subjects: LCSH: Simpson, Bland—Travel—North Carolina. | North Carolina—
Description and travel—Anecdotes. | LCGFT: Anecdotes. | Travel writing.
Classification: LCC F260 .S46 2021 | DDC 975.6—dc23
LC record available at https://lccn.loc.gov/2021015362

The excerpt from Willie Lowery's "Proud to Be a Lumbee Indian"
used with permission of Malinda Maynor Lowery.

To the First Peoples
Who came and cared for this Province
Many thousands of years ago
And to their descendants, who care for it still:
Catawba, Cherokee, Coharie, Haliwa-Saponi,
Lumbee, Meherrin, Occaneechi, Sappony,
Tuscarora, and Waccamaw Siouan

In honor of Jaki Shelton Green,
Betty Ray McCain, and
Alice and Fred Stanback

In memory of William Clyde Friday
and Randall Garrett Kenan

Contents

Places in My Heart

North Carolina, the Old North State, is an ocean wave breaking, a fiddler sawing away in the mountain night, a hundred Ayrshire milk cows lowing in a Piedmont dawn, the sound burst of a B3 organ and joyful voices raised in song beyond the stained-glass windows of a city church. It is a line of sandbars, some nearly thirty miles out into the Atlantic Ocean, some less than a mile from the mainland; a set of broad, flat terraces, vast farmlands, and timber stands broken by willow-clad rivers both black-water and brown and by their deep gum and cypress swamps, occasional bluffs, and green and golden marshes; a host of hills made of red clay and sand, growing pines called loblolly and longleaf, oaks called white and red and turkey and blackjack, red maples and river birches, and hickories with shaggy bark; and then a profusely eruptive land of tall folds upon folds, peaks, ridges and rocky tops, domes, cliffs, grassy balds, and gorges, a host of mile-high mountains, too, with a vast quilt of blue haze laid out over it all.

Water everywhere is my first lingering memory of North Carolina, for home meant water in the Pasquotank County ditches, in the yards flooded with hurricane rain, in the creeks and lagoons, in our river and the sound below, and, always, in the endless deep blue ocean beyond. At times, my family was a set of westbound travelers with a hilltop lookout over a great range of fields and forests, the two-lane blacktop undulating over long stretches, ribbonlike toward Chapel Hill, and when we reached this terrain in late afternoon, the low western sun would be saturating the clay of those roadcuts, a rich, deep, ocherous color I could never look away from, knowing we had left the sound country and were now in a very different place, gliding into the hills of Carolina through long, topless tunnels of red clay. A few years later, I was among a group of men and boys in three cars pulling canoes up and over the Blue Ridge, and then we all saw, many of us for the first time, the high blue mountains that were even bigger and taller than the men had said and that went on forever. As our small caravan passed Asheville at sunset, I could hardly believe at twelve what a vast province North Carolina was and how long it would take—how many journeys and returnings there *must* be—before I would have even the very beginning of a sense of it.

If this is a tale of stories, sights, and glimpses drawn from a relentless traveling presence over many a year, pray let it be, for a lifetime of music, teaching, theatre, literature, and conservation has carried Ann and me, and Scott and Tom too, all across our great state. Let it be a world of powerful passing looks at handmade Canada goose whirligigs at Powell's Point in Currituck, at a biplane crop duster in a hangar just waiting to fire up its Pratt and Whitney engine and take to the air down in Scotland County below Laurinburg, at cloud-enshrouded Chimney Rock almost invisibly towering over Lake Lure in Polk County out west, and at the fall and flow of water everywhere. From sea level to sky-high, from pickles to peaches and cabbage to corn bread, here's to the land: North Carolina.

North Carolina

I
This Wet and Water-Loving Land

Classic moth boat on the Pasquotank River below the Narrows

Northeast, the Albemarle

FIRST WORD

My father's voice, a tideland tenor full of warmth, first put the word *sound* into my head when he returned to Elizabeth City, our river-port home, from a first-light hunt just as I was eating breakfast in the kitchen and getting ready for school—he in dull khaki hunting clothes and a rich pungency, the smell of marsh and mud, about him, with a couple of ducks for our evening meal.

"Where have you been?" I asked.

"Down on the sound. Currituck Sound. Out in the duck blind, before dark, and you were still asleep." Then, laughing, he went off to shave and change into suit and tie for a day in the Pasquotank County Courthouse, where he practiced law.

This was a lot for a small boy to take in, all that my father had done since 2 A.M., up and dressed, 12-gauge shotgun in the trunk of his maroon 1952 humpback Dodge, driving most of an hour to a dock at Poplar Branch or somewhere on the western shore of Currituck Sound, and, once there, putting his gun and gear into a juniper skiff and pulling the cord, starting the outboard, and motoring in the dark and cold morning mists that he could somehow see through, finding his way over the water to the rude planks and the brush thrust in and around them that made his duck blind. And then, after laying out some decoys, killing the motor and tying up and climbing into the blind, still all in the dark, and waiting. And when the ducks then came in low once the sky had grayed up, a few booms from his Browning was all it took. A few moments to reflect on a lifetime of doing this, being out in it, up and down this wet and water-loving land in all seasons and all weathers, and then firing up the engine again and collecting the ducks off the surface of the sound and heading back to the dock and then for the river town and home.

And I was sleeping all that time, till moments before he drove into the garage and opened the door and came on in. There was something incalculably mysterious about his movements made well out of my sight in the dark and dim light, and about the watery world in which he made them, and I deeply wanted, and would in time come to gain, some small purchase upon the Carolina sound country.

A SOUND COUNTRY SERENADE

When a then-unknown marine ecologist named Rachel Carson took pen in hand back in 1941 and wrote of shad running through a coastal North Carolina inlet by night and birds in vast numbers moving "into the sound country," she gave us a great gift, something big to sing about. She laid out the new sense of a *land* truly unified by the very waters—the sounds, their rivers, streams, and creeks, and the pocosins and bottomland swamps between them—that so long seemed to so many to separate this territory all into pieces and parts.

There is nothing like the sound country anywhere else on earth. Waters of the White Oak River brush the docks and wharves of Swansboro and flow off mixing with those that some past time have washed by Corolla on Currituck Sound or rolled by Murfreesboro on the Meherrin River. Only eastern Carolina boasts such a vast, varied, yet fully integrated estuarine world.

This magnificence has long inspired and haunted me, too, in the best of ways. It lifts my imagination and sends me flying up and over its broad wet lands and open waters, from state line to state line, over prongs and branches and

3

Deep Creek tidal flats, Bird Shoal in center, Beaufort Inlet beyond

forgotten sloughs and small-town streets and lonely country crossroads, over places I saw from a car window or walked about or boated past maybe long ago, maybe only last week.

The first time I remember doing this — actively ginning up 15,000 square miles of this flat, wet province in my mind all at once — was early one Eastertide evening at Bogue Inlet years ago. Alone there, I stared out of a dark cottage into the inlet's deeper darkness beyond, channel lights toward Dudley Island the only illumination, and for a pure spell of perhaps thirty minutes I could see it all: the judge's white farmhouse in Currituck where I had overeaten strawberries when I was five; the country store at Tar Landing where an old man, showing off, stood on his head on a basketball and then got a dog to eat fire by batting out a burning bag when I was twenty-four; the cool bankside spot along the Dismal Swamp Canal where my love and I stood and watched the mists gather in the darkening pines when I was forty; the waterway landing at Hampstead where great friend Linwood Taylor and I put his Simmons Sea Skiff in and went out to drift fish New Topsail Inlet for blues in my fiftieth year.

A thousand points of memory laid into this cherished land lit up brilliantly and formed like constellations, and still do.

As the winds sough through the bright, green springtime freshwater marshes of the lower Roanoke and Trent Rivers, or the golden autumnal salt marshes of Roanoke and Cedar Islands, of Bogue Sound and Bear Island and beyond, now from the northeast, now from the southwest, I have been hearing, and have sensed even before hearing, a host of great sound country songs coming over the rushes and the waters, songs as fresh as the given moment yet no less venerable than those our forebears heard and knew. In deep swamps, the tunes are the howls and cries of owls and the high trilling of peepers in the early spring evenings, just as, around the

shallows of Mattamuskeet and Pungo and Swan Quarter in the dead of winter, they are the high honkings of snow geese and the plaintive moans of tundra swans. From muddy burrows and slides near the Buffalo City ghost town in Dare County down to Lockwood Folly River in Brunswick, bull gators set up deep reptilian rumbles, baritone underscorings of springtime love and lust.

Someone should pen a stirring hymn to all those creatures and more, and, while at it, to our ancestors as well, all those who made it possible to follow the waters from Elizabeth City down to Manteo; from Harkers Island out to Diamond City and back again, even to the Promise Land in Morehead; from Washington by the Pamlico and New Bern on the Neuse out to Ocracoke; from Richlands and Tar Landing down the New River and then by sea to the Cape Fear River and on up to Wilmington. A hymn, too, to those who have cared so much for all the wild wet lands betwixt and between, for all the life in them, that they set aside our natural reserves, and to those now in our midst who are still hard at work saving so much of our low-lying east, from Tull Bay at the top of Currituck Sound all the way down the coast to Bird Island below Sunset Beach.

What we have been given — and what we are being pledged and promised at this very moment — is nothing less than a great glorious chain of refuge across the sound country for all God's creatures, for fin, fur, and feather, and for all of us, too, for we are in no way exempt from the need of what we may find in these far-flung places: dark, clean water we might drink in an April or October moment, a tannin-stained handful scooped skiff-side right up out of Sawyer Lake; brisk, mind-clearing air to breathe, clean and free, from the stiff breezes of December or January blowing through longleaf pines or loblollies in the biggest eastern wilderness, with its osprey-haunted lakes and dark creeks and shallow ponds, the great Croatan Forest.

Someone should do this. Someone should fly

Tundra swans in flight, Pungo Unit, Pocosin Lakes National Wildlife Refuge

over this great territory, pulling in all these songs, both the natural and the imagined, and winding them together—for only a cycle of songs could bear full witness to it all, to all these lands Rachel Carson saw as one—and then singing out, loudly and sooner than not, this big hymn to the land of many waters, this sound country serenade.

And then we can ramble about our wide, wet province to melodies of celebration and wonder. One acre out of every ten in North Carolina is water, most of it flowing east of the fall line, and eight of North Carolina's seventeen river basins

are in our coastal plain. In this watery realm, let us honor the ties that throughout its geography and its history have bound us and bind us still.

We should honor and marvel at the great work of boats. At the turn of the nineteenth century, shoal-draft sloops and schooners from Castle Island in the Pamlico River sailed across the sound to Shell Castle Island behind Ocracoke Inlet, offloading crops and lumber from the interior, fetching sugar, molasses, and rum from the Caribbean, fabric and stoneware from England. By the turn of the twentieth century, a rail line had come from Hampton Roads

Shrimp trawlers, Engelhard, Hyde County

down through the cabbage, potato, and game lands of Currituck, Camden, Pasquotank, and west, dropping off passengers at Elizabeth City, Hertford, and Edenton, some of whom were then bound via steamboat for sound and river ports like Plymouth and Columbia, Manteo and Nags Head. This was the sound country knitting itself together: the sharpie turned steamer *Hattie Creef* getting folks (the Wright brothers among them) from Elizabeth City to the Outer Banks, the small diesel mail boat *Aleta* tying Ocracoke to Atlantic and Morehead City the same way the big state ferries *Silver Lake*, *Swan Quarter*, *Carteret*, *Cedar Island*, and *Sea Level* tie that island to the mainland today. Smaller ferries cross the Neuse and the Pamlico and Currituck Sound, even smaller ones move over the Cashie, the Cape Fear, and the Meherrin, and passenger boats smaller yet carry thousands of explorers nowadays out to Shackleford Banks and Cape Lookout, while other vessels haul fisherfolk and campers, as well as rough-country, road-warrior vehicles, out to Core Banks.

We should sing in praise of our coastal bridges and their grace and follow the trails that lead us to them. The NC 45 bridge flies over the braided Roanoke below Plymouth; the NC 32 sound bridge crosses the Albemarle from Sandy Point to Pea Ridge (is it haunted by a hitchhiking ghost, as many say?); the Wright Memorial Bridge lies across Currituck Sound from Point Harbor to Kitty Hawk; the sweeping, silvery Virginia Dare Bridge curves gently over Croatan Sound from Manns Harbor to Roanoke Island; the Roanoke River Bridge at Williamston (and the long causeway to Windsor, which local folks called "the beach" when it was being built out of miles of sand after World War II) crosses the big bottom of Conine Island and its swamps; dizzying bends swoop over both Trent and Neuse Rivers at their New Bern confluence; and, farther south, the high steel of the Cape Fear Memorial Bridge vaults that river at Wilmington, and many spans to the smaller barrier islands fly over the waterway and narrow sounds, where little ferry flats once ran.

And we should sing a rousing chorus of great friendship and love for our Carolina water towns, the ports that boats and bridges have tied together, villages and cities all seeming to be brothers and sisters, all related, yet all different. The long wharf of Plymouth on the Roanoke—Civil War choke point, contemporary entrance to the Purchase Islands paradise of lower Roanoke—dwarfs that of tiny Columbia on the Scuppernong just a few miles away, yet both are similarly tucked away up their rivers only a short distance from the Albemarle Sound. Hatteras and Ocracoke—the antique, legendary fishermen's redoubts—lie a scant twenty miles apart at water's edge, a pair of front doors onto Pamlico Sound, opening westward toward unpopulous sound shores almost thirty miles away. Murfreesboro, New Bern, Beaufort, Shallotte—large or small, they all have waterfronts, and in that way, they all meet the world just the same.

Yes, we have long tried to tie this great territory and its towns all together. In a very real and much larger sense, though, the waters had already done that, and had long done that—for they and whatever they touch are a unity and always have been, which is precisely what Rachel Carson meant by *sound country*, a vaulted, connected world of inland sea and sky, an openhearted spirit running slam through it and its people—the enduring spirit of eastern Carolina generosity and fellowship and helpfulness, the very soul of this serenade.

Wherever one goes, one is buoyed, even moved, by the almost incredible affection folks have for even the tiniest of spots: for a charmed picnic table in the pines at New Bern's Union Point or at Bonner's Point in Bath; for a tent-camping platform lodged between several cypresses on a hidden lake just off the Albemarle's southern shore; for an oyster bar on a side street in Williamston on the Roanoke or one in Windsor on the Cashie; for an old-time chowder house on the waterway at Sneads Ferry; for fading Harbor Island's shell beach and its hunt-club ruin at the top of Core Sound.

Whose heart could fail to be touched by the sweet longing for home that a Hyde County fishing-village native once expressed to his Washington County friend, when both of them were attending an end-of-meeting soiree at the Top of the Mark bistro, high above San Francisco? The Washington County man saw his comrade from Hyde off by himself, quietly staring off into space through a nineteenth-floor window, and took his friend's solitary stance for aloofness or even sadness and went to comfort him, saying, "You all right, Bill?" "Oh, yeah, I'm fine," the Hyde Countian replied wistfully. "I was just looking out over the lights of the city, the bay, the Golden Gate Bridge and all, and I just couldn't help but thinking—this is a *long way* from Engelhard."

A FEAST OF BRICK: ELIZABETH CITY
This half a brick in my hand may have once been red, but its color had long since soaked away, water fading it to brown. On half of its longer side were seven barnacles, and on its break, nine. The same man—attorney Russell Twiford—who pulled it out of the Pasquotank River had later given it to me.

Perhaps the old underwater foundation the broken brick came from—which Russell estimated at 30 by 120 feet—had held up an ancient customhouse, till wooden walls finally fell in around that brick foundation, and slowly the rising waters lapped and rotted it all and sent its remains downriver to the sound. Whatever those dark Pasquotank River waters had chosen to do, they did.

Not to the brick, though. That stayed put, right where now-forgotten hands had laid it, out of sight, scarcely submerged, in the service now not of commerce but of memory.

Harbor Island Hunt Club ruins, north Core Sound

My boyhood friends and I often gathered to play at the mouth of Gaither's Lagoon, where it opened into the Pasquotank a mile or so above the spot where my barnacled brick came from. Near the lagoon, scores and scores of brickbats lay strewn all along the narrow river beach, and in the career of our play we pitched them into the waves with great delight.

What gave me such a truly powerful sense of the brickwork world we lived in, though, was the tightly defined way from school to downtown Elizabeth City that I knew so well as a boy.

Beneath the open, arched cupola of the primary school's bell tower, in that plain, airy brick building, devoted teachers Miss Susie Morrisette and Miss Annie Wood Harris showed us the way to sit up, take notice, and draft our letters onto

standard handwriting-training paper, pages with solid blue lines within which to place the capitals and dotted blue lines halfway between the solids, below which to scrunch the lowercase letters.

When we moved over to third grade in the big S. L. Sheep School—with its Works Progress Administration art deco style—my letters were sagging and bending improperly, and Miss Norris found it necessary to grade me down. No matter: in the Sheep School's auditorium I first trod the boards and spoke memorized lines from a stage, and there began my life in the theatre. In a bright room behind the Elizabeth City High School's dark-brick, colonial revival facade, Miss Audrey Austin read to our fourth-grade class from the tales of *The Black Stallion* and followed these fabulous exotics with mysteries and ghost stories from the coastal and sound country, from our town, and we came to feel and understand that our own land was as important and as full of history and mystery as anywhere on earth.

And so it felt important, too, when I was deemed old enough to walk from the old school, where my father had also studied, to his law office downtown—only several blocks, true, yet to make that stroll under my own will, this was grand. I both witnessed and was overseen by the large and small buildings I passed daily on that way, like the New Southern Hotel at Main and Road Streets, its brick a deep oxblood, and just two short blocks below this corner lay the grand First Methodist Church, a green dome atop it and Flemish-bond courses of brick and Ionic columns holding it up. At four, I had agreed to my own christening here only when promised by my parents a farm adventure, a pledge so vibrant in my mind that a split second after the preacher sprinkled droplets on my head, I hollered out before the entire congregation: *"Now* can I go ride that tractor?!"

On down East Main toward the water, I went walking slowly across the brick pavers of Elliott Street (*Baltimore Block* imprinted on many of them) and then past the Pasquotank County Courthouse, the tall, bell-and-clock-towered brick building and its powerful Corinthian portico, where both my grandfather and father practiced law and held forth in court and where I sometimes got stationed down front on a long, ash-blond bench to watch and listen and hear, over and over again, the words *justice* and *mercy*.

And then I arrived at the city-block-sized Hinton Building, called by everyone the Carolina Building because the movie house—the Carolina Theatre—lay at its street-level heart. Everything was here: a drugstore; a five-and-dime; the Oxena News Stand with papers and magazines, fountain drinks, and small rubber cowboys and soldiers; and that beloved movie theatre. Elvis sang "Love Me Tender" on the silver screen here; a full-sized Robby the Robot took tickets to *Forbidden*

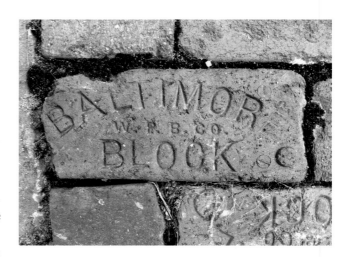

Planet at the door here; a glowing radium-infused skeleton even flew out on a rope-and-pulley rig from the stage-left wings to the balcony and back to the wings during the acid-vat scene in Vincent Price's *House on Haunted Hill* here.

From the windows of my father's law office on the top floor, I watched giant Macy's parade–sized balloon characters float down East Main toward the river during our triumphant Potato Parade each year, and, too, I looked out upon the holiday parades, featuring the elaborately dressed golden Yellow Jackets, the Elizabeth City High School band, and then, always in second place in those segregated days, the purple-uniformed African American P. W. Moore High School band, astonishingly choreographed with its wild breakout sessions that showed true artfulness as they simultaneously startled and thrilled the crowds lining East Main.

What a boomtown Elizabeth City had been— this feast of brick that lay before and below me told so many tales of our river-port world: of produce received, recorded, and shipped north; of logs floated to our local mills and soon shipped out as lumber for joists and rafters, for ribs and planks of boats; of prescriptions filled, bolts of cloth measured and cut to size, jewels set into rings.

Across the street, the elegant 1926 jeweler's building proclaimed *SELIG* near its roof line, delighting the eye with its Delft-blue tiles set about buff brick (fired locally by the Elizabeth City Brick Company, well over 100 years old and still going strong), with a lovely line of sculpted golden waves rushing along a narrow blue field below the second-story windows. Facing Selig's, the side-by-side Kramer and Chesson buildings reflected each other with their tall, arched, third-story windows. Many years ago, I walked through a closet door on Chesson's second floor, straight into the antique past of vaudeville, into the empty, long-unused Academy of Music theatre, its old drapes torn and falling, its seating gone, dust everywhere but no ghost light, or even the *thought* of a ghost light, to keep all thespian spirits at peace.

Now that theatre has been reborn as a fine small venue, rechristened the Maguire Theatre in honor of the renovation's benefactor. On the April Friday of its gala reopening, I was to perform in a small ballroom just off to the side of the Maguire's balcony. Before my set, I stood alone looking out a window to the south, watching a fogbank move slowly upriver, enveloping the old Beveridge house built out on brick stilts above the Pasquotank and the deep-red brick Norman château the Texaco tycoon Miles Clark had built for his bride back in the Roaring Twenties.

From the 1920s came our first and *only* skyscraper: nine stories tall. On McMorrine Street stood the tawny brick tower of the Virginia Dare Hotel, all decked out with a glass-ceilinged arcade and a balustrade above. The Virginia Dare once hosted white-linen-tableclothed Sunday midday dinners (fried chicken, mashed potatoes, green beans to die for, cooked to glory with ham hocks, and iced tea you sugared *yourself*).

Most of all this, what I took in during childhood and embraced forever in my heart, is still there today. Yet an epic fire on March 1, 1967, laid waste to the vaunted brick Carolina Building, and now the very memory of it is older than that great, once-central piece of the town's life was on the cold night it burned.

None of this existed a couple of centuries ago, only the long-submerged downriver foundation whence came the barnacled brick. In a land of vast swamps, the first peoples, the Native Americans, had lived in dwellings of only twining vines and sticks and hides yet still up to the task of keeping them warm and dry enough to go on generation after generation. Into such a land came the Europeans, wanting more permanence to their homes and shops than they perceived the Algonquians had attained in their stockade-encircled tents and longhouses. So they turned to the one handcrafted artifact that they thought could do it all for them: Brick.

No one who called for these old buildings, who laid out their courses and stacked and mortared them into being, still lives—yet the *buildings* do. They speak to us with authority and color, the morning sun rising and lighting up every shade of red on the side streets and on both sides of Main.

Who could see all this, on the way to school see the sunlight warming up all these monuments and all the people going into them to count and order and figure and plan, who could see all this and not love it?

Not I. Brick by glorious brick do I remember and love it all, and I always will.

AFLOAT
Hall's Creek and Little River

On February 6, 1665, under an immense oak tree on the wooded rise just south of Hall's Creek in Pasquotank County, Governor William Drummond, my distant kinsman come young and indentured from Scotland, convened the first Grand Assembly of the Albemarle, the land that would become North Carolina. By *assembly* we mean only six white men, though who the other four were, beyond Drummond and Speaker George Cathmaid, remains uncertain. Early twentieth-century lore spinner Catherine Albertson waxed rather romantic about the affair, imagining wind murmuring in the pines, silver waves rippling softly against the shore, and Indians watching stoically at a distance. The only laws said to have been passed seem merely bylaws: the assemblymen would keep their stockings on during the session, and they would *not* throw their chicken bones under the tree after lunch, which rule does at least have a commendable sense of environmental protection about it.

Just after putting our canoe in at Hall's Creek and lighting out downstream, several blue herons spooked, and my dear friend David Cecelski, the great coastal historian, and I spied an osprey in flight, clutching a frog. Kingfishers flew low and fast, singing their scattershot incantations. A barred owl cried out and cut the blue-sky afternoon air.

Fish rolled, minnows jumped. David spotted a cottonmouth as it slid up under the low branches and leaves beside a gum stump, and we paddled over for a closer look.

This was David's and my late afternoon June assembly in Pasquotank County, just a few years ago.

Hall's Creek soon emptied into Little River, where the Little came down out of its swamps between Okisko and Chapanoke and opened up, flowing due south to the sound. We paddled downriver, into a ten-to-fifteen southwest wind, soon deciding to head back up into the swamps rather than make that difficult pull over open water toward Nixonton hamlet and Windmill Point, several miles below.

Cupping our hands and dipping them, testing the waters, we agreed we tasted a little salt across the river from the mouth of Hall's Creek—but it took us two tastes to sense it.

The pleasures and scenes of this lazy river far from town comprised very little development alongshore: a low-lying brick house with a low bulkhead of timbers and logs and, elsewhere, a lone dock with no house or building on the land—just a bench for two looking out toward sunsets

over the quiet stream—and a dock with a forest-green, single-masted thirty-six-foot sailboat on the west side of the upper river, homeport Hertford, named *Just 'Air*.

Five-petaled swamp rose bloomed along the jungle shores.

A tall, fallen-over, early-summer-green cypress leaned over the river's eastern side like a tollgate, though it collected nothing from us except admiration and smiles.

We imagined small schooners sailing up to Hall's Creek for Drummond's assembly. We imagined the future anthologist of poet Robert Burns, languishing at Nixonton when it was still the county seat and a real port in the 1770s, awaiting a ship back to Scotland and home. And much else long ago and far away.

Cumulus clouds kept building, and the light dimmed. We kept a weather eye and wondered about making it all the way up to the old US 17 highway bridge for shelter if the bottom fell out, but turned ere long to head on back to the Hall's Creek landing, passing a lone fisherman in a jonboat and a couple casting from their nineteen-foot Carolina skiff.

At the landing, a friendly, round-faced fellow about thirty pulled up in his pickup and called out, "Catch anything?"

He said he had never put his boat in at this landing and that his mother had a place downriver where they were catching blue crabs off the dock. Shook his head and told us he was moving here from Hatteras, where he had been living for years.

"Man, I've *had it* with Hatteras—storms! tourists! If I want to see Hatteras, from now on I can just drive down there and look at it. I *like it* up here on the Little River," he said. "It's just so *relaxed*."

Merchants Millpond
Ann and I slid the well-laden canoe—tent, cooler, Coleman stove, four-year-old twins—onto the

swamp water and pushed off about four o'clock on an April afternoon. Our Merchants Millpond campsite lay a mile or two away on a beech-tree hillside—we had a map and daylight to spare. Hunter and Susannah cast eyes of wonder upward as we glided slowly through the duckweed-glossed waters, and they kept pointing and reaching toward the thick, hanging hanks they called *Spanished* moss, Susannah occasionally trailing her hand in the water, though we wished loudly from bow and stern that she would not.

Duckweed, our tiniest flowering plant, ensured that our paddling would go slowly, the gorgeous drowned forest of this reserve sliding by us as in a dream.

Thousands of cypress trees grew closely in the shallow pond that Rufus Williams created when he dammed up Bennett's Creek for saw- and grist-milling power nearly 160 years ago, making a lake three miles long till Lassiter Swamp fully closed in on the upper creek. Two donations in 1973— 919 acres by A. B. Coleman and a subsequent 925-acre addition by the Nature Conservancy— made for the state park's dramatic beginning and its increase, and the popular park now holds 3,250 acres.

The graceful writer Beth Lassiter of Sunbury, my former student, told me years ago that alligators had come to live here—some said two, others said three or four—far above the long-believed northern alligator line about the latitude of New Bern. These migrants were testifying in their saurian way to the steady warming of the temperate zone, as was a cousin of theirs, so Dr. Rob Powell had advised me, haunting upper Knobbs Creek off the Pasquotank on Elizabeth City's north side.

After an hour or so of coasting this cypress sublimity, Ann and the twins and I reached the beechwood slope and got ourselves ashore and up to our campsite in the relative heights, perhaps thirty feet or so above the surface of the millpond.

That night, the full fish moon—the light that

lit shad and herring runs in our coastal streams— rolled up enormously above the woods and the water and got bigger and brighter as our fire died down. A barred owl nearby cried out, *Who cooks for you?* and then the hillside erupted in owl song, an explosion of avian delight in the fresh warmth of spring, in all the breeding to come. They sang out till we four finally turned in.

And, for all I know, the owls may have sung all night.

Devil's Gut and Sweetwater Creek

The May evening before our small film crew took on Devil's Gut in a couple of jonboats and a towed canoe, Lucia Peel, the effervescent innkeeper of Haughton Hall in Williamston, told us about a pair of doctors who came her way, wanting advice on the Gut and the impressive tent-camping platforms the Roanoke River Partners, a crucial alliance Lucia has long served, had built deep back in the big, five-mile-wide bottom.

"Well," she said, "they weren't from around here, *more* than a little nervous about camping back in there.

"'What about bears?' they asked me. 'Bears going to be a problem?'

"'Noooo,' I told them. 'Any bears hear *you* fellows, they'll be gone the other way—nothing to worry about.'

"So they canoed back in, set up, spent the night, and when they came back out, they found me and said, 'No bears? *No bears!* What were you talking about!?' And it turned out that when they woke up in the morning and went out of the tent, there was a big ol' mama laid out sleeping practically *with* them on the same platform. Scared everybody, the bear *and* the doctors—and they *all* cleared out pretty quick!"

So we went in slowly next day, early in the bright sunny afternoon, from Roberson's landing at Gardners Creek, winding north down the dark creek toward Devil's Gut. The Gut was a major distributary of the lower Roanoke River, flowing off the Roanoke along the south side of Conine Island and meandering to the south and east and, having run along some of the deepest wilderness in the eastern seaboard of America, rejoining the main river a couple miles above the old Cypress Grill in Jamesville.

On Bull Run Island back in there, once the last timber was cut out years ago, lay a dinky, a narrow-gauge railroad engine that a logging

company had decided was easier leaving behind than recovering. This was the sort of territory where trouble (a sprained ankle, a snake bite, a broken locomotive) went a long way. If folks nowadays were venturing into this wildlife heaven because they wanted to, they would all do well to remember that they were in the heart of a vastness haunted in the past by folks who went down into that bottom only because they had to.

At the mouth of Gardners Creek, just across Devil's Gut up in a tree, was a sign: *Barred Owl Roost, Beaver Lodge*, to the right. The winding black-water creek put us out onto this brown-water piece of river, and you could feel at once the higher power of the great Roanoke, which drained much of southside Virginia and then poured its waters into the Albemarle Lagoon. Soon we cut back north on Upper Deadwater Creek, another black stream that led us right into a gum-and-cypress cathedral, flat and lazy dappled water that sunshine had a hard time finding.

A couple of platforms and plank pathways made this human roost, but as far as a six-foot water snake was concerned, coiled comfortably in a corner, all the efforts had been for him. He paid us no mind, and for the hours we were here at Beaver Lodge, he lay sultry and satisfied and did not move.

On Good Friday 2000, we (a group of Carolina environmental students and fellow travelers) had floated nearby Sweetwater Creek, held an impromptu class about these bottomlands, and then, after a good meandering spell, paddled back up the lazy stream, passing the same cypress sentinels we had seen in the cool morning, now lit up by the warm western sun, every third one of them with a big cottonmouth coiled atop one of its knees.

We rounded out that fine day with a visit to the justly venerated Cypress Grill (a night fire would burn it to the ground in spring 2018) hard by the Roanoke River not far below Devil's Gut. Every

Tent-camping platform, Devil's Gut, Roanoke River bottom

January till April for eight decades, the air here had filled with the thick smoky pungency of fried herring, which for most of the nineteenth century and much of the twentieth was not only the harbinger of springtime in the eastern estuarine rivers but also North Carolina's big fish—our forebears barreled and sent salt herring across our province and out into eastern America by the million pounds.

Just after we made it inside the low-slung, cypress board-and-battened, tin-roofed fish camp, the bottom fell out and a wild, heavy-hail thunderstorm pelted and *bombarded* the place. *How do you like your herring?* the menu asked, the choices being *Fried*, *Fried Hard*, or *Cremated*. When the herring came out of the fryers volcanic hot, you let them cool just a bit, then held them like corncobs and ate them like cracklings, bones and all.

Before we had paddled out of the Sweetwater depths, my writing students Pat Fox and Holly Herweyer, from Montana and Minnesota, respectively, who were on the first date that would lead them to the altar, canoed up alongside Ann and Cary and me, and Pat, ever the westerner, smiled and gestured broadly in awe at the grandeur of these gorgeous cypress wilds as he said, "You know, we just don't *have* this in *Montana!*"

AROUND THE ALBEMARLE

Just after sunrise one morning in May 2018, the *Belle of Washington* took in lines and pulled away from the Water Street docks in Elizabeth City and plied the Pasquotank River down toward the Albemarle Sound, the way thousands of vessels— dugouts, schooners, scows, tugboats, cutters, yachts—have done for so many years before her.

The *Belle* passed, in turn, the Elizabeth City Coast Guard Air Station, whose orange-and-white beacon, planes, and helicopters all stand for safety and good sense on the many waters and serve sailors in distress in all weathers (as did two brave helicopter captains and crews and an HC-130 that went to the rescue of HMS *Bounty*, sinking 100 miles off Hatteras, and saved fourteen of sixteen aboard at the height of Hurricane Sandy in 2012); the Navy's clamshell blimp hangar at Weeksville, the only one remaining out of two there, a key part of World War II's East Coast submarine-chasing operations, now a manufactory for unmanned weather and reconnaissance blimps; and Newbegun Creek, site of one of Pasquotank's earliest courthouses and one of its largest plantations, Westmoreland, where on Christmas Day circa 1820 the enslaved freight boatman Capt. Moses Grandy (later an abolitionist leader in Boston who toured the United Kingdom) learned that the freedom he had bought and paid for twice had been stolen back from him again.

The *Belle* met the Albemarle at Wades Point late that sunny, breezy morning and cruised west, her top speed eight knots. In the drowned cypresses near the mouth of Big Flatty Creek, epic long-distance canoeist Dickie Conant's empty canoe had turned up, flipped and floating among cypress knees, without him, in late November 2014. Conant, known for extraordinarily lengthy water transits during his peripatetic life, had come all the way down from upstate New York (bound for Florida), across the Delaware, down along the Chesapeake, and through the Dismal Swamp Canal to Elizabeth City, and then came to a mysterious end hereabouts—for Dickie Conant has never been found.

From the foredeck I watched closely as we first passed Big Flatty, the Frog Island fishing shanties on long docks standing gaily just inside the creek's mouth, and then Little River, a waterway so important to eastern Carolina's early European settlement days, now the quiet backwater Cecelski

and I had floated years before. The *Belle* soon swung far out to the south-southwest to avoid the large, patrolled, navigation-free zone in the sound south of Harvey Point, where the U.S. Navy has long maintained a presence, first as another World War II antisubmarine air base, and much more recently as a top secret military staging base for the Central Intelligence Agency and other federal operatives. A model of Osama bin Laden's Pakistani hideout was built here and mock raids rehearsed here in the months prior to the 2011 Navy SEAL Team Six attack in Pakistan that found and killed bin Laden.

Huge concussive blasts from Harvey Point rocked the air of the sound, and heavy black smoke rose slowly from that land's end, while we carefully turned northwest and approached a large north-shore marina just inside the mouth of Yeopim Creek. The *Belle*, though drawing only two feet, at eighty-five feet length overall needed a substantial face dock to come in safely.

A bus hauled us—sixty strong—north a few miles to one of the oldest brick homes still standing in North Carolina, the Newbold-White House, a modest "story and a jump" dating to 1730, a Flemish-bond, grand-for-its-time building set back just a ways from the Perquimans River. A round-hulled periauger, the only extant replica of what was once the prime commercial vessel of North Carolina's rivers and sounds, lay upon a modern trailer—the boat shop at Beaufort's Maritime Museum had built it, and late one summer morning years before, David Cecelski and I witnessed its water test, the first time it touched the waters of Taylor's Creek, seeing whether it was tight enough for its June 2004 launch.

Now David, tired from our early start and hours of helping narrate the wonders of our round-the-sound cruise, lay out under the big pecan tree near the periauger and took a nap.

Later, Judge Terrence Boyle of the Fourth Circuit, Eastern District of North Carolina, met the crowd

in the upper room of the 1767 courthouse in Edenton and set out the story of such eighteenth-century leaders as James Iredell, North Carolina's only U.S. Supreme Court associate justice, and the local leadership of today bade us welcome, and then the wine flowed. A number of us remembered Judge Boyle's sharp questioning of a lawyer for the Navy—during the contentious outlying field case a dozen years back, when the Navy wanted to drop a touch-and-go airstrip on the Albemarle-Pamlico Peninsula, right smack at the western edge of four national wildlife refuges, wintering-over waters and grounds for several hundred thousand large waterfowl: swans, geese, and ducks.

Tom Earnhardt, *Exploring North Carolina* host and another of this tour's narrators *and* the one among us who had witnessed that trial, recalled that great moment with us: "One of the Navy attorneys said, 'The outlying field would actually be a good thing—you wouldn't be bothered by rush-hour traffic morning and afternoon. And once the OLF was there, with a whole lot less traffic, this would be good for the birds.' Judge Boyle jumped in at once, asking, 'Excuse me, sir—have you ever *been* on Highway 99? Have you ever *visited* the location?' 'No,' answered the attorney. And Judge Boyle lectured the lawyer: 'Because if

you *had* ever been on 99, you'd know there *is* no rush hour traffic to protect birds from!'"

Tom and Audubon North Carolina's then director Chris Canfield—the keen and canny man who along with the North Carolina Wildlife Federation and Defenders of Wildlife, all represented by the Southern Environmental Law Center, had first brought the suit against the Navy in 2004—just turned to each other and smiled.

The court later found that the Navy had predetermined the Washington County spot it wanted, then manipulated its environmental impact assessment to support the decision it had already made, which scarcely constituted the "hard look" required by the National Environmental Policy Act.

The Navy famously lost this battle, and the people of the Albemarle *and* all those water birds just as famously won.

We slowly strolled the old town of Edenton, steeped in its own historicity, looked out over the docks where Josiah Collins's ship full of 113 enslaved West Africans docked in the late 1780s and from which they went out, over to the south shore of the sound, to wrest Collins's Somerset plantation from the pocosins and the absolute mud of Tyrrell and Washington Counties, out of the jungles between the upper Scuppernong River and Lake Phelps, a vast farm that for three generations meant great wealth to the Collins family and meant nothing but servitude and farming and milling wheat and corn and punishing, even deadly, canal digging to those stolen away and brought here from Africa.

And we thought also of the bravery of young Harriet Jacobs, born into slavery, hiding out for years in her grandmother's home here from those who had abused her and those who might yet, before escaping to New York and ere long telling the world just how hideous John C. Calhoun's "peculiar institution" had been, in her narrative *Incidents in the Life of a Slave Girl.*

Pound net fishing, Chowan River

Incidents indeed.

The next day, after a stroll past the Cupola House, its gardens all abloom, and the 1767 Chowan County Courthouse with its sycamore-lined green down to the sound, my gaze held upon the beautifully restored metal-facade (all the way from St. Louis, I learned) building on South Broad Street with *J. N. Leary 1894* written across its parapet and columns and sunbursts decorating the front. The affable Edenton attorney and author Sambo Dixon filled me in on just what I was staring at. The name this building bore was that of the woman who had it built: Josephine Napoleon Leary, also born into slavery, gained freedom at nine, married, and operated

the Central Barber Shop along with her husband, "Sweety" Archer Leary. A highly successful African American businesswoman, her name still stands proudly, as it has for almost a century and a third, high over Edenton Bay.

Soon we were away from the Edenton wharf, heading out the bay, and ere long could see, off in the distance, the great Chowan River bridge and, to its south on the far shore, the Avoca peninsula and the mouth of Salmon Creek. Along that creek, during Ann's board presidency, Camilla Herlevich's direction, and Janice Allen's and Lee Leidy's sharp tactical leadership, the North Carolina Coastal Land Trust acquired 1,000 acres

20

up Salmon Creek, including a mile and a quarter of shoreline and "Site X," which *may* have been a stopping and possibly long-term-living spot for some of the Lost Colonists from Sir Walter Raleigh's 1587 Roanoke Island effort.

In a few months, Ann told the *Belle*'s passengers, this marvelous territory would be presented to the people of North Carolina.

We slowly plied the waters of the western sound toward the mouth, or *mouths* as the old maps have it, of the Roanoke River. This was just below the mouth of the black-water Cashie River, where it emptied into the sound after winding its twenty-five-mile way from the tiny river port of Windsor down through swampy Bertie County, and just above Swan Bay, whose adjacent mainland held some of the deepest peat deposits anywhere in eastern Carolina and whose shoreline cypress forest was full of the treetop, stick-built nests of ospreys. Each May, with their young lying in these nests, newborn hearts pumping away against the heat, mother and father ospreys flew overhead in great numbers, circling their redoubts and *scree*-ing out at boaters in the waters with seeming abandon but really with great purpose.

Tom Earnhardt spoke of the fortunes' worth of warblers nesting and living just now in these river-bottom swamps, and he bade all us sailors to look about the water's edges for prothonotary warblers, the black-and-bright-gold birds that shuttlecocked each spring all through the eastern woodlands, brightening them so.

Yet whatever prothonotaries might have been around that day as we slowly wound up the lower Roanoke (or the River of Death, its sobriquet before the upper river was dammed, acknowledging with rueful fear the mightiness of its spring floods), they would have disappeared swiftly once the three-eighths-scale replica of the Confederate ram *Albemarle* overtook us and blasted off several black-powder rounds, massively cracking the afternoon air.

Some years back, one of the reenactors aboard, we heard, had not wet the cloth of the cannon-shaft cleaning rag and, after a couple of misfires on a similar outing, rammed the rod down, setting off sparks that exploded the charge of powder, causing the rod to blast out, severing several of the reenactor's fingers. On this day that man was back in place, we also heard, enjoying his role in this piece of living history—and the *Albemarle*'s captain said of the man's wounds: "It makes him more *authentic*!"

Sleepy Plymouth turned out in force to welcome the *Belle*, and casks of lemonade flowed as freely as wine once we disembarked. That evening, a heavy spread of barbeque, coleslaw, potato salad, and sweet tea made for a fete at Plymouth's maritime museum, filled with shad boats and skiffs and just across the waterside street from the museum's replica screw-pile lighthouse. Bear Festival sponsor Tom Harrison, an energetic outfitter whose work carried him from Plymouth to spots all over the world, gave the *Belle*'s crowd a strong pitch for Plymouth as the gateway to adventure (his daughter, wearing a full bear suit, had been among the riverside welcomers several hours earlier), given all the wondrous birdlife in the national wildlife refuge territory around it and the many and awesome sleuths of roaming black bears.

Offstage, Harrison told me of getting pitched out of his duck-hunting boat one frigid December day down in the lower Roanoke islands and then treading water, fully clothed, till he could catch hold of his circling boat and work his way up the gunwales and pull himself back in.

"I had so much adrenaline going," he said, "I couldn't feel a thing, not till I got back into the boat and started upriver. At least nobody *saw* me, but I had some explaining to do back at home!"

The sun rose the next morning over the trees and river mists lay their smoke upon the water, as the *Belle* sailed outbound now for the sound's south shore and Bull Bay, standing for Columbia up the Scuppernong River a few miles above the bay. Gracious and graceful Marlene True, director of the Pocosin Arts folk school, led the *Belle*'s passengers in an onboard pottery-painting session, and, just for us, Columbians delayed church services that Sunday morning and opened stores, the local museum (where my great-uncle Phil Spruill's popcorn popper and peanut roaster stood as the initial feature, just inside the old movie theatre's doors), and the exemplary Pocosin Arts Gallery and studio, too.

On the way out to Somerset, we stopped a moment just outside of Creswell to look over the old Scuppernong River turning basin at Spruill's Bridge, where schooners once called at warehouses there, and then we came in along the Thirty-Foot Canal Road, the canal itself leading from Lake Phelps out to the Scuppernong. The canal's outlet, David Cecelski and I had discovered by canoe five years earlier, was now all grown over in swamp jungle, impassable for a boat of any size, all that hideous labor now for naught.

At the Somerset historic site, we were greeted warmly by the staff, who fed us hoppin' John and corn bread and walked us through the mansion and the enslaved people's quarters, which *Somerset Homecoming* author (and later site director) Dorothy Spruill Redford had so rightly insisted must be replicated if this place were ever even to hope to have any sense of accuracy as to what it was, who really made it, and what happened here.

A young person named Crystal, in antebellum dress, apron, and cap, led us through the main house, pointing out the locked wine safe and medicine chest on one of its upper porches and the bedroom of the last generation of Collinses here, Josiah III and his wife. After identifying them in their photographs, Crystal remarked: "People say she looks kind of sad and worn out, but I say, 'After having all those children and losing two of her sons on the same day, I think she looks *pretty good*!'"

Dawn on the Roanoke, looking downriver from Plymouth

About those sons: the two Collins boys along with two young African American boys, playing together just outside this main house, all drowned in the Somerset Canal.

"Where were they laid out?" I asked Crystal.

"Here in the house," Crystal answered.

"I mean, in what room?"

"Oh, in the parlor, downstairs, the Collins boys, anyway. The slave boys ... nobody knows about what came of them."

We left Somerset that May afternoon and returned to Elizabeth City, not by boat but by bus (the *Belle* having begun her return to little Washington via the Alligator River, the Pungo Canal and River, and the Pamlico River), all aboard agreeing that the time for a renewal of North Carolina's interior navigation and its sound country maritime life was at hand.

Green barges being pushed by towboats up the waterway from the state port at Morehead City to Nucor's steel plant at Tunis on the upper Chowan were already a part of this. Several thousand cruisers and sailboats that moved in seasonal migration up and down the Dismal Swamp Canal and the Albemarle and Chesapeake Canal were too, and the new passenger ferry from the Hatteras ferry slip to Ocracoke village was as well.

Perhaps the *Belle of Washington* and this Natural and Cultural Resources around-the-sound tour would be too, if only as a proof of concept.

Perhaps.

BEAUTIFUL BERTIE

On a gray morning in January 2019, three of us—the visionary coastal geologist Stan Riggs of Eastern Carolina University, Tom Earnhardt, and I—began our long day in Bertie County at Hoggard's Mill Pond outside of Windsor. Or former pond, I should say, since, though the old mill still stood, housing rusty gears, and the milldam lay before us, the pond's waters were all drained away, blown out by Hurricane Matthew in 2016.

The old mill dated to about 1722 and sat where the pre-Windsor village of Cashy once was. Cypress and river birch grew all around us, a twenty-five-foot magnolia near the road. The ebullient Riggs was undeterred about the empty pond, for the dam could be restored and, he allowed: "The drainage is available for eight miles upstream, *without* interfering with anyone's agriculture!"

Riggs did not say this simply as a casual observation, for in recent years he had become a consultant, a *counselor* really, to Bertie County and the Town of Windsor, which have suffered three so-called 500-year floods in less than twenty years. As he described to us how he, with his group North Carolina Land of Water, helped community leaders come up with a series of ecotourism sites, he quoted them in their collective spirit as saying, in essence, "The river has about *killed* us—now we're going to *live off it*."

We came down off the Wicomico Terrace, the "Windsor Ridge," into the county seat itself, and Riggs took us in to see a pair of those very leaders, then county manager Scott Sauer and Windsor mayor Jimmy Hoggard, of the same family that ran the mill three centuries ago. They greeted him warmly, enthusiastically, seeming to match Riggs's own spirit of adventure and exploration, and then we were off again, Riggs pointing out where Matthew's waters had risen to on the front of the Windsor post office: "Right up to the *zip code*!" He sagely noted how close we were to the edge of the flood zone (though the post office would in time move out of it). "Inches matter down here," Riggs said.

Then we walked the planks of a long dock, looking in on the town's set of ecotouristic tree houses (all for rent) downriver from Windsor and the Roanoke Cashie River Center, four of them, clapboard cabins built around enormous trees along the river's north shore high above the level of the river and its swamp.

(Later that year, Jimmy Hoggard—who grew

up squirrel hunting on the Cashie River, floating down from Hoggard's Mill two hours or so back to town—would share with me his lifelong dreams for Bertie County, even giving me a look at his high school paper on the Cashie River, which concluded, "Although the river is not as vital to our economy as it once was, in years to come it may be one of our greatest economic assets." Now, he said, citing the quartet of tree houses, "I didn't think we could get Toyota, but ecotourism, I figured we could grab *that*!")

We rambled east toward the Chowan River, down Bal Gra Road and overland in Tom's four-wheel drive, down and up two deep creek-cut canyons ("Small, but *canyons* nonetheless!" Riggs laughed), arriving at the new county beach just a couple miles below the great Chowan River bridge over to Edenton. As we walked the beach's cypress-sentineled tide line, Riggs waved at the shore's fifteen-foot bluff and said: "The county folks were wondering if they should take that bluff down, and I said, 'No, don't bulldoze that bluff. If you want this beach, leave that bluff, because that's where the beach comes from!'"

Riggs's wondrous depth of knowledge of North Carolina's natural history and his generosity in sharing it came shining through all day long, as we kept on touring "water hubs," as he called them, all around Bertie County. At an age when most college professors have been retired for years, Riggs was very much in the field, leading us on a sunset climb on the high yet sea-level shoreline bluffs on the western side of the Chowan River, the old Pleistocene coast, emerald moss growing and bits of iron leaching bronze color into the clay and curves of coral in the clay walls, too, left there by the ocean long ago, the senior geologist at work past dusk in service of the people of Bertie, helping them find and meet a better future.

At the dedication of the North Carolina Coastal Land Trust's 1,000-acre Salmon Creek gift to the people of North Carolina a couple of months later, I sat near Mayor Hoggard and next to County Commissioner Ron Wesson, just 100 yards or so from the cypress-lined mouth of Salmon Creek into Albemarle Sound. In light-gray sweater and black slacks, Ann as president stood and spoke happily as she presented the deed to this magical tract to North Carolina State Parks: "Now that much of Salmon Creek becomes a State of North Carolina natural area, we may forever find ways to connect people from all over the state, nation, and world—and especially people from right here in Bertie County and the surrounding area—with this precious landscape and with these precious waters."

Magical? A fair call, in terms of the confluence of cultures that has happened here: A former Indian village, Mettaquem, sat in this place; Lost Colonists, some if not all, may have sought shelter here after abandoning Roanoke Island in the late 1580s, and archaeologists led by the First Colony Foundation are literally digging into that matter; and Nathaniel Batts lived in his trading post here in the mid-1600s (a "rude and desperate man," proselytical Quaker George Fox called him). Two centuries afterward, a massive Capehart family herring fishery anchored itself hereabouts.

Just a short way up the shoreline from Salmon Creek lay Bertie County's nearly brand-new beach, nicknamed "Tall Drink of Water," and Ron Wesson—who as the African American chair of the Bertie County Commission had signed the deed for it—spoke to me later with real pride and emotion about this first ever public-water access in Bertie for *all* people. He himself (a Dun and Bradstreet executive who worked all over the world before retiring back home) had not been able to learn to swim here in his own then-segregated home county, so his mother, a schoolteacher for forty-two years, had driven Ron and his cousins over to Rocky Mount to kin and to the Tar River every weekend till the boys *did* learn. When the county held the May 2019 grand opening of this Bertie beach, featuring food, games, and *swimming*, Ron recalled 900 people showing up and one scene in particular: "This touches my heart—one little lad was in the water and he says, 'Commissioner, thank you for letting us come to play at your beach!' and I said, 'This is *your* beach, and as you grow up, you have to take care of it!'"

The little beaches of Salmon Creek and nearby waters may be small and not of great length, yet they were every bit as important and meaningful to the people of Bertie as the beaches of Australia that look out upon the Great Barrier Reef or those of the French Riviera. In the Albemarle, this is land we love, can throw ourselves upon, and can believe in and enjoy with a mighty passion.

The winds soughing through the tall pines and over the low winter-wheat fields were lovely in sound and touch as Ann and I walked up from Salmon Creek that dedication day, the mile back to our car. Something very fine had happened here, and in the shushing winds a sense of peace

was beginning to come down over the old land, perhaps an atonement or a piece of one, perhaps not, but still a better day in this place than the one before.

Would the prothonotary warblers returning from the tropics not wish to see the noisy species they met in their yearly returns—us humans—*together* at last?

The answer I heard was *yes*, and the place was Bertie, beautiful Bertie.

CHANGING COASTS

One recent September evening in Columbia on the Scuppernong, after a chicken chimichanga supper at Tienda Peniel, the Mexican restaurant on Main Street, I sat on the Pocosin Arts Riverside Lodge's front porch and awaited my colleague, sunny, sandy-haired Brent McKee, a marine sciences professor who had grown up in the pottery world of Seagrove, and our Changing Coasts students from the University of North Carolina.

I loved being alone in this tiny, ancestral port, lost for a spell in familial reflections: of my grandmother Evelyn Spruill, who grew up just around the corner and who met my grandfather just up the street when he was building the new county jail in 1909, the docks where they courted only a few yards from where I sat; and of my cousin Nancy Meekins (Ferebee) at age ten, skipping along and whistling joyfully down the street with her friend and being scolded by an old woman on her porch, who called out at them: "A whistling woman and a cackling hen, is neither good to God nor men."

I could see and hear all this and far more in the small town's intense September riverside silence, and I sat most pleasantly lost in this Scuppernong reverie.

After a bit, Brent and the students arrived and all at once enlivened the town and filled the lodge, and Brent and I left them to it, went to

our quarters on the river, and toasted the dark gorgeous night.

The next morning, we were across the broad, cypress-lined Alligator River and down in the national wildlife refuge, moving up the canal from the landing at Buffalo City toward Sawyer Lake and its freshwater marshes and occasional deep-green juniper on the fringe. Through the woods and back out on lake-like Milltail Creek, from which the long-gone timbermen and liquor makers had sent their wares out to the world, the

keen Kelsey Qua paddled thirty yards ahead of me around a point of marsh. Just before I rounded that point I heard an alligator's slap and splash and a shout of delighted alarm from Kelsey—her goal for the morning: to see one.

Seconds later I saw her back-paddling away from a pressed-down alligator wallow where the reptile had lain sunning itself till she slid by and spooked it.

Later that afternoon, after passing the ghost forests near Manns Harbor, intruding salt water having killed the trees, we spent a few moments

Milltail Creek at Buffalo City landing, Dare County

Yellow-bellied sliders sunning, Milltail Creek

on a Roanoke Sound pine-and-live-oak hammock assaying the broad brackish marsh, then headed a couple hundred yards into the Nags Head Woods. The leaf litter lay thick upon the ground, and when I remarked about the woods being a huge set of remnant maritime-forested sand dunes, Kelsey shook her head, her dark hair, smiled, and said: "How do you *know* it's sand?"

"It just *is*," I replied, an answer not quite good enough, so Brent McKee dug past the leafy dirt into the hillside, till the dune's underlying sand was finally showing itself. Precisely why we were here, to see together what this world—*these* worlds, for the terrains and the waters we visited were so varied, even though so close together— was made of, how it was changing, and to talk about it all together, *in that place.*

Through the marsh and myrtle prairielands of Bodie Island, we went down next morning and then crossed Oregon Inlet on the Marc Basnight Bridge, honoring the late, longtime, progressive Senate leader, great friend to our university, and creator of the Clean Water Management Trust Fund; this new 2019 bridge dwarfed the relic, almost sixty-year-old Herbert Bonner Bridge below it. On Pea Island, we strolled the empty

NORTHEAST, THE ALBEMARLE

seabeach. My head was again full of memories, for I had halfway grown up in Dare County, walked its strands all my life, found kindred spirits of a Kitty Hawk night sitting around beach fires and not a one of us yet turned twenty, courted Ann on this very beach, and stood here with students of an earlier time upon the dunes staring into the teeth of a full gale as it ripped the tops off inlet waves and blasted us with sand.

Now Knoxville's Blythe Gulley, with a fine desire for this maritime moment, found herself smitten by the old boarded-up Oregon Inlet Coast Guard Station and was taking pictures, asking questions. When Blythe wrote her story for class, she did so in the voice of the old station telling what all it had seen across its good long life.

This great coast—settled seasonally by Native Americans seeking fish and oysters for millennia before the first Europeans ever laid eyes upon it—still had the power to hold and haunt, as it had always held me and as it now haunted Blythe, moved the lyric impulse within her, asking her to feel and to tell of the old yearnings and the old doubts and the old visions of tides rolling in and tides rolling out and the deep blue sea that never ends.

After we trod Jennette's Pier with its tall wind turbines and then ate fried fish and crab-cake sandwiches at Sam and Omie's locals' bistro at Whalebone Junction, South Nags Head, its walls festooned to the gills with photographs of men, women, boats, and fish, we headed west.

At Columbia we stopped again, this time at grand old friend Willy Phillips's Full Circle Crab Company shop on US 64. Our students got a look at the soft-shell-crab shedder trays out back and all the fish in the freezers there too, our affable and self-confident young guide a high schooler from Edenton who said he, too, wanted to come to school at Carolina.

I wished they might have met Willy, for after thirty-some years in Tyrrell County he knew

the sound country as few did, and one always found him friendly, compassionate, talkative, funny, and sage—yet his and his artist wife Feather's grandchild in Brooklyn had pulled them northward that weekend. I also wished that the wind-powered sandwich shop in the Full Circle parking lot had still been open—for many were the big, fine soft-shell-crab sandwiches I had enjoyed there.

Now, from out of the glass cases inside Full Circle, my cooler took on bluefish and river catfish filets, a couple of crab cakes, some scallops and smoked mullet, and big scoops of ice to get me back to the short hills and to Ann by early evening.

With a gator seen, sandy soil turned, and many rivers and an inlet crossed to show for this trip to our changing coast.

On our second class outing, we docked in river port Plymouth after pulling forth Roanoke River–bottom muddy sand with an Ekman grab sampler and running up Broad Creek to Cypress Cathedral and its six-foot-diameter cypresses, and then cruising down Middle River past Wood Island all the way to the Albemarle Sound in a pair of UNC's Institute of Marine Sciences bateaus. Back on dry land, we got a top-drawer tour of Grace Episcopal Church from Rev. Hank Burdick and Amy Barsanti. In this brick antebellum house of worship, with white stucco and an arresting dark wooden interior, the pews had been cut up and built into coffins after the Civil War's Battle of Plymouth in April 1864, and here in our day the preacher let two of the students drop iron hooks into a heavy piece of stone flooring, lifting it and revealing urns bearing the remains of worshippers whose last wishes were never to miss a service. In the apse's curved ceiling, bright white stars shone upon a blue field, while a golden anchor decorated a red cloth hanging in a forward corner.

Outside in the graveyard, the reverend brandished a pair of yard-long brass rods and

Marine sciences professors Tony Rodriguez (center left) and Brent McKee (center right) rig an Ekman grab sampler, as students (left to right) Brad Walter, Patrick Mulqueen, Sydney Thomas, and Hannah White (seated) look on. UNC Changing Coasts class, Roanoke River upstream of Plymouth.

held them close together, as if he were conducting water witching. As he moved slowly about, he told our students that the rods would react and turn apart from each other whenever he stood over the spot where a body was buried. When he invited the students quite literally to try their hands at this investigation, Sydney Thomas from Jacksonville, on our coastal New River, turned to me with the strangest smile on her face, a lambent look in her eyes, and said quietly to me: "*What is happening?*"

The preacher moved our group across the street to a half-acre empty lot, where local lore held that an unmarked mass grave from that fierce Civil War battle lay. Again he invited our students to give dowsing for bodies a try, and one after another soon found the brass rods fluttering

outward as he or she walked slowly over the grassy yard, the long dead speaking their presence to us through the thin rods the young hands held. Soon, we strode back downtown and occupied the Garden Spot's upstairs oyster bar, no one quite believing what we had just been party to, as if we had all stumbled into a séance and then found ourselves morbidly attracted to those lonesome yet highly communicative ghosts.

While out in kayaks next morning on the dark Cashie River in Windsor, student Brad Walter, a short man with a tall, powerful wit, paddled over to me and said: "You hear we went over to the Sunny Side after we got back to Williamston?"

We had all been staying in a motel just a twenty-two-second walk from that epicenter of easternness, the Sunny Side Oyster Bar.

"I did, Brad, but nothing more about it."

"Well," he said, "we kind of stumbled into a meeting of the North Carolina Shag Dancing Association."

"Do tell."

"A man named John introduced himself and pointed out a woman who was dressed up as the Cape Hatteras Lighthouse and told me she was the Queen of Shag and that I should go dance with her. Which I did," he said. "She was over fifty-five. They *all* were."

"Was she a good dancer?" I asked.

"Well, *yeah*! I mean, I *guess* she was—I don't know much about shag dancing, but *they* all did. And after the dance I was talking to John some more and he pointed to her again and said, 'She's a powerful woman, a *very powerful* woman!' and I thought, *Hey, wait a minute, what's going on? I just came over here for a beer and now I'm dancing with the Queen of Shag and hearing power narratives at the Sunny Side!*"

And we laughed and paddled on, into the duckweed that curved and slithered in patches and at times grew shore to shore and filled the Cashie, passing the tiny tree-house village hanging aloft in the swamp cypress trees along the riverside. Brad kept looking over at me, seeming to expect further word.

"You're in eastern North Carolina now, Brad," I said at last. "*Deep* in it."

PASQUOTANK SUNSET

After a wonderful long day's float back in the Great Dismal Swamp with the fine, exuberant naturalist Lindsay Dubbs and her ready outdoorsman colleague Andy Keeler (these two professors serving as codirectors of UNC's Outer Banks Field Site on Roanoke Island) and their students—all of us delayed a bit due to a dredge at Arbuckle's Landing, still clearing wreckage wrought almost a year earlier by Hurricane Matthew—I found myself at George and Blair Jackson's Pasquotank riverside dock, boarding their single-masted skipjack, *Applejack*.

Just before a warm September dusk, an unexpected invitation and a moment of true grace.

In white shirt, tan shorts, and a light-brown, broad-brimmed straw hat, George got us away, motoring slowly out into the middle of the Pasquotank. Beyond the crowns of riverside cypresses and pines lay the setting sun.

I had known George for over thirty years, and we had long shared our love of the Pasquotank and the lore of the coast. When I brought the North Carolina Writers Conference to Elizabeth City in 2002, George and Blair most graciously sailed *Applejack* upriver to the Water Street docks, took writers from all over the state aboard, and gave them a good look at the old port town as sailors first saw her: from the river itself.

To hear their laughter and the tender ways they spoke to each other way out on the broad river (and later, too, as Blair held lines and George slowly docked: "That's right, darlin', that's right") was a simple delight, a pure joy. A second joy for me, too, to have gotten out upon not one but two such beautiful bodies of water on the same day, first on Lake Drummond and now upon this river of my heart and dreams—or was it *one water*, really, since the lake flows into the Dismal Swamp Canal and the canal flows into the upper Pasquotank?

As we lay to and as evening shadows fell, I recalled another time on this big stream, a few miles downriver, and in a different season many years ago:

One cold bright sunny mid-1950s Sunday morning, my father drove us down to the river below Shiloh, over in Camden County way downstream of Elizabeth City, to meet fellow lawyer Russell Twiford at a hunt camp near where Portohonk Creek flowed into the Pasquotank. Russell wanted to show my father, still a prodigious duck hunter (he was a frequenter of the Penn brothers' Monkey Island Club on Currituck Sound), three duck blinds at the mouth of Portohonk.

So we climbed into Russell's runabout at the camp, eased down the creek into the drowned cypresses, checked out the brushy, reedy blinds nearby, and then spun out onto the big winter river itself. Across the way stood the Navy's two huge blimp hangars at Weeksville.

We spooked a duck that flapped and sped along over the water, yet never quite gained the air.

"He's hurt," Russell said. "We'll pick him up."

The young lawyer knew his way around boats— he would own fifty of them over the course of his lifetime, and he was descended from a line of boaters and hunters and Coast Guardsmen. Breedlove Tillett, who raised Russell's father, had cut the masts off the celebrated wreck of USS *Huron* at Nags Head, quartered them, and had eighteen Canada goose decoys carved out of one of these mast sections. Russell's great-uncle Bill Tate helped the Wright brothers so much when they first came to the Outer Banks to learn to fly.

One of Russell's kinsmen, who hunted a great deal out of the Portohonk camp, would during hunting seasons boat out and pick up crippled birds and keep them in a pen at the camp, nurse them back to health, and turn them loose again. This is what Russell envisioned for the hurt bird we were now encircling, going round and round it as it kept trying to lift up and fly away.

"He's tired now," Russell finally said, maneuvering the craft closer in, slowly so, to where my father could lean over the gunwale and bring the fatigued duck into the boat. Russell would indeed take the injured creature to his kinsman, though my father would later bring me word that the duck had not survived.

Even so, it was an invigorating, thrilling morning for an eight-year-old out in the great, bright wide open, out in the astringent cold that was always colder on open water, out where two men—neither of them long out of law school— took a winter's morning just to breathe the big estuarine air and coincidentally show a boy how much larger life was out here than back in town.

Applejack felt the lightest of breezes puffing over the water, two knots at most, shifting us around and pulling me out of this reverie, and as the sun sank behind a cloud bank far to the west, lighting up the high cumulus clouds as it did, faint pink on the edges, burnished gold on the thin cloudy reefs, the water tower and the old hotel stood silhouetted against the clouds.

On this September evening, in dusky dark we drifted slowly shoreward, the sheet in George's hand, the lights in riverside homes winking on, and the magic hour out on the dark river waters came to an end and did not linger.

Nor would we love it so if it did.

PASQUOTANK HARVEST MOON
One evening I went down to the Pasquotank River at Moth Boat Park, to sit on a riverside porch with a couple of wonderful friends and fellow thespians, Peter and Sue Thomson, he from Canada and she from Wales, both long here because of the sailing. We sat and watched the full harvest moon appear from and disappear behind smoky clouds, sometimes dropping a patch of white light way down the Pasquotank, sometimes painting a ribbon of it right up to us. One lone moth boat had been out practicing at moonrise for tomorrow's races, trying to see, as those fine pilots do, how to get the last tenth out of the little craft that was born right here in this town, on this waterfront. As pretty a look at a river as I have ever had, and certainly as lovely a look as ever at the one river I cannot remember not knowing.

Island Time

Outer Banks, Core Banks, and the Central Coast

I know a cure for everything. Salt water.

ISAK DINESEN

ISLAND TIME

I have always held shorelines with deep affection, and the greatest of all the shores I know are our long sandy strands, the last sandbars before Africa, the islands of the Carolina coast. Whether folks go out to them only a time or two, or steadily for sixty years, whether we find fish or first love or family life through the generations, the devotional, even reverential, qualities of voice are in the air whenever we Carolinians mention our jaunts, our stays, at the beach, by which we mean *the islands*.

What a gift of the gods, to have been given time to look out and to stride endlessly upon them, to drift off at night and awaken in the morning both times to the sound of ocean waves crashing, to be in love out in this wide-open world, to all but melt into the ocean-washed sands of islands with names like Bodie, Pea, and Hatteras; Ocracoke, Portsmouth, and Core; Bogue, Bear, and Bald Head; Oak, Ocean Isle, and Bird. There are more, yet even the litany of these few, spoken aloud, has about it the sound of a prayer. An *answered* prayer, indeed, for the many millions of us who have been baptized by immersion in the foamy brine of breaking waves, knowing forever what it is like to long for blue crabs and salty oysters from the sounds, the balm of summer breezes off the evening sea, and the astringent winds out on the beach in late December not merely laced but full well laden with salt.

Because we literally taste the sea when we breathe, and taste (no less than music) unlocks

the past, we could not stay the flood of seaside memories even if we wanted to: the gulls following the ferries from Cedar Island and Swan Quarter out to Ocracoke ... the family car stuck in the sand way too close to the high-tide line, a teenaged driver looking on in mourning ... the sweet soul music of the Tams filling the second-floor dance hall of the Nags Head Casino, while other patrons played bingo down below ... the echoing of footsteps off the spiraling iron stairs as pilgrims climbed up and down the Cape Hatteras Lighthouse ... a ten-month-old taking her first steps in one of the tar-paper fishing shacks on the Core Banks strand above Drum Inlet ... older children joyfully crying out as they rounded the go-kart track's tire-rimmed curves at the Atlantic Beach Circle.

And farther south, the Fort Fisher hermit shaking his iron skillet at us, panhandling for coins or the telling and retelling of how Mr. Lockwood's newly finished ship drew too much water for it to get out from river to sea at the east end of Holden Beach and, sinking there, gave Lockwood Folly Inlet its name. How well I recall the ritual crossings of Mad Inlet at low tide (before it shoaled up and closed) from Sunset Beach to Bird Island (where the Kindred Spirit mailbox full of its soul-pouring-out notebooks stood atilt among the sea oats in all weathers, and where a small grave marker tucked away back toward the marshes memorialized one who died young and whose ashes doubtless were spread over, or in, those dunes) and king mackerel steaks

grilling and shrimp boiling away in Jim and Jane's Bald Head Island kitchen one May.

Well before any of this, way before any of *my* millions of coastal memories formed, what a remarkable lot of people had already fetched up and lived *their* lives on all these very same spots over time. The first peoples found their ways across a whole continent and never stopped till they reached our islands. Ever after, for scores of generations, they came out of the longleaf-pine forests, floated down through the sound country and stayed and feasted from March to October on the islands, such as Huggins Island inside Bogue Inlet or Roanoke Island, where at the Wanchese Thicket Lump they left acres of oyster shells and fish and turtle bones and the charred, buried remnants of their campfires. Long before Ferris wheels and pavilions and shag dancing and pier fishing, Native Americans went to the islands to eat seafood and live simply and well.

In my own time, what thrill could I compare to sitting out at the seaward end of the lonesome *Vesta* fishing pier at Sunset Beach late one August evening long ago, with a teapot full of ice and cool

ISLAND TIME

35

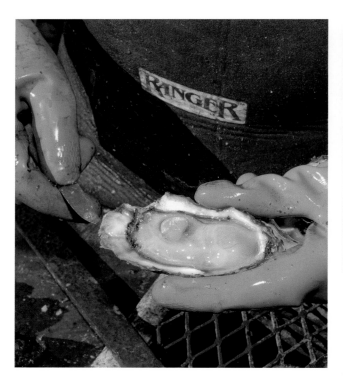

drink and my old friend Homer Foil, the two of us just hanging out, staring up at the universe, the Perseid meteors striking down brightly across the night sky? Or other summer evenings, when Ann and I stepped outside our rustic cottage at the Alger Willis camps of south Core Banks, nearly falling breathlessly to our knees on the seabeach, stunned by the countless stars filling the heavens in this peerless dark-sky realm — our less populous barrier islands and the eastern Albemarle — Pamlico peninsula the starriest places anywhere in the American East.

"Well, I hope you understand," Leon Russell sang, "I just had to go back to the island." Year after year we are borne back to the islands again, our arms stretched out to the sea and to one another, in rhapsodies we share, in reveries all our own. However well we know and *think* we know these gloriously plain sandbars and their grassy dunes, the many winds and waters play endlessly upon them, and whenever we return, crossing bridges, driving low along marshes, or taking ferries to

reach them, we should remember that they will always be different, no less than we will, for time and chance resculpt us all. And so we are always getting acquainted anew with the edge of the sea, Rachel Carson's "strange and beautiful place," no two visits ever quite the same, no two tide lines ever matching, night-time phosphorescence in the breaking waves and miles of spindrift beneath the moon the lights of our lives.

SWIMMING AT DAWN

Before sunrise on warm summer mornings at Kitty Hawk, my father would awaken my first cousin Johnny and me, both of us not yet six, by shaking our feet, and we would come to quickly, put on our swimming trunks, and then follow him through the dunes, dew still on the sea oats and pennyworts, down to the tide line of the Atlantic Ocean.

Sometimes the glow from way out beyond the Gulf Stream clouds would be a deep red, other mornings it might be a faint yellow, with a promising fair-weather pink on the high clouds, nothing yet but the color of ash on the lower puffs closer to the sea. We would stand silently, just we three, for a few moments, till my father, a former Navy navigator, spoke in the voice of command, saying briskly, "All right, let's go!"

And in we went, over the sea-foam and into the surf after him, the plunge always shocking, as our warm bodies hit the frigid waters that had come all the way down to our cottage doorsteps from Labrador. Yet we knew by now what to expect, and to be immersed in those waters and in that moment with him were pieces of an incalculable joy. My father would have already swum twenty yards out and back by the time we got in up to our necks, and then he would pick us up, each in turn, pull us out of the water and toss us, and we would all three splash about a bit till he turned and pointed east and said, "Here it comes."

So advised, we all kept a keen eye on the horizon till the first arc of red glow cut through and laid daylight abroad out over the ocean, and before we knew it the full sun sat itself right up on the eastern edge and fired the sky. Never on these bracing mornings were we out for more than twenty or thirty minutes, yet we knew how pure and how purely important it all was, for no one else was ever up and about.

The sea was ours, and we were the sea's, and soon, after my father got us in to shore and, leaving us there, returned alone to the water, he swam forty or fifty yards out and then kept swimming, parallel to the beach, the quarter mile up to the old fishing pier and back, and we went back up on the porch, found towels and dried off, and stood watching his progress, wondering and marveling over what strength it must take to do that, to be a man swimming powerfully in the sea, and dreaming of a year to come when we might do that too.

Dawn at the fishing pier, northern Outer Banks

THE PATH TO RUN HILL

My cousins and I used to leave our family's
Kitty Hawk seaside cottage after lunch (peanut-
butter crackers and fresh peaches from Currituck
orchards) and tromp away from the ocean,
walking west over toward the soundside woods,
crossing a naked, mile-wide sandy plain behind
and beyond the oceanfront cottages and beach
road, all that was there then. Only a few times did
we go sliding down the loose, angled sand into
the woods themselves, for we were always warned
how difficult it might be to climb back up.

Most afternoons we stopped just shy of
the woods line at a single large teapot dune
absolutely swarming in summertime with briers
and trumpet vines and scuppernongs, found what
small bit of shade this dune afforded, took our
fill of grapes, and stared back at our small, white,
red-roofed cottage silhouetted against the deep
blue sea.

We loved to jump and roll on the sand dunes,
and one of our favorites, of course, was the
biggest, the great sand mountain called Jockey's
Ridge. I once climbed it with my father on a day
the wind was really blowing and the sand stinging
my legs—it hurt, and I was crying, till he picked
me up and sang me a song, carrying me the rest
of the way to the top, making me feel better.

In time I found and strode other ranges of
Carolina sands: the dunes of Shackleford Banks
and the beach and steep live-oak bluff of Durant
Island looking north across Albemarle Sound;
the many miles of low dunes out on Core Banks;
the East Beach on Bald Head Island up where
Corncake Inlet once was; and the half-mile walk
from marshes to sea on Bear Island through
teapot dunes all its own.

Ann and I have lately taken to what on
Ocracoke passes for a mountain range, the piney
woods and live oaks of the Hammock Hills not
far northeast of the village, where a mile-long
trail snakes through the forest in lovely fashion,
first crossing a duck pond by way of a wooden

Jockey's Ridge, Dare County

footbridge, then climbing into the pines and leading out to a marshy cordgrass-and-needlerush cove off Pamlico Sound, replete with a viewing station to rest and muse a bit before making the turn and heading on back. Even higher and larger were the great forested dune ridges, low swamps between them, of the 2,000-acre Buxton Woods, lying between Highway 12 and the national seashore just west of Cape Hatteras, well worth our climb.

Yet after a lifetime of striding and shuffling and threading my way about all these places and many more, up, over, and through the lovely and constantly changing sand masses of our coast, I must own up and play a favorite, hard as it is

to do so, and admit my deep, abiding love of Run Hill.

Such a love does not come upon one lightly, nor does one forget how or when or why.

On the mid-August, Aztec-calendrical occasion called the Harmonic Convergence back in 1987, I found myself yet again on the Outer Banks, on the Nags Head seabeach. Ann and I, new to each other, met up there and drove south, over the old Bonner Bridge at Oregon Inlet to Pea Island, soon found a pull-off that would not sink our borrowed sports car in the sand (thank you, D-Bone), and walked over the dune to swim in the icy Atlantic.

After a spell we sat together in the late-afternoon shade of the dune and she told me about her family—how they had lived on the coast of Spain when she was very small, her father a Navy doctor at Rota there, and then moved to Sea Level on Nelson Bay down our coast when she was only six—and about her younger sister Carolyn, an ecologist, her outdoorsman brother Tad, and Tad's great friends Specklehead and Fig. We laughed and laughed till she reached over into the high-tide scurf and pulled out a big, weedy, olive-and-brown mess and shook it my way.

"Sargassum weed," she declared to one who had never heard of it. "Where the little sargassum fish live."

So I was in the company of a naturalist—and I was charmed eight ways from Sunday and even more.

"This stuff gets loose and floats all the way up here from the Sargasso Sea," she said.

Across Highway 12, we walked slowly down the long, curving sand levee beside one of the big waterfowl impoundments, stilts and herons and egrets all around us, mullet jumping too. I climbed atop an earthwork and stared north toward wading willets and plovers in the marsh shallows, "one of the finest places on the coast to observe the seasonal migrations of the shorebirds," Rachel Carson once wrote of this place. Ann clambered up after me, and we stood together as the brilliant late afternoon sun's long light lay over the tall golden grasses.

Next morning, we took a much longer stroll down the lanes of the Nature Conservancy's Nags Head Woods. Ann had helped put this treasured preserve together, working from both Chapel Hill and out here on the Banks, only a half a dozen years or so earlier, and she wanted to show me places that she had come to love back in the woods: the small, old family cemeteries with chalk-white marble grave slabs, conch shells atop them that meant and marked recent visits of kin;

the steep, involuted sand slopes forested with pines and live oaks; the small dark ponds with duckweed on them at the bottoms of the hills; tiny gum swamps almost within kissing distance of the brackish marshes of Roanoke Sound; and then, last, a very long, slow-rising path ending abruptly—surprisingly—in the twenty-foot-tall face of a vast, living, moving dune, a sand mountain rivaling the more southerly Jockey's Ridge in size, clearly if slowly coming into the western woods and taking it over: *Run Hill*.

The next high dune to the north was Kill Devil Hill, where the Wrights first flew, yet it was the view west from the summit of Run Hill that truly caught me, and I found it simply stunning, first looking down from above the treetops into the steadily sanding forest, next over the broad salt marshes below and the great cove those marshes lined, and at last away across the long reach of Roanoke Sound toward Shallowbag Bay and Manteo on Roanoke Island.

"What's the cove right down there called?" I asked Ann. Smiling, she gazed out upon it for a few seconds, then said exuberantly, "Breathtaking Bay."

Years later, I learned she had made up that name right on the spot.

And just for me.

OCRACOKE
Cuttin' Sedge
Early May, a couple of years ago, we stayed again in the late Conk and Mickey O'Neal's 1913 house, now owned by the writer Kelley Shinn, a great friend of ours and of our lifelong compadre Ocracoke Foundation president Scott Bradley. Out back, across a twenty-foot-wide canal, lay an enormous marsh, several hundred acres chock-full of red-winged blackbirds and egrets, baitfish often breaking the surface along the canal's edge. When I asked native islander and longtime comrade Alton Ballance about it, he said that

Skiff on canal, Cuttin' Sedge marsh, Ocracoke

O'cockers called the whole area Cuttin' Sedge, a variant of Cutting Sage, owing to the tufted sedges that grew in the marsh.

In our kayaks, one orange and one blue, we followed the water to the far side of that marsh, then through a clutch of houses on a whole set of canals, out to the full glory of Pamlico Sound.

One first glided on down past the half dozen or so tiny fish camps, then past the big cottages, all on the sound shore just east of Northern Pond, through a huge bridge culvert and left, or north, on out to the sound. The wind was blowing ten to fifteen on our first outing, so we bobbed just a bit upon the big choppy water. Some stacked crab pots proved that working watermen were still living along that last reach—one younger man was hanging his nets on a cable to dry. Mallards slept in the sun on the docks, a green heron flew

over, and a couple of skimmers went flying along, swift and low.

Another time, a big egret right at Conk's dock watched us put in, and flew off, leading us on down the creek. No dueling country-music radios played on the last canal this time, just a quiet, very light breeze as we made our way out onto the sound, paddling for territory past the cottages, where egrets were fishing the soundside shallows in the distance. Future picnics in mind, we were searching for small sandy beaches, like the one a lone fisherman had kayaked up onto and gotten out to wet a line. As we rounded the head of a marsh, he was wading and fishing not too far out—"Just *practicing*," he called to Ann as she passed by. We were now less than a mile from those gorgeous Hammock Hills woods ("the Highlands," Scott called them) and their languorous winding trail, huge cumulus clouds piling up on one another in the grandest blue sky.

Coming back, each time we veered into Cuttin' Sedge Lake, an hourglass pair of ponds, shallow to about the depth of two paddle blades, just enough water to let us glide along. The first time, a huge egret spooked and flew ahead of us, landing in a live oak, then watching carefully and unmoving as we slid by.

Soon we went on up into the center of the marsh, where we met many dead or half-dead small cedars. Three blackbirds perched and squawked at us and shouted warnings. I went all the way to where the marsh folded in on itself and no further passage was possible, and we came slowly on back to Kelley's place.

That evening, over drinks on Conk's front porch, Kelley got to talking about the fish camps across the marsh and a system of higgledy-piggledy plank walkways and bridges in the past, uneven and leaning thisaway and that as they led out there. She laughed at what she suggested were really saloons built no more for fishing than Fifth Avenue was—"the men liked to go out to have a drink so that 'they don't know back at the house.'" Scott knew the line of small cottages set on the sound shore but said he had not heard about the walks till that evening. A plank bridge and walk array near those little camps could not have been *too* makeshift, after all, for it had worked for those who needed it to.

Rain came that night, and the day dawned cool and gray.

A little before 10 A.M., a bagpipe corps out beyond the myrtles on the road started tuning up with "Amazing Grace," and then a clutch of ancient tunes came piping out through the live oaks, over the shallow creeks and marshes, tunes come all the way to this low sandy spot from the Scottish Highlands and their lochs, from Culloden Moor, yes, and from the Isle of Skye, airs flowing lightly across the centuries, now off into the light

breeze of this May morning, not in martial spirit but in mourning, seventy-seven years after the loss of HMT *Bedfordshire*, an Arctic trawler built in England in 1935, requisitioned by the Admiralty and sent along with twenty-three others to patrol for German submarines wreaking havoc in the shipping lanes along the U.S. East Coast during the first months of World War II.

The high melody of "Amazing Grace" went trailing off as a practicing piper's bag lost its air.

I walked the short distance to the anniversary memorial service at the British Cemetery, where Cdr. Thomas Cunningham and three other crewmen from the *Bedfordshire*—torpedoed May 11, 1942, with all hands lost—were buried. An Ocracoke elder sitting next to Kelley said she remembered watching as a child when horse-drawn wagons brought the dead from such attacks up from the seabeach into the village. I stood with Scott behind the U.S. Coast Guard Pipe Band—seven pipers, one bass drum, one snare, one flag bearer. Coast Guard and Navy folks in dress whites from our services and also from England and Canada (the ship's crew had men from both countries in it) made brief remarks, as did a tall mustached man speaking for the dozen or so American Legion motorcycle riders who were there, dressed in short-sleeve shirts and dark leather vests.

A young man who looked to be a high school senior, wearing a deep-blue shirt and standing erect, slowly called the roll of the ship's crew, along with the age of each man, and then the lead piper played one verse of "Amazing Grace"—alone. When the rest of the pipes and drums joined in full bore at the downbeat of the second verse, there were no dry eyes in this crowd of 200 souls, and over the graves of the four mariners and the live oak above them, over the great Cuttin' Sedge marsh out back of Conk and Mickey's, over Mary Ann's Pond and Northern Pond, Oyster Creek, Silver Lake, and the sound, a light and steady rain had begun to fall.

Marsh pond near Springer's Point, Ocracoke

South Point

Down the sound one October afternoon, our skiff passed the wind-bent and salt-sheared live-oak forest of Springer's Point Preserve, the 120-acre Coastal Land Trust treasure with its marsh-to-beach trail honoring the late Jim Stephenson, our fine, honorable kinsman who, with both the Pamlico–Tar River Foundation and the North Carolina Coastal Federation, had fought for clean water as well and as nobly as anyone ever has.

On down Teach's Hole Channel we plied, over Teach's Hole, where on November 22, 1718, Lt. Robert Maynard of Virginia and his men on the sloop *Jane* with only shot and sword in a six-minute melee put an end to the infamous pirate Edward Teach—Blackbeard—and the crew of his nine-cannoned sloop *Adventure*. Maynard then

stood for Williamsburg on the James River with Teach's severed head on *Jane*'s bowsprit.

Gliding past the low-lying myrtle scrub and marshlands and approaching Ocracoke Inlet, we slowly moved into a world of laughing gulls, pelicans, and plovers, the island's broad tidal flat full of shoals, pools, streamlets, and scalloped sands: South Point.

We came in on the point's sound side and set the anchor in the wet low-tide sand and just walked.

A cleft of shallow water separated this back side of the point from the seabeach beyond, and there a line of jeeps showed us where the bluefishermen were. The lowering sun set a line of diamonds along every light wave that came in slowly from the sound, and in the faraway forest around

Portsmouth village across the inlet, against the glancing light, we could just make out the old Coast Guard station's cupola, the lookout's spot with an eight-mile view.

A few wispy white clouds lay low in the endless blue sky high above us. The Carolina skiff with its green bimini rocked gently in the shallows back up the beach, and the autumn light lengthened over the sands.

Lord, I thought, all that has passed through this inlet, all that it has seen: The restless, the reckless, the rich. All the freight that came in here two centuries and more ago, when Portsmouth was *the* port of Carolina, when the oyster rock named Shell Castle Island (on the deep-water Wallace Channel almost to Portsmouth) had its warehouses all built up on cribbed land, and whether it was lumber going out to the Caribbean or pottery and china coming in from Europe, here it came, from here it went.

Little was moving now in Portsmouth and Shell Castle but wind and water and memories, which have no end. No warning or intimation yet of Hurricane Dorian, the inundator that would put the whole village of Ocracoke under seven feet of water one terrible Friday in early September 2019, a ruinous level of flood no one alive on the island had ever seen.

In the time before names, the ancient first peoples walking east found our wet, jungled, water-everywhere territory millennia ago, millennia before anyone from Spain or England sailed west to get here, a long time before there were any such countries from which to set sail. Perhaps the souls of so many untold generations of strivers in this place float free out over the sounds and rivers on the long sunset light or hang in the mists after sound country rains—if one believes in ghosts, perhaps so.

Something makes us stand at the shallows of rivers, sounds, oceans and stare, something pulls us into a stance of vigil, as if, in the air and light upon the clouds, answers and calls either voiced or set in ciphers or printed as signs and symbols may yet appear.

Who would wish to miss them?

Are we not pulled, ebbed and flowed, by the moon as much as any of these waters and their tides?

If the answers are not on the waves, in the winds that drive them, in the clouds that rise above them, where on earth, pray, could they possibly be at all?

SALTERS CREEK

Between the ages of six and thirteen, Ann grew up living right on the north shore of Nelson Bay in Sea Level, half a mile from Core Sound and just a few steps away from a massive maritime wilderness atop that big cove, much of which has come to be known by the name of the waterway that flows through it: Salters Creek.

Of a childhood day, she used to wander into the piney woods near her home, with no fear either of danger or of getting lost, and she loved the waters she found therein, little rivulets flowing here and there, and the wildflowers she found in these woods. One of them caught her eye and her fancy, and she got a good strong look at it and, once home, delighted that such things could be, and could be right out in the wild open as if just waiting for her, she found it in her book of wildflowers and said its name: *Whorled pogonia,* an orchid.

Years later, as immediate past president of the North Carolina Coastal Land Trust, Ann spoke from our living room in Beaufort to dozens of people, remotely gathered in July 2020, about her youthful moments in the Salters Creek wilds, while announcing that the big—5,482 acres big— territory had now been preserved by the Coastal Land Trust, with help from the Department of Defense (the Salters Creek tract adjoins its 11,000-acre Piney Island bombing range), the North Carolina Clean Water Management Trust Fund, the U.S. Fish and Wildlife Service (whose

45

nearly 15,000-acre Cedar Island National Wildlife Refuge also adjoins the acquisition), the Enviva Forest Conservation Fund, the Duke Energy Water Resources Fund, the North Carolina Native Plant Society, and the North Carolina Wildlife Resources Commission, which would manage most of the Salters Creek tract as game land. The rest—311 acres on the west side of Salters Creek— would remain a Coastal Land Trust private preserve.

One summer morning, with her father in his twenty-one-foot center console, *The Other Woman*, Ann and I had boated up Salters Creek from the landing below the high swooping bridge, north through the stream's narrowing in the marsh, and then on into the big woods, along the cut that tied its headwaters to those of Golden Creek. Once that creek opened onto Long Bay, legions of jellyfish floated in the summer warmth and a big pod of dolphins met us with enthusiasm. Little did we know back then, any more than Ann could have imagined as a girl, that what shows up on the old maps as "the Hunting Quarters" of Sea Level and Atlantic, this world of estuarine marshes, of pocosins, of longleaf piney woods and even some Carolina bays, would someday become a significant part of our environmental

commonwealth, bringing a stretch of seventeen miles of coastal waterfront with it.

We were out that way not long after Salters Creek joined the great eastern Carolina chain of refuge, much to be celebrated and fiercely protected, and we marveled as we always do at the feast of marshes cradling the curving lands of Down East, the green then golden then green again estuarine marshes that in toto nurture half the seafood of the East Coast, the beautiful prairies of marsh that to the joyous eye are endless, and though we know they are not, lo, do they ever seem that way as they lift our spirits into the clouds above.

HARKERS ISLANDER

In one man's life, the heartiness, the fearlessness, and the confident self-reliance of Harkers Island's people could clearly be seen. Tom Earnhardt, who had a cottage on the island's southeast shore for over forty years, from which he could boat down the Drain to Lookout Bight and fish for red drum and false albacore alike, has told me much about his across-the-street neighbor Donald Willis, an American hero then and now.

Once when Donald was a boy of only nine, his mother woke him in the middle of the night. She was one of the island's midwives, and she said urgently: "Mrs. —— is going to lose her baby and she might die herself—you've got to go to Beaufort and get the doctor."

Back then, with no bridge to the mainland, water was the only way. So Donald went down to the dock, mid-island, south shore, to the family's small sailing skiff—"First, I had to break the ice off the sail," he recalled for Tom—and sailed west across the mouth of North River in the dark.

Up Taylor's Creek he sailed on, to Beaufort Fisheries, where he docked. When he rang the bell on the waterside dock, the night watchman soon appeared, a .38 pistol on his hip. "What're you doing here?" asked the watchman, who then heard Donald's story, the need of the woman back

on Harkers Island. They went inside, and the watchman wound the crank on the wall and then started talking on the first telephone Donald had ever laid eyes on.

"The doctor'll be here soon," the watchman hung up and said.

Presently here came the doctor, wearing a long overcoat, with his bag. He walked down to the fish house dock with the nine-year-old sailor and said to Donald, "Where are we going?"

"Harkers Island," said the boy.

The doctor climbed into the sailing skiff, asking nothing more.

All the way back, all in the dark.

The mother in labor lived.

"Plenty of light," Donald would recall. "You had the stars—any boy on Harkers Island could've done it."

Donald Willis made his maritime career in the U.S. Coast Guard.

One day during World War II the chief called his men together and asked them, "Who knows how to fish? Net fish?"

And Donald raised his hand.

"OK," said the chief. "You're a deaf-mute, and you're going to France."

In France, Donald Willis worked with the

French Resistance, indeed feigning as a deaf-mute on fishing boats off the French coast in the face of Nazi patrols, taking soundings with a lead line, triangulating with church steeples, making faint pencil notes on the blade of an oar, and then, when pulling up alongside another fishing boat, holding that oar out and using it to get in close, effectively handing that oar to one of its men, who would file with the Resistance this crucial look-of-shore-from-sea information, Donald getting an imperceptibly different oar in return, one with its blade sanded—a clean slate, as it were—ready for more key nautical inscriptions.

This was March 1944, before D-Day that June.

When June 6 came, Donald Willis piloted a landing craft, which, after putting one company of soldiers on the Normandy shore, as he turned back for his ship took cannon fire astern, leaving

President George H. W. Bush, Donald Willis, and Tom Earnhardt, Harkers Island, November 1997

the boat dead in the water. He spotted, nearby, a Huggins craft with its pilot shot dead and fallen over the wheel, so he swam to *that* craft, set the dead mariner down upon the deck, and piloted on back to his ship and began taking more soldiers ashore.

Decades later, when former president George H. W. Bush was in Tom's cottage after a day of fishing with Tom around Harkers Island, the Drain, and Core Sound, the president said "Of course" when Tom asked if he might invite Donald Willis over. These two old World War II veterans sat up on Tom's upper deck by themselves, looking out on all that water, the great marshes in long sunset light, Cape Lookout Light miles distant, and had a tearful reunion.

"Held up dinner," Tom said, "and no one minded at all."

TOWN CREEK AND BONEHENGE

With a stiff southwest July breeze smacking our small crafts' port quarters, we kayaked from Homer Smith's docks in Beaufort, the nets and trawl doors of the shrimpers *Miss Kayla* and *Capt JP* high over the waters of the Town Creek cove, on toward the upper creek itself, under and past the new bridge, which had knocked out a considerable length of the old causeway and

allowed the waters to flow more easily up into the stream's extensive marsh during flood tide.

This was Saturday, the ides of July.

We floated up a long straight stretch to a stand of pines, then paddled around to the left, spooking egrets, being passed by a chattering kingfisher, a great blue heron, and a night heron. Around a couple more bends, breaching the marsh scarcely above the highest grasses, lay an impressive stretch of massive, aged wooden timbers on low supports, meant for heavy weight, yet clearly having carried nothing for a long, long time.

We were looking, our dear friend Lenore Meadows later told us, at the Town Creek trestle of the Smith Spur, a branch off the Beaufort & Morehead Railroad leading out to what in its time had been the largest commercial fishing operation in North Carolina: Harvey Smith's Fish Meal Company, at the mouth of the Town Creek cove into Gallants Channel. Gallants Point was exactly where a Revolutionary-era saltworks had been: two and a half acres of shops for boatbuilding, for net mending, and for cooking down, *reducing*, oily menhaden to fish meal—a 100-by-250-foot warehouse into which the train came, 600–700 men working ten to eighteen pogey boats with their high spotting towers to go out and find the huge schools and purse seine big catches together by hand, chanteymen singing songs like "Farewell, My Juliana," all the while pulling nets and pouring their songs all over the sea. Though there were other fish factories—such as the plant on Phillips Island in the Newport River where the old redbrick chimney still stands tall and the Wheatleys' Beaufort Fisheries, the last holdout, on Taylor's Creek—none was larger than that of Harvey Smith, whose name rests memorially on the North Carolina Maritime Museum's boatbuilding shop on Taylor's Creek.

This town, as the epicenter of menhaden fishing on the eastern seaboard, was so well known and

ISLAND TIME

this gorgeous grassy space, and the breeze and summer heat back in here sculpted a languorous seclusion, of which we took full, slow advantage.

When I first met lean, mustached Keith Rittmaster, he was running back and forth to the decommissioned Cape Lookout Coast Guard Station with a couple of rough-and-ready volunteers, Bruce McCutcheon and Carl Spangler. Together these men were keeping the old outpost going in good green form, with a small Bergey wind turbine, some solar panels, and banks of batteries inside, all so that students in Scott Taylor's weekend photography workshops and the like could camp out and, thanks to Keith's maritime shepherding of the Cape Lookout Studies Program, have powerful, isolated times out at the cape.

This expansive, energetic man turned out to be an expert in all manner of whales and bottlenose dolphins, and he knew a great number of dolphins personally, given his decades of photographing them individually when they came out of the water, their movements over time being noted and logged. He had assembled a now-legendary collection of images, by which most dolphins working and playing in North Carolina waters could be identified by matching up patterns, shapes, and notches in their dorsal fins.

Keith's wife, Dr. Vicky Thayer, was an expert in marine mammal necropsies, and Keith followed her work with on-site burials on the beaches where the sea creatures had washed up dead, or washed up and died, and much later did exhumations in order to advance scientific study and to recover their bones. When he, McCutcheon, and Spangler got deeply into the total assemblage of a thirty-three-and-a-half-foot sperm whale skeleton, which took three years and finally went on display at Beaufort's flagship branch of the North Carolina Maritime Museum, their effort and their makeshift pole barn acquired the nickname Bonehenge. And when in 2018 a

of such import that the late county commissioner, fisherman, and ebullient Down Easter Jonathan Robinson once remarked: "Beaufort was the Constantinople of the menhaden industry!"

Much water now filled these upper marshes, no longer shaken by the great trains that bore such wealth out into the world, surrounded now by the scarcely visible town and the old, long-closed Beaufort school, where the young Seadogs once studied and played. Our slender blue and yellow boats slid and needled around and through

two-story building went up—near Town Creek and adjacent to the museum's docks and site in the shadow of the new Gallants Channel Bridge—to house a marine-mammal workspace, laboratory, and library, Bonehenge was its name and Keith Rittmaster its founding director.

I visited Keith on August 1, 2018, at his tan double-wide trailer at the Bonehenge site, and he gave me a quick, highly kinetic tour of his trailer lab, full of dolphin skulls, one whole dolphin skeleton, a whole whale skeleton in pieces, and mammalian remains that went out and came back and circulated on loan to museums, including the Smithsonian.

The ear of an unborn fetal dolphin appeared in Keith's hand, and he compared it to the ear of a mature dolphin found near Adams Creek. This showed just how important the sense of *hearing* really was to our maritime cousins, the fact that the ear of the unborn was already almost three-quarters the size of the mature one, though all the rest of the fetus was proportionally smaller—a dolphin's ear, Keith said, was almost fully developed near the time of its birth.

He started pulling teeth from a drawer, one from a whale taken by a Scottish ship decades ago and given to Keith by a former Beaufort mayor's wife, whose brother worked on that ship. He grasped another whale's tooth, which he had made a mold of and then cast whale-tooth bottle openers to give out as swag for donors to Bonehenge.

Then we toured the Bonehenge building itself, fifty-five by thirty-four feet, all dried in, ready for insulation, walls, wiring, and lighting. A little library beneath the stairs had already been named Ishmael's Corner, after the first character and third word in Melville's *Moby-Dick*. "We made the steps wider," Keith said, "thus more inviting," and up we two went to an all-around-the-room gallery, from which future visitors could view all angles of the work going on below.

Returning with Ann two years later, I found

the room full of skeletons, both articulated and in process; of whale mandibles; of a rib cage and set of vertebrae of a pilot whale that ethnomusicologist Paul Berliner of Duke had tripped over and recovered from the beach at Wellfleet and then made a piece of his career playing music on those very bones; and of the entire, unassembled skeleton of a three-year-old humpback whale, dead from a ship strike, named Pitfall.

The upper area had been designed and constructed open enough, Keith said, to hang a complete whale skeleton with its flippers out— for Pitfall.

"They *never* have their flippers up against their sides," Keith said, finally drawing a breath and adding, "North Carolina has more variety of whales than anywhere else on the East Coast put together. . . ."

"This," he said with a wise enthusiasm, "is important for North Carolinians to know!"

SUNNY'S GARDEN

Not 200 yards from the waters of Beaufort Roads, Sunny Newton's garden wraps like an *L* around her two-story home, a white building with a narrow second-story porch and dark shutters, one of three side-by-side Italianate homes built in the late 1850s by one Benjamin Leecraft. Union officers occupied the home during the Civil War, and Sunny will show you the axe marks in the floor of the dining room, where they chopped stovewood down to size and stored it—*inside*.

The garden itself is set off from the street by a short hedge, and Sunny has it organized into various "rooms," which she has planted over the generation or more since her three children—two boys and one girl—came of age and, after wearing the yard bare during their long career of vigorous play, launched themselves into the world.

Once, her next-door neighbor asked Sunny to cut down a small tree in her garden.

"But why?" Sunny asked.

Star at center of Sunny's Garden, Beaufort   *Garden path with English chimney pots*

"It's blocking my view of the street," the neighbor lady replied.

"I should cut down one of my lovely trees so you can watch cars go by?" Sunny answered. She did not accede to the request.

Sunny Newton, as real and right as rain, was an English teacher for the ages, having spent her career teaching mostly in Carteret County. Ann very well remembers the middle school trip she and her classmates took, with Sunny leading it, to England—and to the home of William Shakespeare, where Ann bought a two-by-three-inch miniature book of sonnets she still has. And I remember the first night I met this enchanted woman, when she addressed a reunion of Ann's high school class at the Maritime Museum, calling each of them by name, telling tales about their time in her classes twenty-odd years earlier.

Her late husband John Newton led the team that found the long-lost Civil War ironclad *Monitor*, sunk while being towed in a New Year's Eve 1862 storm off Cape Hatteras. Her sixteen-year-old daughter, Cathryn, who was part of that team, would become a noted paleoecologist and ocean scientist. One of her sons, Jeff, would be named a top North Carolina trial lawyer, and the other, Rett, would captain fighter jets in his Air Force career and later serve as mayor of Beaufort.

And Sunny would step by step build her garden, from which she, as kind and soft-spoken as could be, would offer care and quiet wisdom to anyone who stopped by and looked in or who found her at her other post, the herb-and-flower garden festooning the North Carolina Maritime Museum's borders on Front Street. As she sat near the black-eyed Susans in a neighbor's garden one summer day, I asked her about my making another visit to her own, and she said, giving me way too much credit for my purview and powers: "Of course, of course. Now, could you *please* do *something* about this *humidity*?!"

While walking with her one October morning, Sunny declared, "I want my garden to entertain me—I want something blooming all the time!" And she also acknowledged with a knowing smile, "I've made this a demanding garden."

Here were some miniature pomegranates—"I *love* pomegranates!" Sunny exclaimed, adding that she had used the fruit in classes to show students the beauty and surprise of the difference between the surface and below the surface, once sliced. "See how it grows from the flower," she said. "It blooms all summer."

She pointed to an elongated *S* of brick path, "a portion of a labyrinth," in the curl at both top and bottom English chimney pots she found while living in Norfolk, Virginia. Then to an eight-pointed star in the midst of her garden's rectangular brick-bordered "rooms," where some Beverly Sills pink iris and, in the middle, a Chinese fringe tree grew, and to a now-forty-foot-tall magnolia which she planted in 1964 and which had served as a base when her children played ball in this side yard and wore it bare. Much more recently, her granddaughter Megan, having been proposed to in the garden, climbed high in this magnolia on her wedding day.

The magnolia also serves as the southeast corner of a patio, entered beneath a cedar arch, two other corners being a pecan tree, beneath which sits a Buddha in an attitude of repose and pensive greeting ("I am a want-to-be Buddhist," Sunny said), and a tall cedar tree. In this spot of peace and equanimity, Sunny often sits late of an afternoon, listening to water burbling from a dark copper canister—"part of an old whiskey still I bought at a yard sale."

Out strolling early one summer morning, we turned the corner onto Front Street and here came Sunny in her gardening clothes (an old madras checkered blouse, a round double-roll-brim straw hat: she called them "my colonial costume"), carrying a bag of weeds and trimmings from the garden plots she created and tended for years at the Maritime Museum. She held out a pair of Queen Anne's lace flowers to Ann and told us how, when she was a child, her mother used to put such flowers in food coloring and dye them for her.

"They were so pretty, red, blue—you see, the magic began *early* for me."

PECANS

Not far from the river, just south of Elizabeth City, a large grove of pecan trees once grew, and cattle grazed lazily there. I never ventured into it, only rode past it on my bicycle, stopping whenever I was out that way (some miles from our home near Horner's Sawmill) just to regard the blithe, benign way the modestly spaced pecan tree leaves distributed light to the forested pasture below, the cattle chewing at leisure in their dappled light.

No other large trees growing so closely together, except beeches perhaps, let so much light through their branches and crowns and still maintained shade: a *bright* shade, if you will. Just east of town, across the Camden Causeway on the old Sawyer plantation, stood another such grove, which we passed often, on our way to see our Ferebee cousins in Camden and on our way to the Outer Banks.

At the age of eight, I had not yet fully formed my thoughts about the nature of pecan trees and the properties of sunlight shining upon and through them. That would come much later, when I started rambling around eastern Carolina in my twenties and noticing how many farmsteads, large and small, had pecan groves off to the side—two acres, maybe, or twenty—of the main house or had the main house standing within them. Sometimes only the old groves still stood, the homestead itself long gone.

Here in Beaufort, at our family's house on Orange Street in sight of Taylor's Creek and only a couple miles from the widening inlet to the sea, five pecan trees held down the fort—two small ones out by the street, three large ones in the backyard. Summer evenings we sat under them and listened as ocean breezes and winds blew through them, sometimes mildly, sometimes vigorously with the full authority of Neptune's Atlantic. They made a fresh, brushing sound that

rose and fell, and the little postage stamp of a yard seemed enclosed by the sound as much as by the bodies and branches of the big pecan trees themselves, and I loved the way the southerly breezes of summer soughed through their feathery leaves at night with the softest shushing, insistent, though, like all the sighs of the world.

There was a long view out from under one of them, and through it one's eye was drawn to a pair of massive pecan trees, lovely twin sisters seventy-five yards to our north, whose crowns danced and swayed in the summertime almost with abandon, showing me in their dancing the inlet winds, the winds that have come here unabridged and uninterrupted and unimpeded all the way from the wide Sargasso Sea. How often and how long I stared and wondered: a cleft in the high, billowing

crown of one of those two pecan trees might just be a portal to another world.

So it was (till one fateful night here in Beaufort, when Hurricane Florence felled one of the sisters) that the two dancing pecan trees who were there for so many years swayed, presenting hypnotic delight and delight only, and the hands of the Great Choreographer who directed it all were at play, at play, at play.

ROOKERY

One July evening along about seven thirty, our great friends Belinda and Michael McFee, Ann, and I were all sitting in a seventeen-foot bateau, anchored in four feet of water, high tide in a 100-foot-wide channel curving through the middle of a great marsh near Beaufort, the ceiling broken with gray and black clouds, a few shafts of sunlight now and again falling in the distance. The light kept shifting as the broad, gray clouds moved over us, dropping down and at one point shining up the distant semiglobes and cranes of the state port with cool sunlight. Everywhere, the endless light-green marsh grass stood out brilliantly in the gloaming.

We had been brought to this extraordinary spot at dusk by an equally extraordinary person, award-winning Smyrna biologist-teacher Miriam Sutton, a native Kinstonian whose family had had a cottage on the Neuse River's Minnesott Beach when she and her longtime-fishing-partner brother were growing up: "That's where we learned fishing, boating, all that mess!"

Miriam—a very fit, ever-smiling, sandy-haired recent retiree—had once taught in Asheville for a spell, saying of that time, "I said I needed an ocean up there. Gave 'em eight years, that was *long enough*." She moved back east in the mid-1990s, got a kayak as soon as she returned, and "started exploring—that's what I came back for!" By now, she has been floating these waters in small craft for nearly twenty-five years—a thoroughly skillful boater, she put out a second anchor when a breeze started to push us around, keeping us oriented to the northeast, our eyes on the prize.

To wit: a hammock, an oblong live-oak-and-myrtle islet perhaps 100 yards long and twenty to twenty-five feet high, a small significant spot in great marshes we have gone around one side or the other for many years, yet never gone in. The hammock lay there, an intense deep green, with the broader light green of the marsh grasses stretching out around it forever.

Yet the hammock was getting whiter by the moment, for this was a serious rookery, and more birds kept streaming in as the evening moved swiftly from twilight toward dusky dark and as storm clouds to our south lay rain out over the ocean. By fives, tens, fifteens came the white ibises, the mature birds with black wing tips, the immatures without, all as if led by their long thin downcurved bills right to this very place.

Egrets aplenty greeted them, a couple of big, brown immature night herons too, one great blue heron.

And one roseate spoonbill.

Rarity of rarities for North Carolina.

Soon afterward, David Cecelski told us that he almost always saw a dozen, maybe fifteen, ibises fishing back in Morton's Millpond on the west side of upper Clubfoot Creek in Harlowe miles away. "When they're done, they head off to the southeast—do you think they could be going to the rookery you saw? Or is that too far?"

Not too far at all. Walker Golder, the great colonial water-bird authority who helped establish Audubon's sanctuary system in our many coastal waters, once tracked by plane mature ibises going from Battery Island off Southport all the way to Lake Waccamaw just to fish for their young back in those Cape Fear River nests, a flight distance of *forty* miles each way!

And here this night near Beaufort, just before the rain found us and sent us back into port, all the while the ibises kept on flying in, some just above the water, some suddenly lifting above it to five and even ten feet, Miriam observing this and saying wisely: "Because of us."

CODDS CREEK

Only once had I been out to Codds Creek before, one August many years ago with Down Easters Lida Pigott of Gloucester and Capt. Dennis Chadwick of Straits, to lay out a mullet net and see how we might do. Dennis had played the net out, then bade me get into the shallow water just out from the marshes near Codds, broiling hot from sitting there in the sun and soaking up heat all day. I felt like a scalded dog with nowhere to run.

We did catch us some mullet, though.

This years-later summer afternoon, slender, bearded, Hatteras-raised Dr. Bill Garlick piloted his May-Craft into the winding coastal creek, following a line of white PVC pipes all the way to a dock and plank walk leading seaward. "Some boys from Marshallberg came out and built this one weekend about twenty years ago," said Bill. The dock, which Hurricane Dorian would later do in, then ran about 120 feet or more over shallows and marsh up to the sand and scrub of twenty-mile-long South Core Banks. A pair of ibises was stalking, hunting, fishing in the extreme shallows off to the dock's side.

Once we stepped onto the land—Bill, mountain Christmas tree farmer Mike Pitman, and I—we had only 500 feet left to the dune line, so our walk from the boat to the Atlantic Ocean took us no more than five minutes—scarcely a tenth of a mile from soundside creek to high-tide line, then nothing in either direction for miles up and down the beach, only the flashing beacon of Cape Lookout Lighthouse seen through a smoky haze.

As we slowly boated back out of Codds, knowing I would return as soon as possible to this special spot, I lined up a distant radio tower and a very bright roof along the Marshallberg shore north of Bill's place, my key, my way to come in south of the mile-long pound-net stakes, and

THIS WET AND WATER-LOVING LAND

thereby find the line of pipes—and the creek's mouth.

August a year later, I brought Ann out to Codds Creek.

We had more water this time (I had timed our crossing from Bill's place to the creek for maximum depth by averaging Drum Inlet's and Cape Lookout's high-tide times), and we had a slightly shallower draft boat: our fourteen-foot Whaler. So we eased on in and made our way slowly up to the creekside dock, tied up, and walked the long, undulating wooden path to the sand and the scrub.

And to all the wildflowers growing there: red-and-yellow gaillardia; bright, gleaming, green pennywort leaves big as doubloons; marsh grasses stretching off as far as one could see; and tiny light-yellow and light-purple five-petaled flowers … a big glorious soundside bouquet.

On the seabeach the tides had cut a long, even, one-foot shelf of sand halfway between surf and dunes, and we sat down upon it and took off our shoes. Ann in her white hat went spinning and almost dancing in the surf, holding the hem of her light-blue shirt out like wings, the late afternoon sun diamonding the shallows all about her, and the Gulf Stream summertime clouds all piled up in a line many miles out beyond this lovely woman at such ease along the seaside.

The ocean face of the sand shelf, in shadow now, was a long, charcoal-dark ribbon stretching away toward some Core Banks vanishing point, challenged by the curving lines of white surf every inch of the way, while all manner of small shells— white, tan, brown, black—lay together upon the shelf's face in a wild, variegated mosaic. A joyful, rife-with-romance beach, simply wide open for it . . .

Back at the boat, Ann sat on a dock step, smiling, holding the bowline as I started the engine, the marshy shallows all green behind her, her sea-wet shorts sticking to her legs. In half an hour we were across Core Sound at Bill's dock again, and I stood staring back out over the watery miles we had just covered and wondered for a few moments.

What makes us head so quickly to the sea? We had been out upon an inland sea, the sound, and yet we were so easily and rapidly drawn to its marge and then on beyond it, across that pinch of land to the edge of the *real* sea. The greatest force on earth moved and rolled before us, Swinburne's "mother and lover of men, the Sea"—did we think we had stepped lightly across the hot sands to stand in awe once more and take *her* measure, or had we always known deep down that we were pulled there by the Sea herself, so that she could take our own?

East by Southeast

HOLT'S POND

One glances at Holt's Pond when crossing it near Princeton, just beyond the old stockyards on US 70, our great boulevard through the bean, corn, and cotton fields of Carolina's central east that loosely follows the valley of the Neuse River, and sees that some oddly out-of-place Italianate houses have been dropped onto the pond's formerly wooded shores in recent years.

Change has been afoot here in Shelby Stephenson country, where our great friend and former North Carolina poet laureate, author of *Plankhouse* and *The Persimmon Tree Carol* and much more, has long remarked of houses sprouting where fields of corn once grew.

The wide-swinging US 70 bypass, far to the north of Goldsboro, helped send Wilber's Barbecue, for decades the home of most excellent holy-smoked pig on the town's east side, into the mists. Its packed parking lot with the split-wood piles out back and the fighter jets from Seymour Johnson Air Force Base screaming overhead became only memories to generations of Carolinians who had long marked their coastal-plain, seaward travels with stops at Wilber's. Our lamentations were large, till enterprising Goldsborian businessfolk, banded together as Goldpit, stepped in and reopened the chopped-pork epicenter in midsummer 2020 to sincere applause.

Farther east, folks stopping in Kinston, picking up beer or soda or Nabs or pimiento-cheese sandwiches along with new camo clothes and ghost line and sinkers and lures at the Neuse Sport Shop, that prime eastern emporium, might also be looking for the Mother Earth brewery or the sly, animated public-television host Vivian Howard's Chef and the Farmer downtown.

If they could get downtown on a given day.

For there were new times now when the Neuse River came out of its banks, times that would surprise even those who lived with it and were used to hurricanes passing over the Carolina east and driving the Neuse to overflow, such as Matthew in 2016, which crested fourteen feet above flood level, and Florence in 2018, twelve feet above flood level, both cutting US 70 and the south side off from downtown Kinston. Yet before either of those storms, a huge spring thunderstorm in Raleigh had also pushed the Neuse to flood, sending the mayor out into the streets, almost shouting at reporters: "*This* is not a hurricane, it's just a big rainstorm up in Raleigh! We need help! We need help!"

Kinstonians were not ready for Durham's and Raleigh's ever-increasing storm runoff to put them into the drink any more than New Bernians were ready for it or for Hurricane Florence to fill both the Neuse and Trent River basins in September 2018 and flood them out like nobody's business and like nobody's memory either. Historic New Bern—town of legendary jurist William Gaston and of Tryon Palace and of a great Union Civil War victory and just as great a freedmen's gathering after that—suffered historic deluge and inundation and ruin, as did Lumberton far to its southwest in that same storm.

As did so many communities in between.

The Carolina east was now caught between rising sea level in the sound country waters and stepped-up runoff, in both volume and rapidity, from the Triangle.

Much of our coastal plain—not only its small towns and farm communities but also its myriad low-lying hog farms, its chemical, superfund, and coal-ash sites—now lay in the jaws of a closing vise.

I remember a cold, misty, early-spring morning years ago, when the water stayed in its rightful place at Holt's Pond, Jake Mills and I pitching the jonboat up into the bed of my old blue-and-white Chevy pickup and heading down there. "Holt's Pond is full of fish," Jake said, having fished there before and done well. "Very little pressure on it, we'll come back loaded with bream and bass."

So I was convinced. We were bound to bring home a cooler full.

We first stopped at a short-order fish diner in Smithfield, near the dip under the train trestle downtown that often flooded, and got enormous fish sandwiches, big flounder filets as much sticking out on either side as was within the bun, and these generous rations we took with us and ate, still warm, parked out by Holt's Pond in the late morning damp.

On the water we tried beetle spins, we tried rubber worms, we even tried Rebels—though Jake admitted to a long-standing troubled relationship with Rebels, owing to his once yanking one that was stuck on a willow bush off it, and, as he told it, the double-bow action of his rod and that willow bush propelled the Rebel at him, its treble hooks catching and lodging in his right cheek and right earlobe, occasioning a visit to the nearest emergency room, where the doctor enlarged each hole where the barbs had gone in with a novacained stylus, then wrapped dental floss around the stems of the hooks and neatly pulled them right out.

When Jake surprised the doctor with a University of North Carolina health insurance card and reported that he taught at Chapel Hill, the doctor said derisively, "*You?!* What do you teach?" and when Jake told him, the doctor went off in gales of laughter over "English!?!?" then caught himself and with ridicule said: "Did you quote any *Shakespeare* when that lure got hold of

your head?" to which Jake replied: "Yessir, I did," remembering what Romeo says when he first sees Juliet at the ball. "See how she hangs on the cheek of night, like a rich jewel in an Ethiope's ear."

Jake said the doctor looked like he'd been hit with a ton of fertilizer.

So we tried most all the lures in Jake's well-appointed tackle box, but nothing did the trick. We slowly worked the entire shoreline of Holt's Pond from the dam on up under the bridge and into the short, young drowned cypresses at the upper end, an almost spectral scene, every one of trees in the water covered with heavily misted spider webs, which the gray light lit up like silver from Taxco.

By the time we pulled the jonboat back out at the dam that afternoon, those two outsize flounder sandwiches from the diner by the tracks back in town proved to be the only fish we had caught on that gorgeous gray, early-March day down at Holt's Pond.

But that was all right, too.

That was just fine.

LAND OF FIFTY SWAMPS
Land of the Lumbee

Though one sees flat land everywhere in Robeson County, the land does not see, or know, itself that way.

With hill-country rapidity, the dark Lumber River passes just above Wagram, home of John Charles McNeill, the turn-of-the-twentieth-century poet who called the Lumber "a tortuous, delicious flirt."

This sinuous river courses through Wagram at 266 feet above sea level, down through Pembroke at 171 feet, Lumberton at 131 feet, and Fair Bluff at sixty-six feet—an average drop of about four feet per mile over fifty miles, which is why folks advise canoeists and kayakers on this black river to figure for every *one* minute of floating downstream, allow at least *two* minutes for coming back up.

Not for nothing is Robeson—our state's largest county bar none, the Lumber River flowing through its midst—known for its waters: this one county holds within its big borders fifty *named* swamps. One need only look upon the wonders (and mixed blessings) of all these wetlands in the service of the swift-flowing Lumber and Pee Dee drainage and marvel that the river and its county have not flooded even more often than they have, as they did, grievously so, during both the 2016 and 2018 hurricanes. Native Lumbertonian and beloved author Jill McCorkle and her husband Tom Rankin, the celebrated photographer, heard only the first word of Hurricane Matthew's flooding out the Lumber, then packed their pickup with bottled water and raced to Robeson, knowing the need before it was ever spoken. As hard-hit home folks came to say as in mantra, it was "Matthew and Florence and now Michael," with the Lumber River becoming "an invasive threat" and Lumberton "a town in constant recovery," in the words of the *Washington Post*.

The roll of wet places: Aaron Swamp, Ashpole Swamp, Bear Swamp, Bluff, Burnt, Contrary, Coward, Flat, Flowers, Gum, Hog, Horse, Jacob, Little Bluff, Little Hog, Mill, Moss Neck, Old Field, Peters, Raft, *two* distinct River Swamps, Saddletree, Thorofare, and White Oak—the rest of the swamps here being ovoid pocosins called bays: *two* Big Bays, Blounts, Butler, Buzzard, three Cypress Bays, Gabriel, Green Bay, Gully, Howard, Jacob, Juniper, Little Juniper, Mill, *two* Panther Bays, Pigeon Bay, Pinks Bay, Rafe, Sewell, Shanty, Shelly, Tupelo, and Warwick Mill Bay.

With a few branches and ponds also figuring into the mix.

Especially Waterhole Swamp, formerly Campbell's Mill, Scuffletown, and now Pembroke town: epicenter of the Lumbee Indians.

This largest tribe of first peoples in North Carolina have found themselves misnamed and *re*named—they have been called the Roanoke, the Croatan, the Cherokee Indians of Robeson County, the Siouan Indians of the Lumber River—yet only *Lumbee* comes forth from the Lumbees themselves, is *their* name, is who they *are*.

And they were mistreated and conscripted—or rather, *kidnapped*—during the Civil War by the Confederacy's Home Guard, Lumbee men forced to leave their Robeson swamps and families and go off to the seacoast and build the huge fort named Fisher with its two-mile-range cannon that would keep Wilmington open after all other southern ports had fallen to the Union by mid-1863 and thereby sustain and prop up the Confederacy for over a year and a half after the simultaneous battles of Vicksburg and Gettysburg, till the doomed Rebel turf shrank to two patches of surrender, Appomattox Courthouse in southern Virginia and Bennett Place on the west side of Durham in North Carolina.

The Lumbee were no friends to the Southern faux nation and the slaveocracy it aimed to perpetuate, and their war with those forces, declared and led by the famed outlaw Henry Berry Lowry (after he witnessed the deep-woods Home Guard murders of his father and brother, who were forced to dig their own graves just before their executions and to then stand at them, awaiting the bullets that would drop them into these shallow gashes), lasted into the 1870s, far longer than the Civil War itself.

In 1887, the Lumbees got an academy from the state of North Carolina, Croatan Normal School, which grew into Pembroke State College for Indians and, in 1972, became UNC Pembroke, an honored part of the University of North

Carolina system. With a population of nearly 60,000, North Carolina's largest tribal nation still needed to gain one more all-important item, which it rightly deserved and always had: Federal recognition.

"Yes, I'm proud to be a Lumbee Indian, yes I am," went the late Willie French Lowery's 1975 anthem, "Proud to Be a Lumbee," continuing:

> When I grow up into this world
> I'm gonna be just what I am.
> My mother and father are proud of me,
> They want me to be free.
> Free to be
> Anything I want to be.

Four times in that verse did lyricist Lowery employ the infinitive *to be*, also the first words of our state's motto, To Be, Rather Than to Seem, and his uplifting use of it rings true every time. The eloquent, gracious author and UNC leading light Malinda Maynor Lowery, widow of Willie Lowery, who has chronicled her people, their history, and their purposefulness in such fine detail and spirit, said it best when she declared clearly and succinctly in her recent testament *The Lumbee Indians*: "Having existed as a coherent society for nearly 300 years along the Lumber River, we will not forsake this place."

One Christmastime Near Panther Branch

Into a ten-degree night, snowing and sleeting, the southbound Atlantic Coast Line passenger train to Florida pulled out of Rennert in Robeson County shortly before midnight, December 16, 1943. A few minutes later, most of the way between Raft Swamp and Panther Branch, a rail that had cracked from the intense cold pitched the last couple of cars off and over onto the northbound tracks, and crewmen rushed to evacuate the passengers.

Miraculously, almost no one was hurt.

In this lonely place they built fires to stay warm and to alert any trains approaching from behind or before them of the wreck. The conductor dispatched a brakeman to get down the tracks with flares to warn an imminent northbound express. The ground was frozen, the crossties and rails covered with ice, and on his way the brakeman slipped and fell and broke his flares and they would no longer work.

At 12:45 A.M. *The Champion*, the Atlantic Coast Line's fast passenger train from Florida, carrying 1,000 people, among them many scores of servicemen headed home for Christmas, emerged from Panther Branch of Richland Swamp northbound at eighty-five miles an hour. Only 1,000 feet out, *The Champion*'s engineer Frank Belknap saw the fires and the wreck ahead and applied his emergency brakes even as he was blinded by the headlights of the derailed locomotive, but he could not stop—his train plowed into the empty cars on his tracks from the first wreck, his locomotive cutting through them, going off the rails, and gouging out a 600-foot path before it stopped, while the cars behind him jackknifed and accordioned and in one single car crushed forty-seven servicemen.

Slowly, in the dark, in the worst winter weather the Carolinas ever had, the dead and the dying and the injured were rescued, often by servicemen who had been spared. The Red Cross came, as did military men and women from nearby Fort Bragg beside Fayetteville, and a field hospital went up. The wounded overflowed Baker Sanatorium, a tiny one-doctor hospital in close-by Lumberton. At first light, the two ruined trains sprawled upon and beside the north-south rails, and wrapped-up Christmas gifts and broken toys lay scattered about in the dirt, too.

Yes, there was a war on, and America was just about midway through it. The worst train wreck in the history of southeastern America had just occurred here, between Rennert and Buie, between Raft Swamp and Panther Branch, and

it would take the coroner and the medics and the Red Cross folks, all of them, a whole week to identify every last one of the seventy-some dead, and they would not finish up till Christmas Eve.

The Wood Storks of Warwick Mill Bay

A short distance from the Lumber River below Lumberton lies an enormous Carolina wetland named Warwick Mill Bay, an oval nearly two miles long on its southeast-to-northwest axis, on its eastern end a white-sand rim and a slender curve of open swamp paralleling it. Though one could not see into the swamp through the brushy woods beside Old Whiteville Road, running along the top of the bay, the rich refuge is there nonetheless: a healthy pocosin where 1,000-pound alligators share the bay's damp and drowned arena with 250 pairs of nesting wood storks, the largest nesting colony in southeastern North Carolina, having adopted this bay only in the past twenty years after a hurricane knocked out the milldam and lowered the water level in the bay.

In December 2016, an alliance of some of North Carolina's best natural habitat protectors—the Conservation Fund, Audubon North Carolina, North Carolina State Parks, and others, including the noted environmentalists Fred and Alice Stanback—put together $1.3 million and saved nearly 1,000 acres of Warwick Mill, one of our last remaining large and intact Carolina bays, an absolute water-bird paradise supporting all those wood storks and hundreds more pairs of ibises, egrets, and herons and even a few rare-in-our-state anhingas. Each spring, neotropical warblers fill the pocosin.

"The size and diversity of Warwick Mill Bay makes it important alone," said Walker Golder, long Audubon North Carolina's coastal water-bird expert and now leader of the North Carolina Coastal Land Trust. "Warwick Mill Bay is one of North Carolina's great natural treasures."

Tom Earnhardt enthusiastically agreed,

THIS WET AND WATER-LOVING LAND

remarking on the bay's cypresses, their "bent limbs just from the nests, ten to fifteen stork nests in the same tree, plus other nests, great egrets', anhingas', yellow cattle egrets'. Every available crack and notch and flat space has a nest. How much does a wood stork chick eat? Answer: 440 pounds of protein to raise a brood of three or four chicks—fish, crayfish, a few snakes thrown in, insects." And he laughed about the huge alligators and what he called "their protection racket— they keep down egg predators like snakes and raccoons."

P. R. Barker, the patriarch who protected this wild kingdom within Gallberry Farms all his life, while tilling its surrounds, proudly told Tom Earnhardt a few years back:

"I've been over it with a mule, been over it with a tractor. My bootheels have touched down on every bit of this land."

Would that there were world enough and time to do likewise, to touch all the sandy soil, to paddle every prong, to ramble all of wild wet Robeson as these our forebears have. I bless every moment that I have had a chance to try, as my father long ago showed me how.

I have learned and come to love this river at many places along its curving flirtatious way: Ann and I worked our white canoe through the flooded trees way upriver toward its headwaters, Drowning Creek and Naked Creek, when the bright white flowers were all out on Carolina bay trees yearning for spring in the air, and years later, I paddled alone in the cypress shadows near

64

Turnpike Road over the Lumber River where part of Sherman's army crossed,
March 1865, border of Hoke and Scotland Counties

the Turnpike, where Sherman's soldiers crossed
the Lumber, northbound in the torrential rains
in March 1865, as they inexorably wrote the last
scenes of the Civil War.

Ann and I have stridden slowly about the little
river-fed watercourses on the lawn at McLean
Castle, the faux log cabin fashioned from striated
cement that Margaret French McLean, late
governor Angus McLean's widow, built in the late
1930s just above Lumberton. In a kayak, I spent
a fine hot summer day exploring the river right
in town, on a long reach between the Fifth Street
bridge and the raucous old nineteenth-century

traders' and mule skinners' seasonal camp, Mud
Town. And I put the bow of the kayak head on
into the slow-moving yet powerful vortex of
Griffin's Whirl, felt its hold, and was turned by it
in a bend way downriver at Princess Ann. On the
dark water at sunset in Fair Bluff, I have glided
past catfishermen and late-day streamside walkers
and been blessed by their waves and their smiles,
feeling once more the friendliness of river people.

Should you ever float it, anywhere along its
slender length, pray remember: its name is
Lumber but its earlier, more lyrical name was
Lumbee, owing to the people, according to

the poet McNeill, and his nickname for it was Sweetheart Stream, a river pulling its beautiful, abundant black water from all over Robeson, from the bays and bogs and branches that lie and rise and fall all over this land of fifty swamps.

And pray, remember too, my fellow boaters: *One minute down, two minutes back up.*

HOLLY SHELTER

Northeast of Burgaw, southwest of Maple Hill: We were away about ten o'clock one late June morning, my great friend Scott Taylor and I, bound upstream in the jonboat on dark Shelter Creek, the major drainage in the upper 50,000-acre Holly Shelter pocosin. We were looking to see what Hurricane Florence, which had torn up eastern Carolina so badly from New Bern and Pollocksville to Pembroke and beyond just the autumn before (2018), might have done here in Holly Shelter.

A thick breezeless heat lay upon us, and little

was moving in the pines and cypresses and water oaks in the forest, though we spooked blue herons now and again and a few white egrets, and inevitable crows showed up and sounded off. We drove the little boat through many a stretch of shore-to-shore duckweed, a soupy and luxuriant growth, and passed under one tree hanging out over the creek, covered in red trumpet vine, and what a standout that was against all the hot green of the creek.

"Beat up," Scott said, shaking his head.

Many trees were down in the woods along the Shelter Creek shoreline, some fallen into the water, whose level we made to be about two feet below normal.

"*Really* beat up," he kept saying of Florence's storm damage, for pier planks perched up in branches fifteen feet *above* the surface of the creek, and downed trees lay over in confused crisscross every whichaway, and funky little creekside cabins had their screens blown out, some canted over by flood and wind, while up on the bluffs, bigger houses with decks and gazebos had fared a bit better.

Five miles upstream a hawk flew over clutching a field rat, and taking that as an omen, deciding we had had enough of wrack, ruin, and duckweed, we turned the boat around, hoping our track through the green would not have closed behind us already.

Yet it had.

Back at the Shaw Highway dock midafternoon, we were cheered by the fact that our prelaunch, electrical-tape, field-modified fix on the fuel clip had performed admirably.

We had not spilled a drop.

A few miles south, Lodge Road, a long white lane through pines and wire grass, led into the heart of the Holly Shelter pocosin. Scott and I drove slowly between the dry ditches, willows on the banks and fortunes of bay and cattails.

We stopped four and a half miles in, startling more herons and egrets, delighted to find a colony of huge yellow pitcher plants growing on a ditch bank beneath and around a metal footbridge. Scott got right up on them with his lens, calling them "crispy and burnt," while I watched red dragonflies flying and lighting, lighting and flying. I picked some yellow asters and a strand of flowering grass Ann later called "lady's tresses."

The midnineties summer heat felt heavy, palpable there on the white road, and we stared off toward the forest wall miles distant to the east, the road's vanishing point. We drove farther in, walking the last 200 yards to where Ashes Creek, rushing north, had washed out Lodge Road in several places, a testament to just how much water Hurricane Florence had laid down way out in that wilderness and to how much power it had as it flooded on through.

The first washout we encountered was slight, yet each one got bigger, till the last one we reached we figured to be about twenty-four feet

across and blown through almost down to the level of the water of Ashes Creek in the ditches. Here the causeway was a lost cause.

To our south lay immense open land, a waterfowl impoundment, though holding little water now. The forest beyond stood most of a mile away.

The whole huge pocosin *seemed* tabletop flat, yet in looking off toward that forest, Scott and I were really looking uphill, for Holly Shelter sloped down almost of a piece from south to north, from the long fifty-foot-elevation ridge where US 17, the Ocean Highway, ran to the thirty-foot-elevation of Lodge Road here in the middle and on down to Shelter Creek now miles to our north, where the elevations along the morning run we had just made ranged from four to twelve feet. Where Shelter Creek flowed into the Northeast Cape Fear, one noted with respect, the land lay only one foot above sea level.

These were the lowlands low.

When I asked the Wildlife Resources Commission's coastal ecoregion supervisor, Brent Wilson, who had given us his blessing to explore the Lodge Road area, about Ashes Creek and the Hurricane Florence experience, he reported: "This was the second washout of Lodge Road in the last three years. A wildfire event in 2011 during a dry summer with depressed groundwater levels resulted in a lot of organic soil loss due to ignition. Consequently, the affected area soils have reduced water-holding capacity, so runoff impacts from storms are magnified. There was a limited amount of straight-line wind damage, greatest impact was the flooding event."

Scott and I slowly drove back out of this hot wild spot and parted on the east bank of the Northeast Cape Fear, after a good long day together deep in this immensity. Of our largest coastal wildernesses (the chain of refuge that includes the Great Dismal, the Alligator River, Pocosin Lakes, Mattamuskeet, and the Croatan Forest), I had before this day been in all of them

Lodge Road, washed out by Hurricane Florence, Holly Shelter Swamp, Pender County

a good deal, all except Holly Shelter, so with Scott's help this experiential drought was ending.

And all to the good: there was always something truly affecting about being such small creatures in such a vast place, where never an electric lamp was lit at night, even though when we said farewell, we were standing a mere twenty miles from downtown Wilmington.

WILMINGTON, WRIGHTSVILLE BEACH, AND THE BATTLE OF RICH INLET
At the Battleship

Visitors to the Cape Fear riverbank ruins of Brunswick Town and Fort Anderson, the old,

brick, roofless chapel and the huge sandy earthworks, moved swiftly down to the water on October 14, 1962, to gaze in awe at what was passing by: a World War II battleship being slowly towed upriver to the old shipbuilding city of Wilmington. The nickels and dimes of schoolchildren, mine among them, helped bring USS *North Carolina* to its Eagles Island home right across from downtown, though it would take considerably more coinage to repair its rusted, paper-thin hull these days.

Early one Saturday afternoon in the spring of 1990, before Jim Wann and I were to perform at Thalian Hall's gala reopening that evening, Ann and I toured this great ship, which had seen truly meritorious service in the Pacific during the Second World War, in the company of our twins, then five years old. We went deeper and deeper into it, marveling over all the narrow passages and companionways, and I recall a moment in a mess hall, where the soup ladle was big enough that the twins in turn could set it upside down upon their heads like a hat.

Once we resurfaced on the deck and came down the gangplank to the small visitor center, we bought a few sodas and snacks there. We four sat at a picnic table and talked, and Susannah pointed out a small sign and asked me what it said, and I read it aloud: "Please do not feed the alligator."

"What alligator?" she asked, and I told her there was one living in the channel off the river where the ship lay, an unofficial mascot of the place, just a few feet away from where we sat.

"What do they do to you if you feed it?" she asked on.

"Oh, honey," I said gravely. "You remember those dungeons in your books *Creepy Castle* and *Mouldy Manor*?" I went on to remind her of how the tourists to the castle and manor in these cartoonish, comically ghoulish children's books would happen upon shackled skeletons in basement rooms, and I advanced into scenes where people caught feeding the *North Carolina* gator were similarly hauled off at once and taken down to the brig of the battleship and left there for pretty much ever after, verily a *Creepy Castle* fate.

A light breeze came across the visitor center's deck, quickly lifting half a dozen of Susannah's spherical cheese puffs into the air, dropping them onto the deck, and spinning them over it and under the *do not feed* sign and immediately into the alligator's moat. Instantly she screamed: "No, Daddy, no! Don't let them put me in the brig! Please don't let them haul me off and put me in the brig!" She fell to sobbing uncontrollably, more begging for protection, convulsed by fear of the fate I had painted all too well for her.

I was very nearly in tears myself, and I pulled her tightly to me and spoke as quickly as I could: "It's all right, sweetheart—that was just a joke— nobody's going to take you away, it's all right!"

But it was not all right.

Susannah had believed every false word I said, and, though she could hear well my denials, she now had to sob her way through the moment as the only way to reckon with and recover from the hideous power of the vision of abandonment, imprisonment, starvation, and darkness. Bright as the day and the riverine scene were—the beige customhouse, the Coast Guard's cutter, the fine old waterfront over the way—I sat for many minutes holding my dear child, whose powerful upset was entirely my doing, and I was deeply and justly chastened.

On the Waterfront

On a cool December midmorning a few years back, my old friend Philip Gerard—the vigorous

Water Street, Wilmington, along the Cape Fear River

writer, musician, and UNC Wilmington professor—and I strolled the waterfront talking, admiring the small, newly finished craft sitting outside the Cape Fear Community College's boat shop, looking out on the river of which Philip has become the grand chronicler with his *Down the Wild Cape Fear.* We passed the big Coast Guard cutter *Diligence* still, till its 2020 reassignment, at its customhouse dock, where a federal craft named *Diligence* has been stationed almost as long as we have had a republic, and, at the foot of Market Street, we remembered and spoke of the early 1900s ferries—the old *John Knox* and *Menantic*—that worked the Cape Fear River, crossing over from here to the rice and coffee and naval stores warehouses on Eagles Island.

We stayed with the big river on down the boardwalk to the low-slung riverbank restaurants Elijah's and Pilot House, both below a high bluff. It was Philip Gerard's clear-eyed 1994 novel *Cape Fear Rising*, that, like the telltale heart perceived as mystically beating through the floor of Poe's story, helped open the door in the modern moment to the real facts of the 1898 white-supremacist Wilmington coup, in which at least sixty African Americans were murdered in the streets by a well-armed white mob, stoked to a heat by cold-blooded politicians who had scripted it all. In the 1998 truth and reconciliation gatherings, author-editors David Cecelski and Tim Tyson declared in the title of their essay collection that the 1898 coup was nothing less than "Democracy Betrayed." LeRae Umfleet's full account for the North Carolina Office of Archives and History called the event "A Day of Blood" (2009), and David Zucchino's recent landmark Pulitzer-winning reportage *Wilmington's Lie* (2020) laid it all out beat by bloody beat, as if he had been on the streets of the old port town, pen in hand, while that horror played out.

"You wouldn't believe," another old friend, Gerard's colleague and wonderful novelist Clyde Edgerton, said to me later on this same day, "how much 1898 still looms over this town."

Just now, Philip Gerard was deeply concerned by both the Teflon manufacture's GenX chemical wastes—the "forever chemicals" in the dangerous PFAS category coming *down* the river from the DuPont spin-off plant called Chemours near Fayetteville—and the ever-increasing saltwater intrusion coming *up* the Cape Fear like a tongue from the sea.

"Every time they dredge the shipping channel," he said, pointing downstream, "the salt moves farther upriver. We're seeing salt-tolerant plants and the birds that depend on them moving on up." As this great river's tidal flows push and affect watery terrain for another thirty miles or so above Wilmington, the aggressive Atlantic sea-level rise has profound implications for the whole world of the lower Cape Fear.

We spoke of other environmental matters, such as the nearly decade-long battle against foreign-owned Titan Cement, a Greek company that had planned a massive expansion on the Northeast Cape Fear above this city till it met prolonged opposition from a huge swath of Wilmington's population, loosely yet effectively organized as Stop Titan Action Network and coordinated by the North Carolina Coastal Federation. Titan, whose buildup was mightily challenged on water- and air-pollution grounds, threw in the towel in March 2016, in the same week the Obama administration removed the southeast coast from offshore-drilling consideration.

"There's so much," said author, sailor, and troubadour Gerard when we parted, both hands in the air, feeling the weight yet offering the broad smile of a happy warrior.

"What do we do?" Gerard asked. "I'll help!"

Contraband

A strong and lengthy thread through time has tied our convoluted coast and contraband together.

The pirate Blackbeard salvaged ships at sea, so he said, and brought his goods, contraband sugar, into our interior waters for safekeeping in Governor Eden's Bath Town up Bath Creek on the Pamlico. Two centuries later, rumrunners under chase from federal craft, jettisoning boxes of whiskey close in near Cape Lookout, gave the Harkers Islanders who found that juice something to make a joyful noise about: "The Night the Booze-Yacht Came Ashore," the Carteret County anthem.

A woman I know, out strolling the empty Core Banks strand north of that cape, once tripped over a half-buried Ziploc bag that, reported to the high sheriff, turned out to contain $100,000 worth of cocaine. Twenty-nine thousand pounds of marijuana had been seized off a shrimp boat in Beaufort Inlet in July 1982, and cocaine had come in, too, even at Figure Eight Island, a gated bastion of supposed conservative propriety.

When Jim Wann and I stayed down at the fishermen's motel at Hughes Marina on the Shallotte River in January 1984, writing and playing the shoreside songs that would become our show *King Mackerel*, all we heard for several days was how much more lucrative the marijuana trade had become for shrimpers than shrimping itself. The district attorney for Brunswick County, future governor Michael Easley, in that era even took his battle to shut down the shrimper-smugglers out upon the high seas, as he would later come to tell it.

District Attorney Easley had accepted the Coast Guard's invitation to go out on a cutter with them one damp, fog-shrouded night, their quarry being a drug-running shrimper they had reason to believe would be making his move under cover of darkness out to a marijuana-laden freighter lying offshore, in order to bring as many bales as the shrimper could hold back in to the mainland before dawn.

After quite some time, mist and fog and silence, nothing over the air and surely nothing in sight this bleak night, the cutter's radio on the bridge leapt to life.

"Mother, Mother," a plaintive voice cried. "Help me out, Mother, this is Bull Frog!" The shrimper-runner was calling for help from the freighter.

"Bull Frog, this is Mother. Where are you?"

"Oh, I'm lost in the heavy fog over here on the sand shoals. I'm *all* screwed up!"

Before Mother could offer any guidance to the floundering shrimper, the overanxious ensign at the helm of the cutter grabbed his radio microphone and harshly ordered: "Bull Frog, Bull Frog, this is the United States Coast Guard—state your position, state your position now!"

A few seconds of silence, and then Bull Frog responded, laughter in his voice, "Oh, I'm not all *that* screwed up."

A few years earlier, soon after the Bahamian freighter *Sea Crust* was busted off our coast, that craft's huge six-ton cargo of marijuana was, 'tis said, being held by the Town of Wrightsville Beach. An eyewitness told me that one night he was having a beer in the old Wit's End, which back in the 1950s had been a beatnik bar where they read poetry and snapped their fingers and said, "Cool, man." By the late 1970s, it had become the hub of a freewheeling spot—where fights began over whose quarter on a pool table's felt edge held the next game and where, after closing time, a future politician often slept on the pool table, cue sticks stashed akimbo above him, point ends in the corner pockets, while others took the party upstairs and studied "Debauchery 101"

and became increasingly familiar as the nights wore on.

Word came roaring into the bar that the police were *right now* burning all that *Sea Crust* pot in the town's incinerator, and that the THC in it was *so* strong and burned *so* hot that it had just blown the roof off the incinerator and now there was marijuana *everywhere*.

The Wit's End cleared out at once, everybody grabbing trash bags, garbage cans, buckets, *anything*, and went rushing over to the incinerator and started picking up bits, shreds, clumps of marijuana from all over the place.

Because the police had put the fire to it, most of it was singed and partially cooked.

"That's why everybody called it Wrightsville Black," the eyewitness said. "But it got us all through the winter."

At Wrightsville Beach

We drifted, Ann and I, over to reflect and stroll a little at Airlie Gardens, only a mile or so distant from our lodgings at Wrightsville Beach, across the waterway on the banks of Bradley's Creek. The lawns and lanes lay before us, a cold, ghostly gray, late-spring idyll gorgeous and severe with all its lovely follies and offerings: its bottle chapel, there as tribute to visionary artist Minnie Evans, who worked at Airlie for years and who powerfully painted and captured the spirit of its magnificent Airlie Oak ("I just kept on doing that till I got this big old tree," Evans once said); its butterfly house; its pondside pergola (on such a day, none of its entwining jessamine anywhere near blooming yet) and curving steps down to the water, where all the brides come summer would be naturally beautiful in their sleeveless white gowns.

From a creekside deck my own bride and I looked out upon the broad cold waters, toward the waterway and legendary Money Island just down the way, a sandy little acre whose buried-treasure myth abides, though nary a doubloon nor silver plate has ever been found there. And then the cold sent us back over to the seabeach hotel, the Blockade Runner, and to our reunion crowd.

Old friends who had known one another since about the age of eleven had earlier regarded Wrightsville Beach's small set of restorative waterworks appreciatively: new swales sponsored by the North Carolina Coastal Federation that led storm water away from Lee's Cut and the waterway and a series of enormous tanks, collecting rain from city-building roofs, with which later to water the big green town commons and the playing field. All in our gathering could see how such a relatively small effort and redesign could go such a long way, all agreeing that yes, indeed, the health of the water was the same as the health of the people. And when we would meet up that evening, in the reunion's conviviality and the old music from our younger years now called *beach* but then called *soul*, we could all hear a little more meaning and perhaps a little more soul, too, when Brenton Wood cried out yet again—"Just gimme some kind of sign, girl!"—because we had taken time, spent a few Wrightsville moments together that morning, and we had seen a sign.

And that sign said *clean water*, something to sing about, something worthy of our praise.

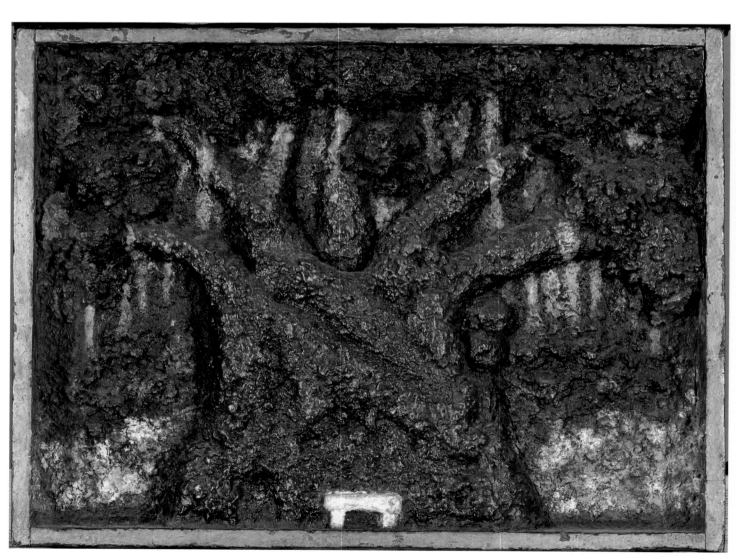

Children's sign toward protecting black skimmers, near Masonboro Inlet,
Wrightsville Beach, New Hanover County

The Battle of Rich Inlet

Several of us met about six years ago at the North Carolina Coastal Federation's Fred and Alice Stanback Coastal Education Center, our regional headquarters in Wrightsville Beach, and went on down with the federation's skiff and put in at the Lee's Cut landing. Just after nine on a hot, blue-sky, late-August morning, we motored on up the waterway, the federation's genial and skillful advocate Mike Giles at the helm, to the southern channel that would lead us over to Figure Eight Island's sound side and then on to Rich Inlet itself.

First we would pick up Derb Carter, rock-steady leader of the Southern Environmental Law Center, with his powerful ringing baritone, and Audubon North Carolina's coastal water-birds champion Walker Golder at Figure Eight and continue past the huge, growing, 100-acre tidal flat to a spot where we could film and tell a tale: why this natural inlet did not need that billion-dollar community's board-of-directors-proposed, 16,000-ton, rock-and-sheet pile wall (a *terminal groin*, in engineering and political parlance) cutting through it.

And putting an end to the tidal flat and the living, breathing inlet as we knew it.

We beached on the upper back side of Figure Eight Island long enough to collect Derb and Walker and to wish a *top of the morning* to one of our state's most noted conservationists, Fred Stanback of Salisbury. Fred, lean and wry, stood at ease in the morning sun right at the shallows.

"Sure you don't want to come on with us,

Fred?" asked Tom Earnhardt of *Exploring North Carolina*, who was directing and producing this project. Fred smiled and shook his head.

"You all have a good day out there," he said, standing still and unwavering, an elder statesman by the water's edge as we pushed off, waving and calling to us when we were twenty yards out:

"Good luck!"

This honorable man and his wife Alice split their time between the island and their home in Salisbury. They had staked much of their family's resources on preserving and protecting North Carolina's natural world, and no one close to the task believed our state's environmental movement would have been so strong, or accomplished so much, without them.

Soon, under Mike Giles's sure piloting, we were on the far side of Rich Inlet, looking back at the enclave that seemed small and unthreatening at a distance, the sun climbing now and the wind picking up, and Walker pointed to the tawny sea oats waving in the breeze and recalled: "I was out here recently, last October, very early in the morning with my son. And the shaft of every one of these sea oats was covered with monarchs that had spent the night on them, as they were migrating. When the sun came up and as the day warmed, the monarchs climbed slowly up the sea oats, till the top one on each shaft reached the tip, and then it'd take off, singly, and fly away, and that just kept on, till at last they were all away."

We would stay out on the lower, southwest end of Lea-Hutaff Island (which Audubon North Carolina would later preserve in the summer of

2019) for over half the day, finding different spots to shoot, moving around and up the back side of the island, staying out of the wind, walking in the creeks. Minnows swam around my feet, gulls swept in to caw and check us out, white egrets glided by without comment.

Our argument was compelling: Rich Inlet had a 200-year history of migrating back and forth within a half-mile range, now close in to Figure Eight, now close to Lea-Hutaff; a groin channel would finish off the inlet's tidal flat forever and its abundant wildlife would disappear; *all* the island's homeowners would have to finance privately the multimillion-dollar jetty, not just those whose homes were proximate to it; and, should it later be judged environmentally deleterious, a high likelihood, we thought, *all* the homeowners would also be on the hook for the groin's future multimillion-dollar removal.

Once we wrapped, several of us boated back down to the Dockside Restaurant on the waterway near the Wrightsville Beach bridge. After more than half a day walking around in the shallows out in the great wide open, telling the story of just what was in the balance here, barefoot and pants legs rolled, sitting down for a few minutes in the shade felt right good to me, face-to-face with a tall glass of sweet tea and an agreeably large crab-cake sandwich.

That moment would live in my memory as one of the truly grand days I have ever been given, the broad green plain of marsh and all those interwoven creeks we worked in, the purpose that had brought us there, the pitched battle to preserve North Carolina's last natural inlet that was moving and flowing just as God had flung it there, and then, too, just being out there together with these wonderful cohorts, bonded by it all. I simply sailed up through the flat eastern terraces and back to the hill country of western Orange County that evening, replaying the moments and thinking a good long while about what it might mean, what it could mean to so many—

men, women, and children who loved this inlet, boated to it often, and were joined in this effort; fish, turtles, birds, and butterflies in migration, stopping off by the thousands in that small patch of Rich Inlet sea oats for one good night's rest—for all those devoted to keeping this piece of the Lord's handiwork intact, simply to have done the right thing for the right reason.

When word came forth a year and a quarter later that the Figure Eight homeowners had taken stock of this potentially ruinous plan and at long last flat voted it down, people all over the state who love our wild Carolina coast stopped and smiled, remembering their best and oldest hopes.

WACCAMAW

One hot, steamy July day four years ago, Ann and I left Beaufort early, driving along NC 24 just below the pine-and-wire-grass Millis Road savanna and sweet Patsy Pond in the powerfully lovely Croatan Forest (which some call "the Croatian Forest"), then southwest around Jacksonville, where she was born at Camp Lejeune on the banks of the New River, and on down through the broad farms and deep woodlands along Highway 53, cutting slam through the wilds of Holly Shelter and Angola Bay.

This was the home territory of two of North Carolina's great African American literary artists: the inspired thespian Samm-Art Williams, whose Burgaw became Crossroads in his deeply loving play *Home*; and the late Randall Kenan, whose Chinquapin turned into Tims Creek in his signal collection, *Let the Dead Bury Their Dead*, and to whose cherished soil the brilliant, beloved country boy, as he called himself, returned on a broiling early-September day in 2020, at his service's end four white doves (representing the Trinity and Randall) flying away high into the Carolina blue.

And then we bridged the Black River south of Atkinson at Larkins Cove, just a few miles

downstream of the vaunted, internationally celebrated Three Sisters Swamp: all of it big, beautiful, empty country.

In Three Sisters less than two years hence, David Stahle, professor of geosciences at the University of Arkansas—the same scientist who back in the 1980s had laid hands upon the 2,000-year-old Methuselah tree and showed us just how aged the Black River monarch cypress trees really were—and his team would find a tree of even more ancient age, declaring it to be over 2,600 years of age and dating it to 605 B.C.

"This," Stahle would tell the *Charlotte Observer*, "is one of the great old-growth forests left in the world."

We were bound even deeper into our state's southeast, carrying a gift that morning, heading for dark-water, off-to-itself Lake Waccamaw, where Ann, as board president of the North Carolina Coastal Land Trust (NCCLT), would present the deed for 197 acres of land by the lake to the state park system, increasing the size of Lake Waccamaw State Park by 10 percent. For the park, mostly along the southeast side of the 9,000-acre lake, for the people of North Carolina, and indeed for all forty of us gathering in the park's museum that morning, this was an unalloyed wonderful day.

All the more so considering what else the Coastal Land Trust had done and was yet to do: NCCLT would hold on to 1,143 adjacent acres to manage as a nature preserve and to restore a stand of juniper, or Atlantic white cedar, on it. And only a little over a year after this July day, NCCLT would acquire almost 3,000 acres along the Waccamaw River, transferring 1,000 acres of it to the state's Wildlife Resources Commission for game lands, with the other 2,000 acres (comprising seven miles along the river) tying into what keen Coastal Land Trust strategist Janice Allen called "a vast landscape of game lands that runs from the Waccamaw River along Juniper Creek for twenty-nine miles to the Nature Conservancy's Green Swamp Preserve."

In short, beyond the gift to the park, the Coastal Land Trust has protected over 4,000 acres of natural lands here and increased a magnificent wildlife corridor.

Back inside that modest park museum, perched in a glass case lay the skull of a baleen whale, and at a glance one might have thought it out of place. This old whale head, reckoned to be 2.75 million years old, was clear evidence of a time when the seas were much higher than now and washed much farther in and over the Carolina coastal plain. Back in 2008, in Lake Waccamaw's shallows, the two women who found this, stubbing their toes upon it, first took the old baleen's skull to be a cypress stump or log.

Surprise.

This bay lake and the swamp world surrounding it were the ancient watery territory of the Waccamaw Siouan, and their creation tale was tied right to it. In the time before time, tribal ancestors said they saw a meteor trail across the sky, landing in the northern Green Swamp, the crater it left then filling and creating Lake Waccamaw. Ever after, these Native Americans have called themselves the "People of the Falling Star." One of the smallest North Carolina tribes, the Waccamaw Siouan number only 2,600—yet they cohere and endure.

A vibrant Waccamaw Siouan quilting tradition continues to this day, exemplified by North Carolina Folk Heritage Award recipient Elizabeth "Lee" Graham Jacobs, who gave a diamond variation quilt—two dozen eight-pointed star panels, green on green, blue on blue, white on red—to her daughter as a wedding gift in 1963. And did she ever love color and variation, once saying, "The littler the scrap, the prettier the quilt." What an honor it was for me, in the Stewart Theatre at North Carolina State University in Raleigh one evening in 1996, to read Ms. Jacobs's citation and to hand her the very award, given to her "for the grace, color, and originality of her work" and its centrality in the life of her people.

"Try not to put the stitching," modest Lee Jacobs said sagely, "where a toe'll get caught in it."

At the park museum that July day we saw David and Donna Scott, whom I had first met and known as dedicated defenders of the Lumber River and who have lived for a long time here in a trim, green, north lakeshore cottage. They invited Ann and me over after the ceremony, and, once there, we all stepped down a flight of stairs through the big cypresses along the banks to the lake level, and strolled out the long dock to a gazebo over the water. And there we lingered, as did slow-moving turtles in the shallows, casting their murky shadows onto the sands below them, as turtles have done for eons.

The noted naturalist-explorer John Bartram, William's father, had also been here in late July,

252 years before us, and he liked it a lot, too, admiring a "great variety of lovely plants and flowers and in generally ye finest lofty pines I ever saw" and judging the spot right where we were this day "a bold shore and good land." Gazing around at the broad waters (which hold a number of endemic species found only here: Waccamaw silverside, Waccamaw fatmucket, and Waccamaw siltsnail among them) and the cottages tucked upon the bluff, one found it easy as sunrise to agree with Bartram.

And to understand why Archie Ammons of Whiteville—this being very much his country too, for though the great southeastern poet spent his life teaching at Cornell in the northern gorges of New York, he never left this territory in his imagination—sang of the "alligator holes down along about old dock" and of "traipsing, dabbling in the slipping laps of Lake Waccamaw." Another fine Carolina writer, my dear friend Katherine Proctor of New Bern, grew up with just such dabbling, in memory-treasured summer visits with her grandmother here, going to and even joining in shows at the religious camp, playing red rover all day long, swimming in the great lake, and being a mite piqued at having to wear a life jacket even though the lake was so shallow forever, and

Catesby's lily, Green Swamp, Columbus County

then finding fried fish, hush puppies, and coleslaw at Dale's Seafood, the only restaurant for many a mile around.

High summer now, and deeper in the Green Swamp the wild yellow-fringed orchids and Catesby's lilies were all abloom in great profusion. We left this lovely place and moment reluctantly, and on our drive back up the long, straight, log-truck turnpike through the pine plantations of NC 11, we stopped for a sandwich at a small roadside grill run by a mother and her daughter, where I toasted Ann with a tall sweet tea for a job very well done. All the rest of the way home, through the lengthening summer light over the flat river valleys of the Black and the New and the White Oak, full of good feeling over what the

Coastal Land Trust had preserved and given to the people, all seemed right with the world. For as the old Halifax County revenuer Garland Bunting used to say: "A purpose accomplished is sweet to the soul."

SOUTHPORT: BRUNSWICK COUNTY

In the old Smithville burying ground in Southport one warm, still, mid-August morning, I walked lazily about, remembering the tale of how the living, on the night of the Wilmington earthquake of 1898, rushed from their houses, thinking Judgment Day had come at last, and ran as a mob out here to this small, haunted place. Men, women, and children, they all came to see the dead rise and be made whole and live again, to see their dead mothers and fathers appear and talk and walk among them and tell them righteously just what it was on the other side.

With torches and lanterns they looked on and waited and waited still and finally marveled not at what had happened but at what had not. The earth had stopped shaking. The headstones had not moved but still stood, some aslant, some not. The dead were still as buried now in the middle of that night as they had been the afternoon before and as they had been when their kin had interred them long ago.

Not a one had arisen.

And so I saw the little graveyard much as the earthquake mob had, still and undisturbed, though in a summer morning's light.

Here lay Capt. Thomas Mann Thompson (1831–1907), blockade runner.

Here lay the two wives, each one a Sarah, of Dr. Walter Curtis, director of the Southport Quarantine Station out in the Cape Fear River (only its concrete supports were left and visible out of the water now, now lit because of a fatal boating accident in the 2010s).

Here lay the children of Richard and Sue Dosher, three infants.

And here stood the Pilots Marker, set in

memory for those lost in two shipwrecks, back in 1872 and 1877, with its legend a sad, clear, declarative hope: "The winds and the sea sing their Requiem and shall forevermore."

Later, down along the busy old Southport docks, I saw that the cedar I had long recalled was no longer growing in the middle of the old octagonal Whittler's Bench, done in by Hurricane Bertha in 1996, and that the *Frying Pan* lightship, long moored here, was gone too. Happily would I partake of the liveliness and jollity of the

open-aired Provision Company, a fine, low-lying waterfront shebang where the taps were well engaged, yet even from within that warm communion a man might still be forgiven for raising his glass to the sweet sadness of sundown over waters and marshes and to those unrisen folk back in the old burying ground, the infants, the wives, the mariners, beneath the bending and yearning live oaks, the small sassafras, the unmoving Spanish moss.

II
Short Hills and Sand Hills

Gimghoul Castle, Chapel Hill

IN BATTLE'S WOODS

One of the finest of my father's gifts to me was an inborn desire to light out walking in big woods, and one of the best given me by my mother was her family's hometown, Chapel Hill, second of the two small Carolina towns I grew up in and one of the few towns anywhere, of any size, that has an honest-to-God forest at its heart.

I cannot recall who prompted me to climb up the big hill that summer of 1959 when we had just moved to Chapel Hill, but I do remember hearing that I would find a castle at its peak. No one need tell a ten-year-old boy any more than that to encourage him to head for the clouds, so I entered Battle Park from the low ground east and underneath the great mountain head called Piney Prospect. I followed a twisting path that is certainly one trod by Gen. Joe Wheeler's retreating Confederate troops in April of 1865, where for a few hours they dug in at the top of this steep slope and prepared to stave off Federal cavalry, till that plan was scotched and this branch of Gen. Joseph Johnston's army passed through heading west and vacated Chapel Hill.

At the mountaintop, I found a semicircular rock throne. Two boys my age, the Scott brothers, Bobby and Bill, were sitting there, and as they knew the lore and were willing to share it with me, we became immediate friends. They told me about the Gimghouls, some mysterious line of phantoms who built the small castle, with its little turreted tower and baronial hall, that I saw just up the rise from the stone seat. (I would learn that the phantoms were in reality a fraternal order and the builders were Waldensian stonemasons from Valdese, North Carolina.) And they told me about Peter Dromgoole, a college student, a Virginian, killed, so they said, in a misty midnight duel over a woman and thrown into one of the most fabled shallow graves in our state's history, right out in front of the castle under a rock at the center of a ring of boxwoods.

Upon the curved rock throne, facing eastward toward Raleigh thirty miles distant, was a dark bronze plaque that read:

In memory of Kemp Plummer Battle
(1831–1919)
Who Knew and Loved These Woods As
No One Else

A thousand times or more since then I have been back to that spot, always stopping to read those few last words again. The Scott boys had no idea who Kemp Battle was, and for the longest time neither did I. Much later I learned how he had ambled time and again to a large poplar in the woods ("Monarch of the Forest") to rehearse his 1849 UNC valedictory speech; how as a state leader he had joined in signing North Carolina's secession ordinance, foreordaining the ruinous Civil War; and how, upon his return to Chapel Hill as the university's president when it reopened in 1875, he sought a lost innocence by cutting a path to that special poplar from long before. "The exercise was agreeable," Battle wrote in *Memories of an Old-Time Tar Heel*, adding, "This led to others until I finished the park in a rough way."

From my earliest encounter with this wilderness enclave, I was captivated. It was only ninety acres or so of mixed pines and hardwoods, but it seemed like 50,000; a rocky creek rose up the slope in Coker Arboretum and made a small wetland before it poured forth just backstage of the Forest Theatre—another stone medievalism, one incorporating a Roanoke Island ballast stone in an upper wall—and then ran below a line of redbuds along South Boundary Street and carved a steep valley into eastern Chapel Hill.

One spring a student of mine told me she had glanced out her dormitory room and seen a hawk gliding by with a squirrel in its talons and that this had made her remember that nature was all around her and always at work, whether she was paying attention or not. We dwell so much in the built environment that it is easy for even the most

thoughtful to forget what a remarkable chain of being links us all. Even the university's sylvan central campus, with its lines of spreading oaks, is a made and manicured place. That hawk was heading for the relative wilderness of Battle Park with dinner at hand, about to be, in Tennyson's words, a part of "Nature red in tooth and claw."

A plan to cut Battle Park and thereby reap timber profits—supported by popular early twentieth-century professor Horace Williams ("a Hog-lot Hegelian," Jake Mills called him)—fell by the way long ago. Nowadays the North Carolina Botanical Garden cares for Battle Park and the Forest Theatre, and my students and I have had many grand classes and walks there over the years.

One of Horace Williams's best students, Thomas Wolfe, would later write of Chapel Hill that "the wilderness crept up to it like a beast."

Most of what is left of that beast in Chapel Hill is in Battle Park, and one of the great pleasures of walking in this town is still just stepping off a gravel road shoulder and entering our biggest woods. One spring evening, my son, Hunter, and I were abroad in the park, and on our way back out to the Forest Theatre he ran ahead of me, into a quarter acre of periwinkle off which the late-day sun was reflecting. At my transfixion he stood there laughing like some wild sprite in a field of silver, till a cloud came across the sun and sent that vision forever into memory. And one hot summer day, as Hunter ran up the mountain to

Piney Prospect for the third time, just to test his nerve and his blood against the high hill, I waited with a watch in hand at the southeastern edge of Battle Park, wondering as all parents do about the future and their children's future.

And well I might.

The older of the two boys I met at the stone seat atop the hill, Bobby Scott, who taught me to play the piano a year after that first meeting, was now dead, having collapsed years ago while out for a run in his neighborhood not ten miles from where I stood. Yet I see him—and myself at Hunter's young age—whenever I visit the stone seat, and I am flooded with gratitude that Bobby and his brother were there, glad for their meeting and for their enthusiastic telling of the old Dromgoole legend and their including me in the spirit of this forest. Looking beyond my own time, I am glad, too, that the commanders of Wheeler's army called it a day on Easter 1865 and shed no more blood here in these woods, for already they bore with them the wounded and dying from a skirmish in the New Hope Creek swamps below this mountain, one of whom was buried in a garden in town just a few days before Johnston's surrender to Sherman at Bennett Place.

And I am grateful for those few moments that July, when Hunter was a boy running alone and nothing spoke to him except the exuberance and vitality of the deep-green summer woods, and when the last time running he bested himself in the contest he had invented, he did so pounding apace past his father, shouting over his shoulder a winded "How'd I do?"

I told him and he was thrilled, and when I gestured at Battle's woods as we were walking out of it through a pine stand, saying "Ain't it great?" he nodded yes, still too winded to talk. So it was, and so may it always be, for the paths blazed in this forest lead not only to its other side but also to a wilderness of the heart where all of us must linger from time to time.

POLITICS

On the last Saturday in March 1963, a month after I had served as a page in the state senate, my father came and collected me in Chapel Hill, and we headed east on narrow, lonely NC 54 to go to Raleigh and get into politics. Just a few hundred yards shy of Nelson (then no more than a solitary filling station), we stopped to help a woman standing alone beside her car on the road shoulder—she had a flat tire and stood there desultorily making no move toward changing it.

Nor did I, but my father did.

I stayed in his car, a big Buick LeSabre, as he got out and walked slowly back to her, waving, smiling (I watched out the back window), and then bending to the task, which seemed interminable, the getting out of the lug wrench, the jack, the spare. Not that I felt unsympathetic—I was simply too excited by the fact that we were heading for Raleigh and the Hotel Sir Walter on downtown Fayetteville Street, where we would soon meet our visionary governor, Terry Sanford, and Vice President Lyndon Johnson.

This flat that needed changing: my father, who never seemed to be in a hurry, was in even less of one now—he had been diagnosed with MS and now walked with a slight limp and carried a black, silver-handled cane. Still, he was relaxed and confident, and he was quite strong—those many years he had gone swimming in the ocean at dawn, out beyond the breakers, the quarter mile between our Kitty Hawk cottage and the old Kitty Hawk Fishing Pier and then back, all helped him. He had no trouble with the tools, or the flat and the spare, and he clearly had no worries about what time we might see the governor, let alone the vice president.

When at last he got back behind the wheel of his own car, I saw that he had scarcely broken a sweat, had not gotten his suit or shirt dirty at all, and only his hands, sooty from handling the tires, needed washing.

"Why did *we* have to stop?"

"She needed help, son."

"Somebody else could've done it."

"You don't know that—not a lot of traffic on this road."

"But sooner or later—"

"No," he said evenly, "it fell to us."

To *us*. Suddenly he had brought me into his Good Samaritanism, as if I, who would have let the brief mission go to someone else, had been a party to it, an actual help, and I was all at once both proud to be his son and proud of something I did not even do: *we* had helped a woman in distress. "And now she's on her way again," he said.

Next thing I recall, we were in Raleigh, at that time just a great big country town, and he had found a men's room off the Sir Walter's lobby and washed his tire-dingy hands, and then we were in a hall upstairs, where a very short line was controlled by a couple of secret service men and state troopers, almost natty in their gray shirts and crimped, charcoal Smokey hats. When they ushered a pair of blond women into the corner room where the two politicians were holding court, one of the troopers said, "Keep it short and sweet." To which one of the women answered, over her shoulder as the hotel room door closed behind her, "We *are* short and sweet."

At our turn, a few minutes later, the governor and the vice president seemed extraordinarily relaxed, informal, friendly. Just the four of us in that room, where, mostly, my father bantered with the two leaders—he already knew well and supported Governor Sanford, and the ham-handed Texan seemed little different from the soybean and cabbage and hog farmers my father politicked with back up in Pasquotank County, where he was solicitor.

"Are you a good Democrat?" the vice president asked me.

"Yes, sir."

(Though likely *not* as good a one as Wilsonian Betty Ray McCain's grandmother, of whom Betty Ray told us once that a man had accused the grandmother of being such a yellow-dog Democrat that if the Democrats ran the devil she would probably vote for him, causing the grandmother to pause and think for just a few moments before declaring, "Not in the *primary*!" Or as good a one as Betty Ray herself, who remarked in Chapel Hill one time that she had made it clear to all and sundry that she wanted to be buried up in the mountain kingdom of Madison County, "so I can keep on voting after I *die*!")

Soon we were off to a cocktail party at a home elsewhere in Raleigh with a dozen folks I did not know, where my father and an attractive, young, sweet-natured woman with brown hair spent most of the soiree talking merrily together, while I watched the clock move slowly toward the time of the Jefferson-Jackson Day dinner, a fifty-dollar-a-plate affair being held in one of North Carolina's most modern buildings, the glass-walled, swooping-arched Dorton Arena at the fairgrounds, where they held rodeos and country music and rhythm-and-blues concerts and championship wrestling, when the politicians were not in there holding sway.

I devoured, if not inhaled, my high-piled barbeque plate, dearly wishing for another one, had they not been so expensive. This was hardly my first mouthful of chopped pork cooked with holy smoke, but it was certainly my first taste of political fundraising. Yet my relish toward my plate held no candle next to Lyndon Johnson's toward his crowd—he was proud to be here, he said, proud to be an American, and so was President John Kennedy, and they were two proud Americans who couldn't wait till the 1964 election, when they would be back in North Carolina, this proud American state, which they intended to carry by a landslide, because North Carolina was *full of great Americans, like every one of you all here tonight*!

We shook a lot of hands, talked loud and proud about the day, piled back into the Buick and kept on talking. "Would you like to go to Washington?" my father asked me after a while, meaning to go be a page in Congress. Yes, I would, of course I would, I said, in the grip of a political swoon — why shouldn't I wish to go to Washington? I had worked in Raleigh, had met the governor, had now shaken hands with the vice president, and yes, I would very much like to go to Washington. (And before I knew it, my father would see to that, too.) And so we rolled our way on back the thirty miles west to Chapel Hill, and every once in a while when we would laugh, he would pat my knee, as he always had when it was just us two riding in the car, and I am glad I did not feel I was too old for that.

For the main event of the day, as it turned out, was *not* the politicians or the Hotel Sir Walter or the cocktail party, whose good man and woman energies were still too strange and foreign and intricate for me to grasp just then, or the lusty handshaking and backslapping of the hundreds at Dorton Arena bonded by barbeque and yellow-dog Democratic faith. But I knew what it was before my head hit the pillow that night.

It was my father, and his kindness to the woman beside NC 54 near Nelson.

It was his kindness to me, a mere fourteen-year-old boy who scarcely knew how to act with him, as he spoke with me in the car, treating me as an equal.

It was his kindness, period.

KERR LAKE
Summer 1966

The first time I ever saw Kerr Lake, I was the seventeen-year-old lake-cottage guest of Dr. Fred Patterson, our family physician and a keen dispenser of wisdom in the life of midcentury Chapel Hill. Once, when I had refused to go see him about a serious ankle malady, he showed up at our home at 7 A.M., banging on the door, my mother letting him in, whereupon he marched into my room saying, "Let me see this damn thing!" and yanking the lower covers off me and grabbing my leg, eyeing my ankle, and fairly shouting, "Just like I figured — we're going to have to *amputate*, come by my office later on today!" and vanishing.

Another time, my great friend Jake Mills went to an office visit, sat down before Dr. Patterson and, when the good doctor said, "Well, Mills, what's bothering you?" Jake answered, "I don't know exactly — I just feel kind of … fat." Dr. Patterson looked him up and down and said, "Hell, you *are* fat! Lose some weight." Never one to mince or waste words.

We got to Kerr Lake northwest of Henderson about sunset, and he and his middle daughter, Susan, whom I adored, and I walked down the high hill from the cottage to the dock and looked out on the broad, muddy water, the single most significant impoundment on the Roanoke River. The Roanoke's headwaters drained some of North Carolina over by Mayodan and Hanging Rock and the Sauratown Mountains and then much of Virginia on its way back into North Carolina by way of Kerr Lake and the lower Roanoke below Roanoke Rapids, Weldon, and Halifax, down around Occoneechee Neck, beneath Rainbow Bluff (where the Rebels had kept a big cannon to hold the Federals at bay) and past Williamston and Plymouth, its way to the great Albemarle Sound.

At the dock lay Dr. Patterson's runabout, and while we were there, a single dim light came on at a small building I could just make out on the distant shore. "That's Townsville," said Dr. Patterson. "We'll gas up over there in the morning." Then he wheeled around and led us back up the hill to supper. Everyone turned in early, and I repaired to my small guest room on the end of the cottage and went back to reading *The Great Gatsby*.

By the novel's close, Fitzgerald's prose had left

me too unsettled to sleep, so I slipped out my side door onto the lawn and made my way by starlight alone down to the dock, where I sat for the next couple of hours trying to make sense of things. Maybe my imagination did the work, maybe not: yet I was certain the cast of that faraway lamp at Townsville landing was green, and that I had somehow, here on the side of this huge muddy Carolina lake, entered the world of Gatsby, haunted by love.

No boats were moving, probably midnight now and nothing moving except my heart and my eyes, striving for a place to land and finding only the weak glow of the Townsville lamp. However weak and far away, it was still strong enough: I felt I had my very own orgiastic green light, just as Fitzgerald had warned or promised me, and I sat staring till I risked falling asleep right there on the dock, and yet I would not let go of it, any more than that faint emerald light would let go of me.

Summer 1967

The next summer, we were tent camping on a wooded point on Kerr Lake's western shore, my longtime friend Bobby Schwentker and I, with an aluminum canoe I had luckily borrowed from lawyer and later distinguished judge Stanley Peele. By day, plenty along the lakeshore presented itself for exploration, and we were given to navigating the tin craft across the lake, about three-quarters of a mile, and poking in and out of the small coves there, watching gulls and blackbirds, dodging willow bushes, and mainly quartering the big wake waves thrown up by high-speed bass boats and runabouts dragging slaloming water-skiers at rapid clips.

Our rations were scant, a pack of hot dogs, some white bread, a little in the way of water and soda, but plenty for a long weekend, and Bobby and I were just plain enjoying the water. Whenever we cranked up our radio, Billy Edd Wheeler's lyric "You've got to prime the pump, have faith and believe" seemed to be playing, and

the song's premise—use the water in the jar to prime the desert pump and you will have plenty more, or go on and drink it and that is it, you will die of thirst—gave us two young men, he in school in Missouri, I at Carolina, plenty to mull over and talk about around the fire after each boating day was done.

On our final night, about nine o'clock, we were letting the fire die down slowly, when suddenly one of the strangest sights appeared: The sky lit up in a huge, vivid, almost furious orange glow, like sunrise in a mist. We quickly doused our fire and nearly dove into the car as the sky got brighter and brighter. Bobby drove out a long gravel lane to the hard road, and then we saw what it was.

A tobacco barn was going up in flames a quarter mile up the road, an enormous burnout, and the night air was redolent, thick and pungent, with the heady smell of tobacco. He eased the car closer, not too much, though, on account of the heat, and we got out and walked closer yet, within eighty yards of the barn burning.

A small rural volunteer fire truck pumped an anemic stream of water onto the flames, to no apparent effect. Only a few others hung around, several white men and a Black man and woman in their thirties—the man of the pair would look stoically upon the unfolding event, then gaze away, then back, away again. We were nearest to him, and as the fire did its work, his countenance assumed an ever bleaker cast. I walked over to him and said, "Is this your barn?"

He nodded yes, sadly, scuffing with his brogan at the road shoulder dirt.

"Oh, man," I said, "I'm sorry."

"Yeah," he said, "yeah."

He stood with his wife, and I moved away from them and the fire, and for a long time they stood silhouetted, unmoving and funereal against the broad reach of fire. Till they gave up and drifted away.

A large, agitated white man threw his weight around near the firemen, cussing, as if his imprecations might hurry their work and gain its success. Yet he knew, as was apparent to all, that soon nothing would be left, nothing but ashes, and a fire-twisted remnant of whatever stove or burner had been in the barn to dry its bright leaf but had instead destroyed it all. This man kept glancing over at Bobby and me, at last coming our way, shaking his head. I gestured in the direction the Black couple had gone, and ventured, "Lost it all—he seemed pretty shook up. Hardly said anything."

"Him?" the white man said. "It don't mean much of nothing to him. He's just a tenant, here on shares. He don't have too much of a stake in this—he don't care, he don't *have* to." Maybe this man was the owner of the farm or maybe he was just a neighbor, mad that anyone he knew had to see his cash go up in smoke. He did not say, and he was too tense and angry to talk to.

"Naw," he said. "He don't care."

For a few seconds, though, I had seen the Black man's empty eyes, his face expressionless as if disengaged. However close to nothing his share of the barn's holdings would have brought him at market, it would surely bring him nothing now. And someone or ones near and dear to him would not be getting something they had already planned on, had the dried leaf made it down to

the warehouse in Henderson or up in Clarksville and sold: a dress, school clothes, a bicycle, a water pump for the car.

He may not have stayed to watch the bitter end of it all, but he *did* care.

The glow now gone from the sky, we left this dismal scene, went on back to the camp, and called it a day.

DURHAM ATHLETIC PARK: SUMMER 1985

A crack of the bat and a high, reversing foul ball at the old Durham Athletic Park often presaged the remarkably loud sound of the ball smashing a car roof or hood and sometimes a windshield. Veteran attendees parked out of foul-ball range and never regretted it.

The progressive Left—that is, the poets and novelists and magazine writers, the Triangle's literati—generally sat in a conversational claque down the left-field line, talking, drinking beer, killing time between the rare yet special upbeat moments baseball games afford. Occasionally an organist played "Take Me Out to the Ball Game" or the *Charge!* phrase, but for the most part the games were quiet, almost pensive affairs at times, not scored wall to wall with abrasive sound and with very little activity between innings. A radio announcer sat high up in the stands behind home plate and gave a play-by-play narrative out to the Durham AM station, and one might occasionally hear his voice in the open air.

The Durham Athletic Park was easy to get to, not a project to park nor a project to sit through the game. My only recollection of energetic hollering is that of journalist Hal Crowther, who each season picked out a Bulls player to cheer, regale, and occasionally be sad for. One year it was a fellow named Bob Tumpane, first baseman and left-handed power hitter whom Hal cheered (never jeered) in lusty outbursts: "Way to go, Tumper!" "Tum-*PER!*" And then we all went back to watching the two-dimensional bull down past first emit smoke through his nostrils, Bob Burtman's work, and to the talk and the pints of watery yet highly pleasing ballpark beer.

The old park had quite a tale behind it: Kenesaw Mountain Landis rode onto the field on a live bull to dedicate the place in 1926; in addition to the Bulls, teams like the Negro League's Durham Black Sox and one much later named the Durham Dragons played here. When the stands burned down to cinders in 1939, banker John Sprunt Hill funded an almost immediate rebuilding—a 1,000-seat grandstand in two weeks! The place could seat 5,000, yet it did not feel that large and seemed to draw only a thousand or two.

Till the 1988 film *Bull Durham*, which changed the minor-league game for Durham and everywhere else too.

I recall taking our twins there when they were very small, once by myself when they were two and a half, without much forethought as to knowing what to do when Susannah had to go into the lady's beneath-the-stadium restroom and I, of course, could not help her there. She fared fine and was quite ready for more popcorn upon her return.

Once, earlier than that, we sat far down the left-field line on a high-attendance night, when the twins were only a few months old, and about six innings into an uneventful game, here came a line-drive foul ball, right toward our party, where I held baby Hunter in my lap. Even that far from home plate, one had less than a second to react, and, as the ball was coming straight for us flaming hot, I leaned back and tried to make Hunter and me as small as I could in open bleachers, without also slipping and sliding through them.

"Whoaoooww!" the great *Rocky Mountain News* columnist John Coit screamed out.

Coit, on my right, had thrown his left hand out to block the ball and succeeded. It had slammed into the heel of his palm, then fallen through the seats, and he was rubbing his wrist and hand, wincing from pain.

"Whoa, oww, man, man," Coit went on but only briefly. For he then put on his game face, looked up, held his beet-red left hand aloft with his right, and started performing for the crowd: "Hey, y'all, you saw it! I saved that baby's life, saved his life! Oh, man! Saved that Simpson boy's life, I did, I did! Damn!"

A young woman, a ballpark official, appeared at once.

"Sir—will you come get looked at?"

"Naw, naw, I'm all right—saved that little boy's life!"

"But won't you let us look at your hand?"

"I'll be all right, whoahhh, man, be all right!"

The woman, quite skeptical, lingered.

Someone returned from beneath the stands with the baseball.

Coit took it and held it aloft to great cheers.

"Saved that Simpson boy's life, this ball woulda killed him, took his head off!"

More cheers.

"Sir, are you really sure?"

"Yeah, yeah, course I am, be fine—anybody got a pen, I got to *sign* this baseball!"

Which he did. But not before grimacing through his pain as he tried to hold the ball with his left hand tightly enough to sign and *date* it with his right. Everyone around watched him lay the ink to it, then hold it up again.

One more round of noisy crowd worship, and then folks went back to watching the game, while Coit, a large man, shifted his weight, handing the ball around for everyone to witness, squeezing his left hand under his upper right arm, with more grimacing. He appeared to need an impressive sedative, a stiff whiskey in a venue where only beer was served.

"How 'bout a couple a cold beers? I saved that little boy's life!"

A great deal of beer quickly appeared, the game played on, and the ball went into John Coit's pocket.

That was all thirty-six years ago, and Coit at

the game that night had done what he always did, made a huge lot of noise and had real fun despite acute pain, going with bluff and bravado all the way, full out in the moment.

And it may have even been true; he just *may* have saved my son's life—that was one blistering *hot* foul he stopped, before he stopped himself.

For John Coit died in Denver the next January, of a heart attack at thirty-eight. We buried him at Arlington on a cold sunny morning a few days later, and a hillside piper played "Amazing Grace."

And I wish I had that signed and dated baseball at hand just now.

A GATELESS GARDEN

If the world is divided, as Max Beerbohm suggested, into hosts and guests, then we who had long been guests bade a sad farewell to one of the best and most creative and original hosts of our time and place. Before his death in 1991 at the age of forty-one, Bill Neal had presented his community with two restaurants as popular and appealing as they were different from each other. And he had published four books on the southern kitchen and garden, works he called "my affirmation of an active Southern heritage."

With Moreton Neal in the 1970s he took the rambling Fearrington farmhouse in Chatham County and turned it out as La Residence, a wonder of French cuisine and quietude that two moves and nearly five decades later still thrills the town. With Gene Hamer in the 1980s he took on a modest pig-and-ribs place called Crook's Corner (itself the renovation of Melton's Fruit and Produce, an extremely down-home tippler's haven said to have occasionally drawn Beat author Jack Kerouac to town way back when) on the cusp of Carrboro, cranked up the rhythm and blues on the menu and over the speakers, and then sat at Crook's bar greeting the fleet of cheerful southern boulevardiers his culinary enterprise and expertise had helped create.

Effectively utilizing Crook's Corner as his laboratory, Bill filled the tables with collards, biscuits, black-pepper corn bread, sweet potato pones, fish muddle, shrimp and grits, and much, much more. Nearly 120 of his recipes appeared in Bill Neal's *Southern Cooking* (1985); in his words, these were "imaginative and original reconstructions of historical dishes that were prepared in the antebellum South." He spent the rest of the decade helping maintain the quality and atmosphere at Crook's, as well as writing *Biscuits, Spoonbread, and Sweet Potato Pie* (1990) and, with our dear, mutual Ashevillean friend David Perry, *Good Old Grits* (1991). His reputation as a prime renovator and rehabilitator of southern cuisine transcended his hometown and region, as did that of his brilliant successor, Bill Smith of New Bern.

"The *gathering* was Bill Neal's focus," Gene Hamer once remarked to me. "The gardening and the cooking were all interrelated—plants were the basic ingredients going into the final presentation. He wasn't into rare plants or things that were going to be hard to grow, but things that he grew up with, producing gardens, mainly vegetables." Gene likened the exchange of seeds and slips between growers to recipe trading between cooks and observed that Bill enjoyed how "the whole exchange brings people together."

It brought Bill Neal to Elizabeth Lawrence, the gifted southern gardener and horticultural writer whose *Charlotte Observer* columns he edited and published as the elegant *Through the Garden Gate* (1990). I remember poring over that text and saying something to Bill about her close and tender observations on so many plants and flowers and Bill responding, "All her columns were like that. It was so hard to choose."

His numerous talents and interests must have often made it hard for Bill Neal to choose what to do next, or what not to do, and his unfinished works were varied. He was at work on a vegetarian cookbook, on a horticultural Latin dictionary, on a work of fiction. "He was very discerning about fiction," Algonquin Books' Shannon Ravenel said, allowing that she had regularly sent her house's books his way. "He was hard to please." She recalled that at some point Bill reacted to a book or books with the remark, "I can do better than this!" Soon, Bill was showing Shannon the beginnings of a work set on a Depression-era family farm, written in the voice of a young girl. "The new story," she said, "was very, very promising."

There was another unfinished project that Bill and I both thought promising and intended to collaborate upon, a contemporary version of the Works Progress Administration's *North Carolina* guide. During one of our sessions about the guide, an afternoon at Crook's where we were cheerfully divvying up the state ("I'll take food and plants," he said, "you take music and the environment"), I made a broad remark about this being our chance to make a statement about North Carolina. Bill gave me a screwy smile and said, referring to all the hinterland travels that would need to be made, "Well, yes, *sure*, but the real reason *I* want to do this book is *to take the trips*!"

Bill Neal never did. But he had already brought some of the South he found in other cities and crossroads and centuries back here to the same little corner café where, on that brilliant fall Sunday afternoon long ago, several hundred gathered for his wake. A woman on her way home from church sang a gospel tune. Stafford Wing sang opera. There were home builders, English professors, Mildred Council (Mama Dip) and her family from their Country Kitchen two blocks away. Barbara Tolley, who earned a doctorate in French while working at Crook's Corner, stood on the bamboo-bordered patio and read Edna St. Vincent Millay's "The Blue-Flag in the Bog" and "Journey," which concludes:

But far, oh, far as passionate eye can reach
And long, ah, long as rapturous eye can cling

The world is mine: blue hill, still silver lake,
Broad field, bright flower, and the long white
    road;
A gateless garden, and an open path;
My feet to follow, and my heart to hold.

One long road, most certainly a two-lane blacktop, once carried Bill down east to the Grifton Shad Festival. He wrote of Grifton's fish-muddle men, yet this serves as an unintended comment about himself as well: "They know the success of the stew will be reflected not only in its taste, but in the respect accorded the cook by the entire community."

Our respect Bill Neal long had and always will have. At his end we all did the only thing we could: we sent our last, and fondest, regards to the chef.

COON ROCK FARM

A rolling woodland and a southeast-sloping field of beans and greens and so much more in Orange County, with big chickens and pigs and goats nearby, composes Coon Rock Farm, an exemplar of green small-farm life from which, since 2004, Jamie DeMent and her husband Richard Holcomb had directed provender to their elegantly down-home Durham restaurant, Piedmont, a farm-to-table wonder (just around the corner from a worthy coastal parallel, Ricky Moore's Saltbox Seafood).

DeMent's and Holcomb's purposefulness, their artfulness, and their great enthusiasm for each other and what they have wrought together made for an agrarian idyll here, writ large upon the ground, in the dining room, and in print. To wit: Jamie's joyful 2017 work, *The Farmhouse Chef: Recipes and Stories from My Carolina Farm.*

Two generations ago, in the industrial-agriculture era when Carey McWilliams was writing *Factories in the Field* and Jim "Whole Hog" Hightower *Hard Tomatoes, Hard Times*

Coon Rock Farm on the Eno River, Hillsborough, Orange County

and Wendell Berry *The Unsettling of America*, the oft-repeated, antagonistic imperative laid down by agribusiness proponents upon farm families coast to coast was: "Get big or get out!"

Yet Coon Rock—named for a huge granite outcrop right on the bordering Eno River—was living proof that such a modest, integrated, sustainable enterprise could not only work nowadays but could also *thrive*. Big? In a state of mostly small farms averaging 168 acres, Coon Rock, at 55 acres, came in at less than a third of the average yet still plenty big enough to support Piedmont restaurant, an online grocery named

Bella Bean Organics, and the couple's farmhouse table itself—all in the spirit of the late pioneering, mentoring Chatham County farmer Bill Dow, whose Ayrshire Farm was the first to be certified organic in North Carolina.

A groaning board it all was, too. If the British author Christopher Burney was right when he said, "Variety is not the spice of life—it is the very stuff of it," then Coon Rock's smorgasbord was prima facie evidence of that very right stuff, for the farm grew a remarkable range, including heirloom field peas and potatoes, peppers and corn, onions and melons, eggplants and cabbages, pumpkins and squashes, cucumbers, okra, turnips, and naturally, kale. And fruiting orchards … and a flock of hens laying two-yoke eggs.

In late February 2020, out-of-state investors from Washington, D.C., with little notice bought Durham's old Nash Rambler auto dealership, home of Jamie and Richard's bistro Piedmont, and advised the pair to clear out at once, as the new owners intended to, in their words, "recapture the space." With no recourse but to vacate and no plan to relocate, Jamie sent her last plates out to devoted diners on Saturday, February 22, 2020. As the pandemic would have had it, Piedmont may have only had three weeks or so before closing down for that spring—but serving takeout *and* coming back would have remained an option.

These were two energetic, resourceful people, though. Jamie and Richard lifted up and offered their friends and neighbors a community-supported agriculture (CSA) program for the summer of 2020 and others for the fall, winter, and spring that followed.

Ann and I signed up at once, as hundreds did, and the goods of Coon Rock Farm graced the year.

MILTON

One summer afternoon at Woodside, a home outside of Milton in Caswell County close to the Virginia border, I touched and was touched by the front-hall stair rail's newel coil, and I gasped. For its dark, in-curling circle showed master African American craftsman Thomas Day's hand,

Pews crafted by Thomas Day, Milton Presbyterian Church, Milton, Caswell County

his having wound the rail down into itself much as a chambered nautilus does with its shell, as the golden spiral of a fiddlehead too, a thing of natural beauty Day had seen somewhere and then somehow brought the grand notion in from the sea or the violin or the fern and carved it into the furnishing of a home—which no one could fail to see, for there it was, a foot in diameter large and lovely at the base of the stairs, just inside the front door.

Bravo, Mr. Day.

"A thing of beauty is a joy forever"—for every single Keatsian time one laid one's eyes upon it, this wooden nautilus right there at home, one could not help but be moved.

For Bartlett Yancey, the congressman (whose mother warned him that going to UNC would ruin him) and namesake of the Caswell seat of Yanceyville, the stair rail Day made would come to its lower end with a finial curving sufficiently to be a question mark, to make a man and a woman and their children never forget to wonder, to ask, and to be compelled to thank their Maker for the graces that came their way, most of which may not have been of their own doing or done by their own hands. Thomas Day would remind them by placing that charged mark in the middle of their living space, a piece of wood imbued with meaning that they would touch every day of their lives.

Wooden heads beneath crowns of Gothic arches looked out, one on each side of the Long family home's living room mantel, also in Caswell County—what of them, and who would carve things like that, if not someone with a powerful lot on his mind? Faces with furrowed brows, pursed lips, and serious downcast eyes, these twinned faces stared out purposefully and almost grimly into the future, forever wondering if they were in endless bondage to this fireplace, like most of those who kept it stoked, and who might be entering the room, and whether family, friend, or foe. At other times their questioning might be whether the fire was well set and warm enough to meet the day, or the night, for it could get real cold that close to Virginia. Another sly challenge to his patrons from the heart, soul, and hands of Thomas Day.

If ever a man loved curves and circles and curlicues and cutouts almost to distraction, certainly to distinction, that man was Thomas Day. And who on earth else could that be, or have been, except this free man of color, cabinetmaker extraordinaire, the artist and artisan of Petersburg, Virginia; of Warren County, North Carolina; and, at last, of the little Caswell County village of Milton?

Just look at his chairs, the feet of his sewing table, his bedsteads, his church pews, and his sponsors: Governor David Reid could not get enough of Day's work—each piece made him beg for more till he had no place to put more, forty-seven pieces in all.

And just look at his home and shop, old tawny-bricked Union Tavern, still standing, taciturn yet proud, on Broad Street in Milton.

And then just look at Thomas Day himself, cast in bronze and now standing forever before the main doors of the Museum of History in Raleigh, erect in long coat, waistcoat, and cravat, a plane in his left hand, tool of the trade, his right hand balled into a fist, as if he were about to make a point to a patron not by pounding the plane but by tapping it, thereby showing how well he knew just what a light, firm, knowing touch on the best of wood could do.

A GOLD MINE IN BINGHAM TOWNSHIP

Time which antiquates Antiquities, and hath an art to make dust of all things, hath yet spared these minor *Monuments.*
Sir Thomas Browne,
Urne-Buriall, 1658

The old man and I stood in his backyard one cool spring Saturday morning. I had left my old Buick running but turned it off when I saw we weren't going to hurry away.

"Finally got my new aluminum siding on," Mr. Stacy said. "How you like it?"

"Looks good," I said.

Stacy Thompson's small square-frame house sat atop a slight rise facing Morrow Mill Road in the rolling dairy land of Bingham Township in southwest Orange County, where Ann and I have long lived, not far through the woods from his home. There was pasture across from it, hayfields beside, once, a sawmill nearby, and a great stretch of forest behind. For years I had been driving past, on my way home, watching the bare clapboards of his house gray and weather more and more, till they began to crack and curl and buckle. Then Mr. Stacy got someone to rip the siding off and put insulation into the framing and plastic over that.

But the new siding, the neat oyster-white aluminum stuff, had been a long time coming. Mr. Stacy's house had sat the entire fall and winter season with only the plastic on the outside. Now that the aluminum was here on the house, the place looked pert and tight again. He was proud and pleased, and relieved.

"That boy just couldn't get back to it," he said, "but I reckon it'll be all right. Looks a lot better than that old mess, don't you think?"

"It looks good," I said again. "He did a good job."

"Everybody told me I ought to paint that old wood siding, but I never did—didn't believe in it. So it got all ruint. You don't ever have to worry about this stuff, though. Well, you say you want to go see the gold mine?"

The North State, or Robertson, Gold Mine in Bingham Township operated for a number of years right after the turn of the twentieth century. No one here now knows exactly when it was running or how much gold came out of it or where the people who worked it went once it played out; geologists suggest the mine's short tenure was about 1908–10 and that the amount of gold mined is thought to have been insignificant.

Most of the Carolina gold mines were southwest of here, down in the Uwharrie Mountains and beyond, such as the Reed Mine at Gold Hill toward Charlotte and the U.S. Mint there (active as a coiner of the realm in the nineteenth century, long since a fine-arts museum), and most of them were a long time gone by the time Orange County's only gold mine was a going concern.

For some time before Mr. Stacy took me to it, I had known *about* where the mine was just from hearing people out here speak of it. I had gone looking for it a couple of times but apparently went into the woods short of the mark and missed the mine by 100 yards or so. This hardly rivals Hiram Bingham's search for Machu Picchu hidden by astonishing vines, but, even so, the Piedmont woods had worked quickly to heal the scars of our local mine.

Mr. Stacy was a thin, soft-spoken man in his seventies who had been walking—"scouting," he always called it—these Bingham Township woods all his life. We drove down the dusty Gold Mine Road and I pulled over where he said to.

The woods were full of diggings and shafts, and dark moss on the mounds of earth stood out in the early spring. The shafts have long since filled with water or with leaves and dirt, deceptive and dangerous as false tops. A fox going into the small space left at the top of one shaft had made it slick, and a sourwood tree growing out of the top side of

the same hole leaned crazily, almost parallel to the ground.

Ahead of me Mr. Stacy walked apace down the hill, to more shafts and holes and trenches, stopping briefly at each and saying little. When I returned later that same day with my family, one of us spotted an odd-shaped bottle floating in one of these water-filled pits, which made me think of the ancient whiskey bottles and tin pots set up on planks on posts out in Death Valley, old trash in a *National Geographic* picture marking some spot of former renown. For twenty minutes we tried to swat the bottle out of the pool with sticks, to reclaim this thing the miners had left. Each of us nearly fell in, but we finally got it landed and read what was still clearly legible on the small cylinder: *Amway.*

"This is where they had all the works," Mr. Stacy said. The hillside was like a broad half funnel, and we now stood at the bottom. There were no works here now, but here men once broke and crushed and dragged and stirred quartz and iron and copper pyrites, for the real gold may have been hidden among the fool's.

Now there was only a long ridge of dark blue tailings, a levee of rock dust in the woods. There were other mounds of spoil here and there, most settled and buried by leaves. I kicked a rusty bucket that was full of dirt, and Mr. Stacy and I started up another slope.

In a comical cluster were fifteen or twenty sacks of cement, all of which sat where they had set up decades earlier, the heavy paper bags they came in long ago rotted and gone to dust. A shallow trench where a pipe once lay led up this slope to a tabby-walled reservoir, a sixteen-foot square of concrete about twelve feet deep. Empty of water, the reservoir held only leaves, a beer can, several gray two-by-fours. Moss grew atop the reservoir's jagged wall, quite coarse-grained with its big quartz and all kinds of broken fieldstone. Mr. Stacy looked at the concrete mixture and judged:

"They weren't particular."

The forest was tall here, big oaks and hickories, 100-foot broad-topped pines. A mature pine was growing up out of the reservoir. Just a little ways back down the hillside was a flat square place, earthen foundation and floor all at once for a small cabin, and all over the mound where the chimney had collapsed was more moss.

Never during a number of return trips to the gold mine did I see anyone but those who came with me, though Mr. Johnny Baldwin, an older African American man who lived at the opposite end of the gold mine forest from Mr. Stacy and from me, told me: "Spring is the time the miners come out."

Two men and two women from Winston-Salem, he said, had for years on spring Saturdays come out early and stayed out late. At the end of these days they would cart off bags of crushed rock. "We're gon' carry it out from under you," they would say to Johnny Baldwin. Two other

men used to come to the gold mine right regularly, Mr. Baldwin said. "They had 'em an old-timey windlass, like you used to bring water up out of a well, and one of 'em would lower the other one down into the shaft, and he'd work down there."

"How far down would they go?"

"About ninety feet."

I had expected him to say twenty or thirty feet at the most, and I don't know why ninety feet should seem so deep to me, but it did. Much later, I would learn from friend, neighbor, and UNC geologist Paul Fullagar that the gold mine had one shaft 120 feet deep and 350 feet of drifts, or horizontal tunnels. When the West Virginia artist and writer Porte Crayon toured the Reed and Gold Hill mines down in Rowan County in 1857, he went with a Cornish miner named Mat Moyle down a ladder, step by mud-slick step, to a depth of 425 feet.

Knowing that one shaft went so deep here just added to the sense of wonder I had felt when Mr. Stacy walked me around the gold mine that first time, a sense of the incredible effort that had been expended on this quiet hillside.

Where did the miners come from?

Where did they go?

Whose hands drove the nails into those two-by-fours at the reservoir, and whose tipped the wheelbarrow and poured the cement?

And who got drunk and left those cement sacks out in the rain, right where they would soon set up and lie there and laugh on into time at the marriage they had witnessed between rapacity and waste?

Mr. Stacy said there were a lot of people working and living back here, that there were buildings, a whole little town. Houses, sheds, a store, eight or ten or twelve buildings in all, maybe. They must have been quickly thrown-together frame buildings, because there was no trace of them now—only that cabin floor up the slope.

There was nothing for me to do on a cool

spring day but lean on the tabby wall and look down the hill and contemplate the North State Gold Mine, the dreams and disappointments of these unknown miners from the days of Teddy Roosevelt.

"I tell you one thing," Mr. Stacy said, as we walked back over the gold mine grounds and toward the Buick.

"What's that?" I said.

"All them buildings . . ."

"Yes?"

"They'd all of 'em still be standing today if anybody'd ever just thought to take the time and go on out and paint 'em."

IN AUSTIN'S QUARTER

Spurred by the belling of hounds that regularly ran hard across Cane Creek from the Bingham Township cabin where I first lived in this central Carolina country, I sought them out.

My wonderful neighboring farmer William Morrow, who carried a bunch of us on a hayride the night of my thirtieth birthday ("Down nothing but four-digit roads and roads that've got *no* digits or names, farm lanes," he declared at the start), told me those were Charlie Bradshaw's foxhounds and that I would find him any Friday evening up on the road that ran the ridge atop Austin's Quarter.

I knew it well—this was an enormous tract of cutover timberland on the north side of the Haw River near Saxapahaw, territory that had once been in the final considerations for the location of the state's zoo, a signal attraction that ultimately went to Randolph County, near Asheboro (nota bene: though he spent a third of his life denying it, the right-wing politician Jesse Helms *did in fact* say that all North Carolina needed to do to create its zoo was "put a fence around Chapel Hill").

As had many others, my great friend and mountain attorney Frank Queen and I had made numerous forays into Austin's Quarter to cut

firewood from waste piles and windrows the loggers had left. Driving slowly out after one of these trips, we startled a wild turkey hen and her brood of six or seven poults, all of which ran across the dirt road ahead of us, disappearing into a patch of woods too young to have interested the timbermen. In the spring I often walked up there and loved the old house that had had no occupants for a generation or two at least, though an absolute feast of daffodils had spread out and almost completely surrounded it.

So one October Friday evening about eight o'clock, after stepping out onto my cabin's back porch and hearing, over the ripple of the creek, the distant sound of the hounds, I drove from Clover Garden almost to Saxapahaw and turned off onto the Austin's Quarter lane. Most of three miles back toward the daffodil house, up on the ridge road, I came upon a pickup, front toward me. Stopping, I got out, came around the truck, saw the dog box in its bed, and met a very large man in bib denim overalls and a ball cap sitting on the tailgate.

"Mr. Bradshaw?" I said.

"Charlie Bradshaw," he said, offering his hand. "That's me."

I told him William Morrow had let me know he would be up here and that I had been hearing his hounds down at my cabin for a good while now and just wanted to pay him a visit. He gestured at a friend, another older man, sitting off to the side in a camp chair, as slender as Charlie was large, but I did not catch the other man's name.

"We run 'em most every Friday night," Charlie said. "We just like to hear 'em work."

Several dogs sounded off, quite a distance away.

"They down by the river now," the other man said.

"Yeah," Charlie said. "They onto something."

Without objection, I leaned against the truck and listened with the two men. Now and again a hound would howl much closer to us than the distant ones down the river almost a mile away,

SHORT HILLS AND SAND HILLS

101

but it was hard to get a fix on where this nearer dog was. This was the way of it for an hour or two, with very little comment from these hound-dog men. A quarter hour would go by, and then the voice of one hound in the pack would become more earnest, more insistent, than the others, and Charlie would venture: "That'd be Wheeler."

"Un-hunh. Sounds like."

Another quarter hour of rapturous silence on the ridge, with the bugling and howling of the distant hounds rising up to us from the valley, the occasional chop from the nearer dog, which seemed to be coming closer, but who knew? Neither of the men spoke of it.

On toward ten o'clock, we heard a pickup slowly lumbering on up the ridge, same way I had come, and after a spell its headlights flooded the scene, and the driver pulled to a stop behind my small station wagon, leaving the lights on and the motor running. After ninety minutes in the unlit dark, I was blinded by the beams and could not initially make out who the tall, stocky driver was, though when he said, "Charlie? Charlie Bradshaw?"

I recognized William Morrow's voice.

"Evenin', William," Charlie said.

William nodded as he passed me and shook hands with Charlie and Charlie's friend. Then he stood for a full five minutes without speaking, as if to listen a bit to Charlie's dogs, over the sound of the idling truck, were a common, requisite courtesy, respects any country gentleman would pay prior to getting to his point.

"Charlie," William said at last, "I don't reckon them dogs of yours would chase a deer."

"Don't reckon so," Charlie said.

"'Cause a dog chases a deer might run anywhere."

"That's right."

"But you say yours are broke off deer."

"Yep. Ain't interested in *nothin'* but a fox."

"Well, good," said William, "that's what I thought."

"You growed up on this ridge, didn't you, William?" Charlie Bradshaw said.

"Right down yonder," William said, something they both already knew. William had lived in a two-story farmhouse amid maples well below this ridge most all his married life and was in his sixties now. "That old house. And on past it I got thirty acres of beans I ain't picked yet—I just don't want no dog chasin' a deer into 'em and tearin' 'em all up."

"Understand that," Charlie said.

"Cause the thing is, they ain't *my* beans no more."

"Ain't your beans?"

"That's right. I sold 'em on futures and already took the money—and spent it. I got to deliver them beans or pay that money back one. Dog chasin' a deer get in there'd tear 'em up all to hell."

"You ain't got to worry none, William," Charlie said.

"All right, then," William said. "I'd best get on back up to the house."

And then he passed me again, climbed back into his truck and three-point turned it around to the west and drove off. We could hear him for several minutes, till he dropped down off the ridge, and again only the sounds of the dogs held sway. After some time, Charlie Bradshaw stirred his large self up off the tailgate and spoke calmly to his friend, "Well, then. I reckon we ought to get on down the lane and get that dog out of William's beans."

So that was where the single hound had been working himself to. I knew I had no business being complicit and so said goodnight and that I hoped they would not mind if I joined them again sometime.

"Come on back anytime!" Charlie laughed and said.

"Yeah," said his friend. "We're always here."

"Every Friday night," Charlie said, "'cept when it ain't fittin'. And the weather's got to be *real bad* for it ain't to be fittin'."

From my cabin I kept on hearing those dogs bell and run—it was only a mile and a half downstream to where Cane Creek hit the Haw, and many times they worked their way on up the creek before Charlie and his friend would finally call them on in, crying over and over, "Hock on in heanh!" But then sometime the next year the Fridays fell silent, and I ran into William Morrow somewhere and with honest regret he told me why: "You hear Charlie Bradshaw died?"

"No. I'm sorry to hear that."

"Yep. Last month. He was a good friend of mine, been knowing him all my life. And his wife, she took his dogs, a couple dozen or more, and sold every one of 'em. *The day after he died*, and she sold every damn one."

IN PRAISE OF CLAY

Here lies the remains of James Pady, Brickmaker,
in hope that his clay will be remoulded in a
workmanlike manner, far superior to his former
perishable materials.
Epitaph from the Addiscombe
Church yard, Devonshire

The old Morrow Mill sits on the north side of Cane Creek just above a southward bend, the milldam and pond not far upstream, the millrace still evident. Marie Summers's kiln, studio, and gallery lay against the hillside behind the mill, first converted into a home by the Forbus family, he a doctor and she (Ina) a writer (who set her children's book *The Secret Circle* just downstream of this spot). Marie and her husband Fred ("I'm not a *baby* doctor, I'm a *woman* doctor") moved into the domesticated mill and creekside world the Forbuses had made at the close of the 1960s, when Morrow Mill Road was still dirt and gravel and when their nearest neighbor, farmer and timberman Clayton Rogers, still pulled logs out of the woods with his snaker horse Charlie and still, when he plowed and planted and cut his hillside cornfields, did so driving standing up on his dull-red Massey Ferguson tractor and singing hymns full bore at the top of his lungs.

For many years, the easiest way to tell people in Chapel Hill what part of Orange County I lived in was to say it was not far from where Marie Summers had her pottery studio. Everyone seemed to know where that was, so many town folks having either come out and taken lessons and thrown and turned their first pots with Marie—a small, purposeful, wise, and merry woman—*or* made their ways to her extraordinarily popular fall-of-the-year sales, when people thronged out to take in the autumnal sycamore, oak, hickory, and pine and to take pleasure in the Grant Wood landscapes of Bingham Township, and automobiles by the score would line Morrow Mill Road on either side of the Cane Creek bridge below the old mill's arts center that drew them there.

We have a pair of lavender blue liqueur cups from one of Marie's sales, freckled brown-and-tan cereal bowls with her jaunty signature on the bottoms from another. Whether we use the bowls on a given day or not, their mere presence in the kitchen ensures that she is always there, being an ongoing and essential part of our household, our family's life, always touching us. A clutch of bowls from her final sale stands proudly near the coffeemaker, and another cereal bowl—light gray with a deep-green-and-brown inner rim and yellow and green dots around the outside—bears our younger daughter's signature; this one Cary made when she was fourteen, under Marie's tutelage in what would be the master potter's final class, which she graciously held for Cary and for her good friend, another neighbor child, Rose Peifer.

No one can put a price on such household gods, yet we know their current value full well, for plowshares turn up potsherds from some of the hundreds of generations of first peoples who preceded us here at Clover Garden and remind us. We have seen their sherds, too, in the shallows around the sound country's inner islands, such as Davis Island in Core Sound. There, about twenty years ago, a storm sheared off a face of peat—the topsoil above Davis Island's beach—revealing the halves of three clay bowls nesting in one another, as they must have nested for untold centuries.

We have seen sherds rise, once students dug them up, from the long-buried, charred ruins of Fort Neoheroka near Contentnea Creek in Greene County, testaments to the violent end of the Tuscarora War. Farther west, half a million clay pottery fragments were unearthed at the Town Creek site in Montgomery County. Westward still, where the Cherokee have long made fired vessels of clay dug from Soco Creek, patterns from ancient potsherds have found their ways into the works of modern Cherokee potters.

In the east, in addition to its ancient Native American dugouts, Lake Phelps has yielded fabric-impressed pots and even a boat-shaped dipper. Pocosin Arts founder Feather Phillips has dug local clay for the studio's potters, clay from farms and yards, once a fine yellow clay from a Pea Ridge ditch—the African American artist who led her there sculpted heads from it, Feather told me, "with rhinestone buttons for eyes."

Well before I ever heard of Seagrove, epicenter of the clay "turners and burners" written of and well honored by Carolina scholar Terry Zug, I learned of the Coles of Sanford and drove down one Saturday in 1969 to see what they and their wares were all about. I remember Mr. Cole, the slender patriarch, and his shop and kiln right alongside US 15-501 just above Sanford—he went striding about the shop as if in a trance, moving clay bowls and pots in various stages of work closer to, or farther from, his kiln. His hands were shaking as he approached one five-foot board laden with a half a dozen large pieces, yet I recall that the moment his hands latched on to the board to move it they were firm, solid as iron, and as balanced as a Toledo scale.

Back in the summer of 1993, we were staying with our three small children in a cottage on the waters of Beaufort's Taylor's Creek, and we used to pile into the jonboat and float over, sometimes as often as four times a day, to the little Town Marsh point that townspeople fondly call Cape Carrot. There the children swam, played with shells, made castles and creatures of sand and mud. Once, seven-year-old Susannah dug deep into the beach and collected a bucketful of dark gray clay, which she brought back over to the cottage and went to work with it. Two of her creations were diminutive sculptures of the wild Carrot Island ponies, to which she added grass seeds and shreds for their manes and tails. Many tides have flooded and fallen through Beaufort Inlet since she presented me with this priceless pair of ponies, yet they still ride along a slender strand of beach, up on top of the window trim in our office at home, proof to this day, to both eye and heart, of the absolute, abiding strengths and joys of Carolina clay.

No one can set a price, either, on the abiding spirit of love that lies within and behind Susannah's ponies and Cary's bowl and these lovely pieces of Marie Summers's in our kitchen. For therein is the secret of the wheel within the wheel that Ezekiel saw, and the turning of those wheels goes on forever and always, and they will turn long past the time when even our potsherds appear in the heart of some far future garden and cause wonder, as well they should.

REDBUD STATE OF MIND

Redbuds blooming in the early spring were one of my grandfather's favorite things.

I knew this from early on, but only much later did I begin to appreciate why.

A few daffodils and crocuses may be lured forth by short spells of warm days that are then done in by late February and early March ice storms, but nothing in the Carolina woods above ground level blooms earlier than the redbuds. With light-lavender-pink flowers, they lean out singly and in bunches from forest sides; they stand, thin yet magnificent, in the central dominions of deep woods. One sees ornamental hybrids in median strips, the country come to town, the right size and shape, yet the color of their blossoms is often an almost frighteningly grotesque purple—and these look nothing at all like the wonders that appear at the forest fringes, the wild, slender, bending woodland race that with a sublime delicacy makes pastures and farm-field edges into works of art.

Granddaddy Page liked the redbuds and their yearly arrivals so much because, I believe, to a boy who grew up on a one-mule Onslow County farm, they always meant the end of winter, the end of splitting wood for fireplace warmth and the beginning of the chance to grow a garden and start to make a crop. Time to be outside, to sit on a porch with Page and Armstrong neighbors and kin, to set stump, to walk down the road a mile from Tar Landing the village to Tar Landing the New River wharf, to fish, and as air and water fully warmed, to swim.

These tiny lavender-pink blossoms, thousands to the tree, meant all that and more, and each spring they said all they had to say in a scant three weeks and disappeared for a year as their light-green heart-shaped leaves came on out and supplanted them. In the year 2015, the first buds on the trees we know from our lane and our route into town appeared on March 22 and 23— by April 4, the redbuds everywhere in central Carolina were at their peak, and those earliest blossoms were starting to drop, and it remained to be seen whether or not we would get a full third week out of the lot of them.

Just a year later, 2016, on the first day of March I saw the very first buds on a tree that grew high above the creek in Battle Park and hung out over the South Boundary Street sidewalk—they were small and shy and hardly showy and must have emerged from their branch only in the previous

twenty-four hours, as their width could only have been a sixteenth of an inch. Yet there they sat, ready to expand and open with the coming warmth—after half a dozen days near sixty and on into the seventies, these modest buds had become the most resplendent and dramatic heralds of spring.

Earlier and earlier by the year they came on— in 2018 on the Carolina campus I saw their initial slivers on February 20, and in 2019 on February 19, February 18 in 2020. In other places, some redbuds, of course, still waited till March to show themselves, which meant that for a time redbuds in central Carolina were having a five- or even six-week blossoming spell, twice the long-understood and much remarked period of their ephemeral blooming.

English explorer John Lawson loved to eat their blooms, as he noted in his 1709 advertisement for our state, *A New Voyage to Carolina*: "The Red-Bud-Tree bears a purple lark-Heel, and is the best Sallat, of any Flower I ever saw. It is ripe in April and May." George Washington often remarked in his diaries how beautiful the redbud was, and planted much of it around Mount Vernon, as did

Thomas Jefferson at Monticello, also noting in his meteorological journals (1810–16) that in his redoubt in northern, mountain Virginia "the Red bud [comes into blossom], from April 2 to Apr. 19."

For us they bloomed when, and now often before, the songbirds started coming back to us, to our coastal swamps and deep woods, from the tropics, the Yucatán, and South America. I once went looking for these returning birds out in the glorious longleaf pine savanna of Millis Road in the southern Croatan Forest, on the twenty-eighth of March, and found them not at all. The next morning, in town in Beaufort, a warmer, calmer day, they were everywhere all at once, singing their heads off.

Perhaps all these millions of warblers knew that the wild iris flags would pretty soon be showing themselves in the lowland creeks, the yellow jessamine as well along their banks, and were singing to bring them on. Perhaps they sought and sang for the blooming redbud, which our late friend and Neuse River chronicler Janet Lembke called "a tree to cherish."

A tree to *worship*, say I, and I would join all the warblers in that church and sing "Worthy of all praise!" as loudly as the rest, just to remain for a few moments more in an exalted redbud state of mind.

CHICKEN BRIDGE

Scott McLean, a lean, handsome, mustached southerner from Bowling Green in western Kentucky, handy with a hammer and a nail and everything else related to house joining, was one of the greatest and merriest hosts. He had a sublime, rare gift for friendship and was always gathering his broad circle in sometimes unusual ways to have what he called a big time.

For years he challenged his fellow contractors and subs to build anything-that-can-float boats and run them in a farm-pond regatta in remote Chatham County, and here came PVC-ribbed craft overlain with ten-mil plastic, refrigerator boxes coated with Krylon and duct tape, bathtubs outfitted with bicycle-chain paddle wheels, packing-foam rafts wired together with electrical cords. Very cold beer was involved, and most of the crafts sank before completing a lap, but the ever-smiling Judge McLean oversaw it all with his own brand of even keel and saw to it that everyone—including the first to sink—won *something*.

Yet, as the boat race was mainly for the trades, in the early 1980s Scott McLean enlarged his vision. Believing "if some is good, more is better," he hit on another humor, one that ultimately enchanted countless parents and children. He started convening a host of dedicated pumpkin carvers some days before Halloween at his rustic abode in the Saralyn subdivision about eight miles south of Chicken Bridge (this was a first-generation back-to-the-land spot where residents raised goats and chickens and had hog killings, whether they knew what they were doing or not, and where one blond woman of thirty famously lived in a tent and had her telephone nailed to a tree and did her gardening in the nude for hours each day all summer long, a naturist wonder the report of which ran rampantly from that neighborhood and all over UCLA [upper Chatham, lower Alamance] via intrigued repair- and deliverymen who happened through and bore witness).

Now Scott wanted his flock to lay knives to and sculpt hundreds of pumpkins he imported from a farm down in the Sandhills of Moore County.

By midnight of the carving party, scores upon scores of jack-o'-lanterns lay about his wooded lot, singly, in lines on the porch, and in piles out back, faces both mischievous and malevolent flickering away into the night (they all had to be candled, lit up, tested), as well as spheres sporting hieroglyphics, peace symbols, abstract designs, intricate tableaux with horses, human figures, cattle … if one happening by this scene of bibulous folk working on orange gourds in the candlelit night did not already know that one of creation's merriest men sat as the lord of this pageant, he or she might have been frightened by what looked like a fierce, even troublesome, paganism at play here.

I chanced upon a sculptor of a different sort at one of these affairs, the celebrated river-driftwood artist Clyde Jones, who stood out back off to the side of things, rocking heel-toe with a beverage in hand as he looked over the scene. Clyde lived up on the mill hill in nearby Bynum, high up above the onetime water-powered London's textile mill, his side-yard strewn with a great lot of twisted wood, out of which he crafted lizards, Gila monsters, gargoyles, and all manner of imaginary beasts that he sent out into the world. Champion old-time banjoist Tommy Thompson and I came on him at home one day while out on a walk, when Clyde was standing, head cocked, staring at a big set of tree roots he had just hauled up from the Haw's riverbank the day before. "I hadn't figured out yet what it is, what it's supposed to be," he allowed, adding, "But I will. 'Cause Tommy, you know I'm bad to want to get at the nature of a *damn stump*."

So now Clyde, kind of a visiting advisor, an ambassador from another area of the folk-art world, eased the night away at Scott McLean's carving party, witnessing upward of forty folks as they themselves tried to get at the nature of the pumpkins they were working on. He and his work had only recently been discovered, and he was enjoying the first flush of real celebrity, gallery showings well beyond his tiny hometown—I congratulated him on his richly deserved successes, to which Clyde just shrugged in the dark and took another slug of whatever he was drinking.

"No telling who'll show up at my place these days," Clyde said. "Big limo pulled up not long ago, this fellow clumb out of it, said his name was *Baryshnikov*, you heard of him? Well, he walked around looking at my creatures, finally kind of picked one out and said he'd like to buy it, how much? And I told him no, not for sale, and he looked some more, picked out another one, and we went through the same thing. He said, 'Why won't you sell this to me?' And I just told him, 'Cause you don't look like you *need* it!'"

Midnight now, and carvers were beginning to lay down their knives and scoops and drift away. I bade Clyde and other friends good-night and faded myself. Late the next afternoon Scott and a handful of coconspirators would load the 200-plus jack-o'-lanterns into his dump truck and transport them the few miles north over the Haw River to Chicken Bridge, so named for the 1950s wreck on the bridge of a poultry truck full of stacked wooden cages bearing chickens, spilling the less-than-sturdy crates every whichaway and freeing their cargo—feral chickens wandered the river banks and woods for months.

There, Scott's team would then place pumpkins on the bridge railings, one every few feet on both sides, making sure there was plenty of candle in each, as well as boxes of backup candles on hand. Several of the tribe stayed on to light all these jack-o'-lanterns at dusky dark and to await come what may.

By eight o'clock in the evening, word would have magically spread—"The pumpkins are out on Chicken Bridge!"—and hundreds of people of all ages, particularly men and women with young children, would appear, parking their cars along the road shoulders on either side of the river and walking slowly along the rails, marveling at the incredible variety of carved images and lavishing as much wonder upon them as if they were nothing less than the Chauvet Cave art in France. The sense of collective delight was palpable, and almost none of the admiring witnesses, who came from all over central Carolina, had the faintest idea how on earth this unheralded, unadvertised theatrical affair had come to be or by whose agency this majestic delight of illumination appeared.

Scott McLean and his legion of friends got

the Chicken Bridge decorated with jack-o'-lanterns for many a year and in so doing touched many hearts and souls and spread incalculable, unforgettable joy.

LINDLEY MILLS: YELLOW GRITS FOR DORIS BETTS

On a bright, sunny, cool morning a week or so before Christmas 2011, I drove across the Haw River and through the winter-wheat green hills and dales of lower Alamance County toward Lindley Mills to get some yellow grits.

Big corrugated grain bins and blue silos stood high over a gravel parking lot, down in a Cane Creek bottom below vast rolling pasturelands, the former plank-sided mill right below the modern one on the creekside itself. This spot has hosted Lindley grain millers for generations, since before the Revolution, ever since Thomas Lindley (a settler and Pennsylvania Quaker) set up the first gristmill in the upper Haw River valley in 1755. Right here, on the day after Tory Loyalist "Scaldhead" Dave Fanning's governor-capturing, liquor-swilling raid on Hillsborough in September 1781, a Whig militia battled but failed to stop Fanning's force on its way to Wilmington and Cornwallis—some say the bloodiest battle of the Revolution in North Carolina.

I first became aware of the old mill in the mid-1970s, when my generation's Lindley brothers set about restoring and reopening it, having a great new metal overshot mill wheel crafted up in Pennsylvania and shipped down here. When a few friends and I rolled up to see the mill, one of the Lindleys was there, and he proudly opened the millrace, threw the lever, and let the new wheel roll forward under the water's force. Inside, he shifted other levers into gear, and canvas belts and straps running grinding machines flew into action at medium and high speeds, and one immediately sensed the intense danger and risk inherent in such an operation and pulled one's arms tight into one's sides.

The Lindley millers' goods hit the market at just the right time. Organic flour and big flaky yellow grits found their way to shelves both local and far-flung, and before too long the popularity of the firm's goods caused it to outgrow the renovated late nineteenth- to early twentieth-century structure and to build a more modern mill up the slope a bit, the one I drove to that 2011 morning and had been heading to before Christmas for years. You could hear the mill humming away when you stepped out of your vehicle in the gravel lot.

I bought a twenty-five-pound bag, slung it into the back seat of my station wagon, and then made a call to Pittsboro, to Doris Betts, the great North Carolina novelist (*The River to Pickle Beach*, *The*

Near the summit, Cane Creek Mountains, Alamance County

Sharp Teeth of Love, Souls Raised from the Dead) and beloved UNC English professor who was suffering from cancer. If she would see me that morning, I would turn right out of the Lindley Mills parking lot, head for the Old Switchboard Road, Gum Springs, and Pittsboro; if not, I would turn left and go on home.

"Sure, come on down," she said.

Doris Betts had lit thousands of fires under thousands of students, and under their parents and grandparents as well, as she near-feverishly crossed the state for years giving readings from her growing shelf of stories and novels and advice and counsel at just about every single Friends of the Library group North Carolina ever had.

"How does she do it all?" people asked.

"There are *three* of her," we answered.

In her home, a horse farm not even two miles southwest of circle city Pittsboro's old courthouse, we sat and talked for an hour. As we were Carolina colleagues over many years, she had told me much about her family's life here, about how she held on to the old Arabians even when she could scarcely keep up with them because her late husband—retired, highly respected, Parkinson's-ridden Judge Lowry Betts—loved them so, and about the night her mother was downstairs at 3 A.M. all dressed as if for church and jiggling the front-door handle trying to get it to open.

"Mama!" Doris said when she staggered down. "What on earth are you doing?" And her mother said, "I'm going downtown to meet *my* mama, she's down there and she's calling me!"

"No, she is *not*," Doris said, "'cause she's been

dead for twenty-five years, and she is *not* calling you, you are going back *to bed*!" When Doris told me this, on campus just hours later, mighty fatigued but still preparing for class, she added, "I tell you what—the dead are in and out of my house twenty-four hours a day, and they don't do a *damn thing* to help!"

Doris may have had but four months to live, but her penetrating wit and gaze never slackened, not one bit. When I said I ought to head on, she asked me, "Why are you holding on to that empty plastic bag?" I said I had brought it in to remind me to get her some Lindley Mills grits before I left, and that I would go back to the car now and pour some out of the sack, which I did, Doris following me out to her deck and watching as I pulled the sack forth from the car, set it upon the car's hood, and poured out a pound or two into the bag.

"Not too much!" Doris called from the deck.

"You can give some away," I called back.

When I walked back up to the deck, stood at the bottom step, and handed the bag up to her, I said, "Now Doris, these are not quick grits, these are the real thing, so when you cook 'em—" only then realizing I had walked right into a *You gonna teach your grandmama to suck eggs?* moment.

Doris Betts leaned over me and gave me her dead-level-best stare and cut me off at "when you cook 'em" with her slow steady knowingness, her dark flinty eyes, her voice both warm and steely, "You stir and stir and stir."

WEYMOUTH: HOUSE AND WOODS
Southern Pines

Weymouth Center for the Arts and Humanities, former home of foxhunter–historical novelist James Boyd of *Drums* fame, stands upon the western end of a long ridge on the south side of Southern Pines, an easy walk from the railroad tracks and the old depot and the magnolias downtown. Housing the North Carolina Literary Hall of Fame, Weymouth serves as one of the epicenters of North Carolina's long-running

literary renascence, rung in by Paul Green with his Pulitzer-winning Broadway play *In Abraham's Bosom* in 1927 and by Thomas Wolfe's acclaimed first novel, *Look Homeward, Angel*, in 1929, a ninety-odd-year tide of much-loved novels and plays, poetry, and music that has never let up.

In their time, the Boyds entertained many of the leading lights of the 1930s, including Wolfe (who would show up at Weymouth in the middle of the night, slip into the house through an unlocked window, and sleep the rest of the night on the nearest sofa), Paul and Elizabeth Green, F. Scott Fitzgerald, and William Faulkner. Longleaf pines towered everywhere, over the stables on the grounds and the two-story brick house and its ballroom, where all these folks and more once roistered and frolicked.

Longleaf pines abound and tower across the nearby rolling pine-and-wire-grass woods that also bear Weymouth's name, a 900-acre state natural area lined with trails, a small yet signal place to see and honor what our naturally terraced east once looked like: a 100-million-acre unbroken blanket of pinelands—pine barrens—not only here in North Carolina but also covering the massive coastal-plain country from Maryland down to Florida and the Deep South.

I first saw Weymouth one Sunday afternoon after Thanksgiving, when I had been asked to read there, a true honor that I drove swiftly that morning from Haywood County to Moore County to accept—and to thank *Pilot* newspaper editor and state literary leader Sam Ragan, who as former editor of the *News and Observer*'s book page had published my first literary work, a brief melodramatic lyric, "Chapel Hill: Southern Part of Heaven or Northern Part of Hell?" Ragan was also the key to Weymouth becoming an arts center and home to the Literary Hall of Fame.

On this Sunday, Sam sat in the back of the room, silver hair slicked back and long over his collar, nodding only slightly as I spoke, yet smiling broadly.

Ballroom, Weymouth Center for the Arts and Humanities, Southern Pines, Moore County

Since that time, Ann and I, and our children, have made many returns to Weymouth, some of the most joyous ones being on October Sundays, to celebrate new entrants into the Hall, on occasion even to introduce them. Of Doris Betts in 2004 I said, "In a thousand years, someone will still feel the same clutch of heart we do when reading those final six words of *Souls Raised from the Dead*." And saluting Margaret Maron in 2016, I cited Secretary of State Elaine Marshall telling newcomers that "the best and quickest way to get to know North Carolina was to read our contemporary native writers, starting with Margaret Maron's Deborah Knott series." Judge Knott, that is.

We Red Clay Ramblers performed twice on Weymouth's grounds under the stars in a bright well-lighted tent just 200 yards or so from the house, and a couple of times in the ballroom. My fellow Rambler Jack Herrick's eleven-year-old daughter Skyler, playing all over the old pile, said that wherever she and her friend ran about in the house, "everywhere we look, there's *another* stairway!"

Ann's and my daughter Cary, then six, slept in an upstairs room of her own and said she heard a ghost. The erudite poet, novelist, and historian Robert Morgan and I read together there on a drenched Sunday afternoon so beset with massive thunderstorms that, on the way down to Weymouth, I found Chatham County's Chicken Bridge across the Haw River was so enshrouded it seemed not to exist.

Once, just before Christmas, UNC Press's head

Trail through longleaf pines, Weymouth Woods, Southern Pines

editor David Perry, UNC poetry professor Michael McFee, and I stayed a night at Weymouth to discuss a host of literary matters in this cherished place. Dropping down into town, we wandered through the exemplary Country Bookshop, then toured the Creation Museum, an indiscriminate gathering of articles and items of faith, its most intriguing presentation of all being forty or fifty extant varieties of barbed wire.

Who else in the world had *that*?

We were treated kindly at Chef Warren's fine bistro with the copper bar, where on that evening one of the appetizers was camel bits, small flattened pieces of blond meat.

"Where do you get your camel meat?" we asked the waiter, who seemed to be fielding the query for the first time.

"Not sure, exactly," he said. "I think sometimes they have to, you know, phase the old camels out of circuses, stuff like that."

We bit.

And we shot eight ball at Neville's, the bohemian basement bistro just off Broad Street that my friend Stephen Smith had introduced me to years earlier. A couple of pints, an odd little drink called lemon drop, and soon we were off back up the hill, where we grouped ourselves around the ballroom's grand piano and sang lustily from the *Broadman Hymnal* Perry had brought, and by the conviction and volume of our lifted voices, if there were not really "a fountain filled with blood," there by God should have been and right on this blessed site.

Another time I took a van full of senior honors

Red-cockaded woodpecker at home in longleaf pines, Weymouth Woods

fiction writers from Chapel Hill down to Moore County for the day, a springtime field trip after they had all finished up with their yearlong projects. We all roamed around in the Hall of Fame room and talked about writers they knew of, writers they did not, and there was always a deep warmth about saying, and hearing, the names there—Elizabeth Spencer, Charles Chesnutt, Doris Betts, Clyde Edgerton, Randall Kenan, Jill McCorkle, and on and on—and in speaking of what the students had done, what they had left us, and in reminding these twelve twenty-two-year-olds that they, too, had now become a very real part of North Carolina's literary life.

After lunch we moved over to Weymouth Woods and walked the perimeter path, down into the low ground, the slender swamp on the

eastern side of the woods, then back up the rise to the west, where the endangered red-cockaded woodpeckers lived and flew, and where the afternoon sun really lit up the longleaf pines, and their globes of long needles caught every line of light that came in upon them and shone for us like polished silver.

Sunrise

Stephen Smith—teacher, journalist, poet, and the witty and imaginative inventor of the Bushnell Hamp tales—has over many years graciously kept me involved with Moore County, and for that I owe him quite a lot. Though the doors of the old Pinecrest Inn at Pinehurst or those of the Sunrise Theater across from the vintage Seaboard Coast Line Railroad depot in Southern Pines are each only an hour and fifteen minutes' drive from our Clover Garden home, what a world of difference that short drive always made, as we drifted from the mixed Piedmont oak and loblolly pine and hickory woods to the rolling sandhills and longleaf pine, turkey oak, and blackjack.

An invitation came to me from Stephen and Audrey Moriarty, the fine, elegant Pinehurst archivist and author, to join in and do a short set for a "Raise the Roof" fundraiser at the movie house, the Sunrise, which the community was all about repairing and returning to its status as a small legitimate theatre and concert venue. The multifaceted evening, a musical revue, also included the first-tier Moore County musicians Craig Fuller (songwriter and lead singer of Pure Prairie League's lovely ballad "Amie," which he sang this night backed by Fayetteville's Bill Joyner and Danny Young) and Jimmy Jones (coauthor of "Handyman" and lead singer of "Good Timin'")— the place was packed, and Jimmy sat on a high stool downstage to lay out extended versions of his two major hits, introducing "Handyman" with a tale.

Seems Jimmy had once hit a rough patch in his career and, against his common sense and better judgment, he called upon a New York City loan shark he knew, and he was about to take out an extortionary loan that he knew would be bound to hurt him. But just before he signed in blood and took the cash, Jimmy got an urgent call from a close friend saying, "Jimmy, don't do it—*James Taylor* is just about to release *his* version of 'Handyman'! You won't need that loan anymore!" The crowd, knowing both versions of the song, roared with laughter, and Jimmy then said, "I stood up, said 'Thank you so very much,' and *backed out* of that loan shark's office just as fast as I could!"

And there and then in the Sunrise, Jimmy Jones, still laughing at his own tale, lit into "Handyman" with an unmitigated joy, while a racially integrated cadre of senior women in green and red sateen hot pants, a dancing group from a nearby Moore County fitness parlor, poured forth from the wings and, surrounding the R&B hero, kicked, shuffled, and ball-changed for him from start to finish, as we all sang with him: "I fix broken hearts—I'm your handyman!"

If joy could be bottled, jugged, or jarred, the contents would sound and feel and even *taste* something very like what all was present in this little old Southern Pines theatre that moment, that night. Like one of Faulkner's characters, I felt both humble and proud to be a part of it, or even just to see and hear it too.

RIVERSIDE STAGE: FAYETTEVILLE

On one downstream side of the Person Street Bridge in Fayetteville, on the Cape Fear riverbank stood the Cape Fear Regional Theatre's outdoor stage, and there early one summer we played *King Mackerel* a dozen times or so. Folks parked around a bait shop of long standing, which served the sportsmen launching and landing their fishing boats at a Wildlife Resources ramp only forty feet or so off stage left. As a lot of fishermen and women came in off the river right at full dark, we got used to seeing, and working around, bass boats each night as men and women trailered them, muddy water dripping noisily off them as the pickups pulled them away, almost as if they were part of our fishing-buddy, chowder-house show.

The houses were full, raucous: down-home Cumberland Countians used to director Bo Thorp's riverside shows came ready for a good time, and when we threw rubber worms into the crowd to give them party favors and get their attention at the top of act 2, sometimes they threw a few right back at us.

We sang about the ghost at Maco Station, one of North Carolina's favorite haunts from farther down the Cape Fear valley, just a few miles west of Wilmington, where the specter of a railroad brakeman named Joe Baldwin, decapitated in a double train wreck back in 1867, for well over a century waved his spirit light as he searched for his head alongside train tracks running through swamps. Nightly, during the "Maco Light" song in our show, the riverside stage went nearly dark as we gestured toward a high railroad trestle fifty yards off stage right, where a stagehand waited in the dark for that signal and, getting it, vigorously waved an old lantern around to awed children's gasps and screams and bemused grown-ups' laughter.

Except for one night.

The stagehand had made her appointed round, climbing the bluff up to the tracks and trestle at the beginning of the song to get into position, but as she walked riverward out the trestle, she stumbled over and then positively flew past a man passed out on the tracks in the dark. She shrieked and abandoned the lantern and her post and leapt over the man, startled and coming to, and ran pell-mell down the bluff to backstage, and when the stage went dark and we, unknowing, waved toward the trestle, quite mysteriously *nothing* occurred, except the show went right on till after the closing curtain, when we heard the terrified stagehand's tale.

The real ending of which was likely that, by awakening the slumbering man on the tracks, she may well have saved his life and kept him from joining in much the same way the very ghost about whom we were singing.

STONY CREEK: ALAMANCE COUNTY
A bright summer afternoon in Stony Creek, upper Alamance, Jim Wann and I stood off to the side after the graveside service for Jake Mills's mother. Jake himself spoke to family members and fellow mourners in the heat and, seeing us, drifted our way. He drew a deep breath and sighed, then shaking his head in grief, he looked off into the woods beyond the churchyard.

"Stony Creek!" Jake proclaimed. "This was my grandmother's favorite place on earth—she always said, 'Things ain't really right in the world till I get up to the cabin at Stony Creek and climb in bed and hear the flying squirrels hitting the roof and scratching as they slide down the tin!'"

Stony Creek was where Jake got his nickname when he, only a boy, was standing off to the side of his grandfather's garden there, not helping even when asked, till his grandsire said, "I swear to God, Jerry, you're as lazy as Jake Tate, laziest man in all of Alamance County, so I'm going to start calling you Little Jake Tate, I sure am!"

So Old Man Leath did, and the nickname stuck at once, though Jake—as a university scholar (one of the world's top Spenserians and, too, author of the dead mule theory of southern literature), master teacher, advisor to many contemporary southern writers, a skillful outdoorsman afield and afloat, and an unmatched storyteller about it all—was throughout his life far more productive than the original Jake Tate. During his teenage years, he had spent a few late summers being a "Drive in!" boy at this grandfather's tobacco warehouse, luring or trying to lure in farmers with their leaf-laden trucks down in Adel, Georgia, for which he got a reasonable day rate *and* the mounted skin of a six-foot diamondback rattlesnake his granddaddy had run over on a farm lane—this was before he started hopping curb for Bear Webster at the Oak Grove Café in Burlington, much closer to home, where folks ordered their steaks "guitar big and lightning quick!"

"We were up at Stony Creek one time, Steve Coley and I," Jake said once, "just went up there on the spur of the moment on a Saturday night— I knew no one was there and knew how to get in. Didn't bring anything with us. So we spent that night, woke up Sunday morning, hungry enough to eat the hind end of a mule. Not a damn thing in the house but one single box of stale frosted flakes and one bottle of 7 Up.

"Steve said, 'Well, hell, Jake, let's try that.'

"So we poured the 7 Up over the cereal. Couple

115

of bites each and we went out and threw it all in the creek for the fish to eat, if they even would. Worst thing we ever put in our mouths.

"'Stony Creek Breakfast' we called it. I don't recommend it."

As to gardening, Jake told of a man he knew back in town who had a large empty lot beside his house, empty in the sense of there being no homeplace on it. In fact, the lot was an overgrown bramble comprising privets, smilaxes, young sweetgums and pines, and honeysuckles all woven together, and there came a time when the man finally set out to reclaim the land and grow a garden on it.

This clearing project took him quite some time and effort, though after a couple of years he had cut down the larger plants and hacked away at the smaller ones, finally grubbing out enough of their roots to till it all up and plant a grand spring garden, which he tended assiduously.

And that was what he was doing one summer afternoon, amid his vegetables, weeding and mulching, when a preacher walking up Rawhut Street stopped to study the scene. Being a preacher, he was unable to remain silent for very long.

"Good afternoon, friend," he said. "I see you and the Lord have a very nice bunch of Better Boys growing there."

The gardener nodded.

"And," said the preacher, "the Lord's okra is straight and tall."

Again, the gardener nodded and kept right on with what he was doing.

"I like the way the Lord's bush beans are . . . mighty bushy," the preacher said.

"Thank you," the gardener said at last.

"I really must say," said the preacher, drawing himself up to pronounce, "you and the Lord have quite a beautiful garden growing here!"

"Well, thank you, preacher," said the man, modestly. "I reckon we do. You should've seen it back when He was working it by Himself."

116

TRANE: HIGH POINT

When first I heard "My Favorite Things" through the soul and sax of John Coltrane, I knew at once that this song, which I thought I had grasped intimately for years, I had never really known at all.

Who was this man?

And what were *his* favorite things?

A reed and a club date, an hour-long solo . . .

Son of a tailor, grandson of a preacher, yes, let him play in the high school band, the community band, let him pass through the brass and then live among the reeds, and God almighty let him have and hold a tenor sax and weave a tune, preach a sound. Born in Hamlet, North Carolina, at the east-west and north-south crossing of the rail lines and raised in High Point, the real *high point* of the Southern Crescent, Coltrane grew up twice blessed by the greatest moving power on land, and so in time this man with the power of a locomotive took its name and shortened his own: *Trane.*

Trane on his way to play R&B for Cleanhead Vinson, to swing for Dizzie Gillespie, to bop for Johnny Hodges and Earl Bostic on the way to Miles Davis and Thelonious Monk, a fellow Tar Heel and also train-town raised, Monk on the Coast Line of Rocky Mount (where the hipsters and the jivers, flush, hit up for airtight loans, would say, "Sure, man, how much you need? I got any amount 'cept Rocky Mount").

And then back to Miles.

Was Trane there at the *birth of the cool*?

No, but he was nearby, mighty close.

Was Trane there when all life got *kind of blue*?

Of course he was there, he was one of six, *the* six, Miles's sextet, one point of the most blessed hexagram.

So what?

Trane had sheets of sound in him from babyhood, inborn from roaring clacking night trains and their long whistles, carrying folks every whichaway—all the compass points, he could play

John Coltrane monument, city hall, High Point, Guilford County

rings around every single one of them. High Point, he lived it, in it, of it, not down in the red-clay gullies but up on top of it, which made him the highest point of all.

You can see him still, by city hall there in his old hometown, forever bronze, eight feet tall because he was at least eight feet tall. Holding his saxophone, a hero.

Preaching: "My music is the spiritual expression of what I am: my faith, my knowledge, my being."

Trane going higher: *Ascension. A Love Supreme.*

The power and the glory.

Forever and ever.

Amen.

That's what!

ABNORMAL CITY

My dear friend and colleague Marianne Gingher, the fine fictionist and *Girl's Life* memoirist who grew up in Greensboro, has called her small city, with its low skyline and Southern Crescent train station and its many colleges, "the capital of *normal.*"

Yet is it?

What is normal about a town where its namesake, Gen. Nathanael Greene, inflicted such heavy losses on British general Cornwallis at the Battle of Guilford Courthouse in 1781, a signal part of the Revolutionary battle for the South and for the new nation itself?

Where Jeff Davis, his Confederacy collapsing, spent four cold-shouldered days early in his April 1865 flight from Richmond, meeting his cabinet in a broken-down boxcar as if he might will his defeated, ruined faux nation back into being, fleeing the day Lincoln was shot, for the Union was chasing him down, coming for him for real at last ...

Where four young Black men taking and not abandoning their seats on the old spinning stools at Woolworth's lunch counter in 1960 turned an upside-down world right side up, for the good possibility that a righteous South—and *nation*—might someday come to be ...

Where in more recent times a church with solar panels on its own roof challenged the state's—and region's—powerful monopoly, Duke Energy, till the state supreme court found in favor of the monopoly ...

And where the schools of the self-proclaimed *gate city* were now absorbing children from families all in all speaking an astonishing 120 languages, quite likely more than all the Native American, European, African, Hispanic, and Asian tongues ever spoken here in North Carolina at any time before, an emblematic immigrant town where Southeast Asian Montagnards were fileting big fish so skillfully, so little left on the skeletons, that one could read a newspaper through the residual membrane ...

Some of the state's most progressive politicians—among them John McNeill Smith, Richardson Preyer, Pricey Harrison, and Katie Dorsett, who as Governor Hunt's secretary of administration was the first Black woman who ever served in a state cabinet position—have come forth from Greensboro, and North Carolina Agricultural and Technical State University student Jesse Jackson started coming into his own here as one of America's civil rights and moral conscience leaders during the era of those early 1960s protests.

Some of the finest writers anywhere have called Greensboro home, like ironic O. Henry in the old days, and some have both written *and* taught here to great success, Fred Chappell and

Michael Parker among them. First-tier folk and country singer Emmylou Harris went to school and found her first coffeehouse to sing in here at UNC Greensboro, and the prodigious vocal and song-writing talent Rhiannon Giddens, who came to national fame as a clawhammer banjoist and leader of the Black string band the Carolina Chocolate Drops and who now leads the internationally renowned Silk Road Ensemble, also hails from Greensboro. So does the jug-blues-skiffle-and-swing band the Swamp Cats. So did one of the South's most impressive and genial luthiers, David Sheppard, who for nearly thirty years had a wonderful shop on Spring Garden Street.

New theatre, such as Triad Stage's *Brother Wolf*, and a national folk festival have thrived here, as have the Scuppernong bookstore, whose name honors our sweet native grape, and one magazine that celebrates the city's literary heritage as *O. Henry* and another that excels in revealing North Carolina to itself: *Our State*.

Might not *abnormal* be the better word for this place?

Service

The International Civil Rights Center and Museum in Greensboro memorializes the Woolworth's lunch counter and that all-important 1960 moment, and much else, as it sits in the former Woolworth's itself. And Colin Quashie, a fiercely independent Charleston artist once called by Halsey Institute of Contemporary Art director Mark Sloan "among the best artists working anywhere today," took the story of the Woolworth's four—the *Greensboro* Four—and dramatically portrayed it, and a lot more, in a five-by-fifty-foot mural, *Service*, commissioned by and hanging in UNC–Chapel Hill's School of Government.

In the piece, Quashie painted each of the four men in chef's habit and significantly put them *behind* the lunch counter. In his own words, "they literally took possession of the lunch

counter with their refusal to leave until served. By seeking service they were, by extension, serving a cause greater than themselves." The men are foregrounded, and across the background in eight panels stands a legion of notable North Carolina African Americans who led the arcing way toward justice before them.

Here, among others, are the freed slaves who founded Princeville, first African American town in the nation, in the low ground across the Tar River from Tarboro; keeper Richard Etheridge's all-Black Pea Island Life-Saving Station crew on the Outer Banks; Beaufort's chantey-singing, net-pulling menhaden fishermen; the people of Parrish Street, the "Black Wall Street" of Durham; those involved in the drama of integrating Charlotte's schools in 1957; the U.S. Colored Troops who fought to capture Fort Fisher in January 1865, marched at the Union fore on into Wilmington, and helped ensure an end to the Civil War; the enslaved people of Somerset plantation on Lake Phelps in eastern Carolina, honored in Dorothy Spruill Redford's writing; and the Reverends Martin Luther King Jr. and Ralph David Abernathy coming to Greensboro in support of the lunch counter sit-ins soon after they occurred.

In the artist's mind, hands, brushes, and canvas, the history of a people sprang from that moment in 1960.

When Quashie's masterwork was dedicated in July 2010, Ann, who had coordinated its commissioning, and I were glad to be there among the crowd and bear witness, to hear artist

Quashie speak on the fiftieth anniversary of those fateful sit-in moments in Greensboro.

"A New Well"

On the sunny summer day of Monday, August 13, 2018, I witnessed two remarkable gatherings: one midday beside Belews Lake north of Greensboro, the other that evening in a church in Greensboro itself.

In both sessions, the leading speakers were the Reverend William Barber II, former president of the North Carolina NAACP and leader of a multitude of "Moral Monday" social justice protests at the North Carolina General Assembly, and former vice president Al Gore Jr. of Tennessee, who, after his defeat in the 2000 presidential race at the hands of the U.S. Supreme Court, had continued to devote himself to environmental work as founder and chair of the Climate Reality Project, his effort toward stanching adverse climate change, which he named "an inconvenient truth."

The two men were now allied in Reverend Barber's revival of Dr. King's Poor People's Campaign, linking poverty squarely with the environment, both knowing environmental degradation always hit the poor harder than anyone else.

At Belews Lake, a number of local residents came forth to testify to the long-term effects of unclean air and potential groundwater pollution in the vicinity of Duke Energy's Belews Creek Steam Station, its coal-ash storage, and its smokestacks. One person with pulmonary problems after another spoke; others told of those who bathed only with bottled water. Speaking with those smokestacks fuming powerfully behind him, Gore declared emphatically, "This is a crime scene!"

That night at Shiloh Baptist Church in downtown Greensboro, before an integrated audience, Reverend Barber called for singing early on, citing Elisha, the biblical prophet who could not speak until a minstrel had sung.

Rev. Nelson Johnson, former minister of Faith Community Church, appeared, witnessing to what it had been like to have the full force of Duke Energy come down upon his church, which was buying solar energy from its rooftop solar-panel installer NC WARN at half the price Duke Energy charged. Years earlier, Reverend Johnson had said, "It makes common sense. It makes theological sense. It makes environmental sense and economic sense." (*Not*, though, what the state supreme court would later find: that the church's purchases were against North Carolina law. Even in legal defeat, though, NC WARN would donate those panels to Faith Community Church for its continuing use.)

Al Gore showed unusual energy that night, as he spoke for an hour with few notes, asking and proclaiming vigorously, "You all watched the news lately? It's like a nature hike through the *book of Revelation*!"

Coming nearly sixty years after the sit-ins, these events, which bore little resemblance to the lunch counter times, nonetheless still rang the bell on the theme of justice—*environmental* justice, here in the very state where that movement had begun, in poor Warren County over the state's massive dumping of polychlorinated biphenyls (PCBs) there in 1982—and climate change. Small wonder that the big coal-fired-power monopoly was the target, for only four and a half years had passed since Duke Energy's disastrous, 39,000-ton coal-ash spill into the Dan River at Eden, only thirty-odd miles distant, and Duke in less than a year and a half would be under state Department of Environmental Quality orders to remove the 80 million tons of its massive coal-ash deposits from its waterside sites and put *all* that ash into lined pits well away from our rivers.

At high noon earlier in the day, we had all seen Duke's smoke.

Reverend Barber, whose deep voice in full flourish could make mountains rumble, at one point in these proceedings spoke with great hope, conviction, and determination these prophetic watchwords (which would come back to mind with real power in July of 2020 when Duke Energy and Dominion Power of Virginia, two Goliaths fought by many thousands of Davids, canceled their highly controversial 600-mile Atlantic Coast Pipeline plan): "North Carolina, we are drinking from a *new well*!"

Just Waiting for the Rain to Pass

Once, after a walk up to some stores on the edge of the Greensboro neighborhood where his family lived, a good friend of mine—Jim, let us say—was then strolling on home. The time was just before two o'clock, and a sudden summer rainstorm drove him to run up onto a stranger's porch to wait till the storm blew on through. He had been on the porch for only a few moments, though, when the front door opened and a man in a dark suit smiled sympathetically at him and welcomed him into the house saying, "We're so glad you could come."

A coffin lay within, set upon a stand, surrounded by flowers and several dozen men and women, darkly dressed mourners. "Did you know him very well?" the man who had opened the door asked the astonished Jim, who said: "No. No, I didn't, not very well at all, really."

"Well, then, you're all the kinder to have come."

Among the mourners, Jim took his place, or *a* place, as a home service then proceeded. He listened to the prayers, the homily, the weeping, sang along with the hymns, and simply made his peace about going right on along with the event into which he had stumbled. He would slip away as soon as the funeral was over, as soon as he could. This, though unusual, was not *too* high a price to pay for getting out of a hard summer rain, after all, and not getting drenched. He could manage.

Right after the service, as the real talk and visiting began, Jim moved slowly but deftly for the front door, and, just as he got to it, the man who

had brought him into all this caught Jim's arm and said earnestly, "Thank you."

"Well, thank you too," said Jim. "It meant a lot to me to be here." They both nodded at each other, and as Jim reached for the front-door knob, the man said: "You *will* come to the cemetery with us, won't you?"

The cemetery. He had not thought of that.

"Well, no, I . . . don't have a car," Jim said. "I walked here."

"Oh," the man said, "that's no problem. You may ride with the family. Everyone will come back here after the burial."

Suddenly Jim felt trapped: in over shoes, about to be in over boots. How could he drift away now? The man still held his arm, tightly. He saw that he was going to have to play out the whole ritual with them, and now he was finally beginning to mourn for real. "I—"

"Good," the man said. "We'll leave in another ten minutes or so."

Not till Jim had gotten into the car to which he had been assigned, and the strangers he was among started talking about the family plot and who was already buried there and the lovely oak trees and the old white-clapboard church and the way there, did he fully learn what he had walked himself into on that rainy day.

The graveyard where the deceased was bound lay peacefully in southside Virginia, beyond the green rolling hills through which now they slowly drove, a line of cars all with lights on, toward a lonely churchyard just over 100 miles away.

Littlest Theatre

And what, Marianne, should we observe and say about the littlest of little stages, which you and your collaborator Deborah Seabrooke have devised—Jabberbox Puppet Theatre—and presented to the delight of one and all in many a venue, including your own green craftsman home, perched up on a corner in Greensboro's historic Fisher Park?

That the arts will out and that no stage is too small, no roles or actors either, and that a Greensboro living room whose orchestra seating sells out at twenty-four patrons might be just as important as the Forty-Fourth Street Belasco on Broadway that tops out at 1,000.

In the Carolina world of little and regional theatres and outdoor dramas, of low-budget film in Shelby, Hollywood sound-stage film in Wilmington, and Full Frame documentaries in Durham, a puppet theatre may seem to be the least sparrow. Yet one of the most enduring traits of North Carolinians of all creative stripes has been our deep artesian wells of imagination, another our wholehearted appreciation of *all* those who step out from the wings and find the light anywhere. And if small figures on sticks that tread puppet boards can hold us heart and mind and touch us, too, then anyone anywhere can, and therein lies the inspiration and deep magic of the theatre.

Of *this* theatre: often issuing show warnings of *brief puppet nudity*, fearless dramatists Gingher and Seabrooke took on and adapted one of Fred Chappell's most intriguing tales, *Linnaeus Forgets*, staging it as *Beauty and the Botanist*, wherein Chappell's Linnaeus sees the life of the whole world in the magical fairylike people and creatures all living in a single tree. A time-traveling young woman deals with both Linnaeus and the January 21, 2017, Women's March on Washington in a show by turns musingly philosophical and acerbically political.

In the town of O. Henry et al., Jabberbox adult puppetry in Marianne Gingher's home was thrilling, the thespian work in no way *normal* but rather full of heart, highly articulate, microcosmic, and simply lovely—this, too, was the life of the theatre, which can never die.

Curtain up.

DOC IN MOCKSVILLE

We Red Clay Ramblers booked shows all over: Burlington, Vermont, in January and Kalamazoo, Michigan, too; Cleveland's Palace Theatre and Chicago's Old Town one February blizzard weekend; Winnipeg and Vancouver in the summers. We have driven up and down US 52 past majestic Pilot Mountain, climbed and descended the Blue Ridge above Mount Airy and Toast more times than I have kept count and at all hours of day and night.

Tommy Thompson and I once drove out to play a Mocksville, North Carolina, music festival, circa 1990, in my big blue 1971 Delta 88, pulling up to the pole barn where it was happening, and as he carried his banjo backstage, I walked over to the musicians' trailer after some water. When I opened the trailer door, I did so upon two men in the middle of a conversation.

One was Doc Watson, the absolutely superb singer and flat-pick guitarist, and the other was an admirer who had brought *his* guitar to the festival with hopes that Doc would hold and handle it, maybe play it, and lay his blessings upon it.

Doc was just then lifting the guitar up to his face, by its body, and sighting up the neck, up the frets toward the tuning pegs, and squinting, like he was taking aim and intending to shoot the guitar, fire off a round over my right shoulder.

"I tell you what," Doc said. "This is a fine-looking guitar."

"Well, thank you, Doc," the man said.

"I mean it," Doc said, "really fine looking." The blessing thus passed.

Not seeing a cooler, I backed on out, thinking, *Did I just see and hear the world's most famous blind guitarist, after sighting up a guitar neck, say* fine looking? Yes, I believe I did.

We played with Doc, split bills with him, a number of times—there in Mocksville, up in Illinois at the Schaumburg PAC and in the gorgeous little Woodstock Opera House, where Doc did his vocal warm-ups in his dressing room

Pilot Mountain, Surry County, with Sauratown Mountains beyond

by singing old Baptist hymns — "Rock of Ages," "How Great Thou Art," "In the Garden" — his warm clear voice echoing all throughout the theatre's backstage, and we ate ham sandwiches before the show in the suburban Chicago green room with it sounding for all the world like we were in a country church back in Doc's home of Deep Gap, North Carolina.

At the enormous arena near Carter-Finley Stadium on the west side of Raleigh, we opened for Doc, played a couple of numbers with him, then gave the stage over to him at this appreciation event for our four-term, progressive former governor Jim Hunt. Doc delighted the crowd, as he always did, with his seemingly effortless flat-picking and then gave them a melodramatic rendering of "Don't Mess with My Widder," a jealous dead man's rough-hewn warning from the grave to his old friends back in the land of the living; Doc's comically gruesome, corpse-like grimaces as he sang this threatening song, jumbotronned around the arena, truly brought an old-time vaudeville power and wonder into this early twenty-first-century soiree.

All in good, warmhearted theatrical fun — and I will always recall what a great help and comfort Doc had truly been to me when I was first living in New York City and missing North Carolina deeply.

One of the LPs I kept returning to showed Doc in a gambler's getup—gold vest, tawny Stetson shadowing his eyes, black tie—sitting before paisley wallpaper at a table with cards and chips all over it, staring, *looking*, as it were, at the five cards he had been dealt, and holding one red chip in his left hand, smiling wryly. With top-tier Music City sidemen like Floyd Cramer on piano and Shot Jackson on Dobro, and Doc himself on six- and twelve-string guitars and banjo, this was *Good Deal! Doc Watson in Nashville.*

A fine-looking record.

Fine sounding, too.

Mighty fine.

THE UWHARRIES

When I first started recording in Charlotte with bluesy, gravelly voiced Don Dixon of Lancaster, South Carolina, a musical force of nature, he described to me the best way to get to the city and the studio from my deep-woods home in Clover Garden, Bingham Township, southwest Orange County.

The *shortcut*, he called it, the back way.

"Go over to Eli Whitney, stay on the Old Greensboro Road past the millpond and on through Snow Camp, then straight at the Quaker church, to Pleasant Hill and on to Staley. You have to make a little jog at Staley, over the railroad tracks and then left near the PO and the grill, then right—you'll see the steel fabricator's big building off to the left. A few miles, a lot of farmland, and you'll hit NC 49, turn left on 49 down to Ramseur, shortcut by the old-timey water tower—Ramseur, that's where they burned all the rock-and-roll records that could get their hands on and pile up and light a match to, because they thought there were devil-worship messages encoded in the lyrics and the backbeats!

"Head west on US 64 over to Asheboro and then on the far side of Asheboro you take a left turn on NC 49 and that goes through the Uwharries all the way to Charlotte. Kind of empty and dark and quiet at night, but, still, it's the best way there is ..."

The Uwharries stand tall and proud high above the same-named river that flows through them, a national forest and a mountain range (one of the oldest on earth) comprising the biggest wilderness in the middle of North Carolina, a great wild country scarcely known, if at all, to most of our citizens. South and west of Asheboro, west of Troy and the state zoo and the state pottery center in Seagrove, this 50,000-acre big empty with its almost 1,000-foot peaks lures wild spirits to it, for the Uwharries are full of streams, trails, and ghosts.

Ann and I rambled all over these old hills one January, beginning with a brief stop at the Thornburg Trailhead on the northwest side of Birkhead Wilderness, bright winter sunlight and an enormous silence all around the old Lewis-Thornburg farmhouse, its clutch of old outbuildings, its stacked-log, zigzag fence. We soon passed a large furniture-company sawmill, its lumber stacked vertically in a domino-like line, then drifted on down Pisgah Covered Bridge Road to the bridge itself.

Lewis-Thornburg Farm at entry of Birkhead Mountains Wilderness, Uwharrie Mountains, Randolph County

At the covered bridge, set across the West Fork of Little River just below the two-lane blacktop, two men had already made their way ahead of us to study it, one of them white haired and wearing a ball cap, the other a pepper-gray longhair, smoking a nub of a cigar.

"The bridge washed away some time ago in that flood," said the long-haired man.

"Hard to believe," said the first man, "that water could get up that high."

"You can see lots of people been down here, *graffiti* all over the inside." He looked up and assayed the shake roof of the old wooden relic, adding, "Lot of moss on top—if it grows much more, they gonna have to *mow it*!"

We stopped in Troy for a fine barbeque lunch at the Capels' home (memorialized in song by Chapel Hill and Beaufort guitarist David Robert, whose "Christmastime on Chestnut Street" has been a family favorite for years), where big, friendly, cowboy-booted Jesse Capel fondly told of trail biking with his son, along with many other father-and-son teams, all over the Uwharries. "That was the most I ever knew about the Uwharrie Mountains before or since!" And he also recalled the pleasures of jonboat fishing in Badin Lake, formed by a dam on the Yadkin River on the far side of the forest from Troy: "What a thrill it was when that bass would hit the lure and just *explode*!"

After lunch we got the cook's tour of the family's impressively productive rug-making

factory, in the care of the family firm's marketing director, the witty and stylish Mary Clara Capel. She took us straightaway into the sewing plant, where two-unit flat braid strips were being sewn together, mostly in ovals, to make braided rugs of whatever size for some of the nation's prime catalog retailers—Pottery Barn, Garnet Hill, L. L. Bean. Jesse Capel had proudly insisted we get a good look at his ingenious invention, the "magic air table," which made big work possible for smaller people. These were broad tables set beside workers at sewing machines, each surface featuring a grid of one-to-two-inch holes through which forced air blew strongly, lifting large rugs that were being worked on, braid by braid abuilding, rugs that would otherwise have been huge dead weights.

At the age of seventeen, Mary Clara's grandfather had been making braided reins for mules and horses, under the name of the Gee Haw Harness Company, when he got a good look at the horseless carriage that rocked his young world. Observing that "Mister Henry Ford succeeds at whatever he sets his mind to," Granddaddy Capel knew in a trice that he was seeing the beginning of the end for horse-and-mule gear. And he soon figured out that his Gee Haw braiding mechanism could be adapted to making rugs and so went that way and found his fortune.

Outside the sewing plant, Mary Clara, wearing a white leather jacket and a scarf around her neck, reminisced about a celebratory photo shoot their advertising agency had planned.

"They'd found a donkey symbol, but I said,

Pisgah Covered Bridge, Uwharrie Mountains

'No, no, no, it *must* be a *mule*.'" The ad people asked, as one might have expected, "What's the difference?" Mary Clara went on: "They found a miniature mule named Wilma for the shoot, brought her up an elevator to the fourth floor of an old factory in High Point, but Wilma didn't like that at all and came off that elevator mad as fire. She bit *me*, she bit the creative director, and we got it *all on film*. That farmer who owned her was laughing all the way to the bank."

The firm got to celebrate nonetheless: successor to Gee Haw Harness, Capel Rugs marked its centennial in 2017, a North Carolina company through and through, its agrarian roots ensuring an elegant simplicity in its handiworks.

"All based," said Mary Clara Capel, "upon the figure-eight braid. Just like a girl braids her hair."

Twelve miles up the road from Troy at Eldorado ("el-duh-RAY-duh"), in the big supply house for campers and off-road four-wheelers, we found everything from propane to Vienna sausages, bandanas, camp chairs, fishing gear, western wear, boots, cowgirl signs, stuffed deer heads, and voracious taxidermied largemouth bass up on the back wall. Remembering Jesse's remark about how bass would hit the lures and *explode*, I kept my distance.

Up front, a middle-aged woman, answering the phone and finding nobody there, asked loudly: "Why's that always happen? Wonder what's goin' on?"

To which a younger woman said, "Probably somebody out in the *forest*—'I'm *stuck*, come *get me!*'"

From Eldorado, jumping-off point into the northern Uwharries, we headed up Coggins Mine Road, a slender lane owing its name to the nineteenth-century Carolina gold-mining era not just in the Uwharrie Mountains but all along an east-west band from Franklin County above Raleigh over to Charlotte. Before the Civil War, as many as fifteen gold mines—placer, shaft, and open pit—operated here in the Uwharries, and the most successful, the Russell Mine near Eldorado, was an acre-sized pit, one of whose managers—industrialist Charles Fisher—became the namesake of Fort Fisher near the mouth of the Cape Fear River, the fort with the two-mile-range cannon that kept the port of Wilmington open and prolonged the Civil War. The veins of gold in the Uwharrie rocks proved too slender to sustain the rush, and, nowadays, the old Russell Mine pit grew mature trees whose crowns were not as tall as the pit's sides were deep.

Back on Chestnut Street in Troy, Jesse Capel had talked about contemporary gold mining up in here. "There's a bunch of guys," he said, "still go in and pan for gold. They've all got these little vials, like a pill bottle, with maybe *that much*" (here he indicated two fingers worth) "flakes of gold in there." Jesse reported that so-and-so had gotten a museum set up at the site of the old Coggins Mine, adding that the Carolina gold rush of the 1820s and 1830s motivated a lot of folks to come to Montgomery County, to head down from the North to mine for gold. Then he looked meaningfully at his daughter and said: "The Carbones."

"I thought he was a painter," Mary Clara said.

"Well, he *is*," said Jesse. "He painted houses 'cause he couldn't make enough money mining for gold."

More successful, and more long-lasting, in the mining pursuit were the rhyolite diggings and doings of the Paleo-Indians, the Native Americans who for eons—going back at least 12,000 years—were working up thousands of projectile points, scrapers, and other tools at and around the Hardaway site at the north end of a high ridge overlooking Badin Lake on the forest's western side. Highly regarded attorney and musician Wade Smith of Raleigh, who grew up in Albemarle, once recalled for me with relish camping in the Uwharries and looking for points in the Hardaway area when he was a boy.

We wanted river more than museum, gold, or points, so we bore east onto Low Water Bridge Road and thence rolled slowly down the dark lane to the bridge across the Uwharrie River, a long unrailed concrete affair not shipping, that day, any of the river's brown waters. On we went, through the minuscule village of Ophir and east toward Flint Hill—on this road, one staring off at the mountains to the north might well imagine being not an hour's drive from downtown Raleigh but rather far out in western Carolina beside some vast, awesome range.

Something *haunting* there was about such an empty, high-peaked, dark-hollowed territory, as a pair of gnarly nineteenth-century tales may prove out.

In one story, a man met up with his old friend Alfred Hanes, who was boiling eggs in a bucket at a ford south of Cedar Rock Mountain (950 feet in the Birkhead Wilderness), and then and there heard the indiscreet Hanes's plan to run off with Bob Lumber's wife, the new illicit couple's assets little more than the clothes on their backs and one twenty-dollar bill. Mrs. Lumber appeared later that same day at Rupert Freeman's store, there to buy a pair of shoes and then to leave alone. Now, Bob Lumber was known always to carry a shotgun, and the rest is speculation: Did Lumber catch and confront the new couple and shoot, kill, and bury rival Hanes in a shallow streamside grave somewhere in the Uwharrie wilds?

Who knew?

Mrs. Lumber reappeared a month later at Freeman's store, again alone.

And Alfred Hanes was never seen again.

In another tale, Civil War bounty hunters tracked down three Confederate deserters, the young Hulen brothers, found them between Ophir and Flint Hill near the Likker Spring and the Painted Rock, and summarily slayed the three men. January 28, 1865: the bounty hunters rolled the bodies of these fatally unlucky men into a common grave at a place called Lovejoy.

And the name of the Uwharrie spot right where the Hulen brothers had been killed?

Dark Mountain.

MINT CITY REFLECTION

When Don Dixon grew up in Lancaster, South Carolina, future rhythm-and-blues star Major "Um, Um, Um, Um, Um, Um" Lance was still pumping gas there. By the time Don, a fine tennis player like his father, hit sixteen, he had also taken up guitar and bass and spent many a weekend night playing with the Ardells at Club Adora in wet Kershaw County. ("Hard soul, deep country," he recalled, "and Hack, the owner, would call out a square dance while playing fiddle during the last fifteen minutes of each set!") Ere long Dixon started drifting the few miles north to Charlotte, a magnet for musicians for decades, a town where radio, recording, and live performance had built many a career since the 1920s and '30s, from banjoist Wade Mainer and Arthur C. "Chitlin' Cooking Time in Cheatham County" Smith to the Briarhoppers powering out music to millions over WBT's heavy-duty signal (already at 50,000 watts by 1933).

What really drew Dixon, though, was Reflection Sound, which drummer Wayne Jernigan set up, for over two generations one of the finest recording studios in the American South. Tall, friendly, down-home Jernigan had drummed long and hard for country baritone Ernest "Waltz Across Texas" Tubb, till he saw a better way than endless miles, endless motels, and life in Nashville. Jernigan saved his hard-won road-dog cash and put it into this brick-and-mortar twenty-four-track creative cauldron on Central Avenue in Charlotte.

Because Dixon found his way to Reflection, the world is a better place; because he put his great voice, his wondrous musicality, and his fierce concentration all to work here, *so* much work here, he shared his lifetime's worth of the gifts of creation, performance, and production, as he worked and bore witness to many other musicians coming to Charlotte and passing through. James Brown laid down "Papa's Got a Brand New Bag" at Arthur Smith's studio nearby, and Reflection later bought the U47 microphone Brown used on that hit, Don and everyone else calling it "James Brown" ever after.

Vocalist Dottie Pearson became gospel singer Dottie Peoples and launched her career from here. Crackerjack musicians from fraudulent Jim Bakker's *PTL* ("Praise the Lord") *Club* television show (ridiculed by many Charlotteans, even in its money-gleaning heyday, as the "Pass the Loot" Club and skewered forcefully by Pulitzer-winning cartoonist Doug Marlette) worked here. So did hoarse-voiced General Johnson and the Chairmen of the Board, the inspired southerners of "Girl Watcher" and "It Will Stand" renown.

So did Dixon's popular band Arrogance. And so did R.E.M., the band Dixon and his excellent longtime studio cohort Mitch Easter recorded here in its initial efforts, *Murmur* in 1983 and *Reckoning* in 1984. The afternoon when Dixon

laid down his own epic love-and-longing gospel ballad "I Can Hear the River" with John P. Kee and the New Life Community Choir, he stood, rocked, and sang his heart and soul out in Reflection Studio A, right into that special mike named James Brown.

Dixon showed up at my Bingham Township cabin door one night and knocked me over with a feather when he kindly asked me to come record a collection of my songs with him at Reflection, and so we did. Our friendship at that point covered nearly a decade, and whenever I asked him how he got so much done, he would say, "I know that *if* I get to the pearly gates, Saint Peter is not going to reward me for the things I *meant* to do."

Almost every time Dixon in the control room hit *record* for a take, his warm, enthusiastic voice sounded through everyone's earphones, booming, "Let the big dog *eat*!"

One evening he was out in the studio preparing to lead a seven-member string section in recording the chart he had written for my ballad "Home on the River," a coastal man's romantic fantasy. The players would be overdubbing to my piano and vocal track, and a couple of them had invited their wives to sit in the control room and watch through the glass as the string parts went down. My role this evening was to run the two-inch, twenty-four-track tape, so I was in there with the visitors.

The players were top-notch, all of them from the orchestra of the absurdly popular *PTL Club*. From the studio floor, Dixon at last signaled me and I pushed the red button, and over the speakers in the control room came my piano and vocal, along with the new string parts. We would get what we wanted on about the sixth take.

But after the very first, one of the visiting wives leaned her head back my way and asked me, "God, *who* is that horrible singer?" as her companion added, dismissively, "I mean!"

With as much poise as I could muster, trying not to laugh, I said, "'Tis I."

To which both women, as one, grunted, "Oooagghh," and said no more to me. They did manage to sit exceedingly still through the next hour, and they created no further distraction.

When we had our take, and the players had packed their violins and cellos, they and their visitors headed on out. As soon as I had a private moment with Dixon, I told him about this humorous exchange, whereupon my even-tempered friend got so mad he wanted to go chase them down in the Reflection parking lot and give them a large piece of his Lancaster mind. But I would not let him, just waved it off with a comment given me by a fictional baseball player named Hog Durham: "Don't worry about them, Don," I said. "They're 'the salt of the earth—nothing'll grow where they live.'"

When many years later Jernigan sold the property, its wiring, its Hammond B3 organ and all the rest of its magical gear in the early summer of 2014, he closed the door, regretfully, on forty-five years of great southern music making. And Dixon, who presided over fifty album projects in the plain box near the Salvation Army store and the Krispy Kreme doughnut shop, was the last man out the door, after he polished off the latest beach-music recordings of Dip Ferrell and the Truetones.

"My favorite studio in the world," Don Dixon said.

"I feel more weird about it than I thought I would."

A month and a half after *King Mackerel* played Flat Rock in the fall of 1995, we recorded the score at Reflection and resettled the show in Charlotte's Booth Playhouse downtown. In that deep-mauve-and-gray house we ran nicely, though one critic declared Charlotte to be such a sophisticated town that it had little need for the sort of coastal chowder-house chorale we put forth in *King Mackerel*. Another referred to me blithely as "the poor man's Willie Nelson," amusing me but offending my older daughter, Susannah, no small bit.

In those days Charlotte presented an empty, haunted downtown by night. After our full-house shows, the theatregoers, cheerful coming out of our coastal evening in the Booth, nonetheless rushed to their cars, the College Street parking garage emptying in a heartbeat, and we Coastal Cohorts were left to repair to the one and only pub several blocks north before retiring to our hotel at Fifth and Trade.

This was, admittedly, before the coming of Panthers football and Hornets basketball and the huge Ivey's department store being renovated into center-city condominiums, all of which presaged better, at the very least more populous, evenings for the downtown. When I returned with daughter Susannah to catch a Friday evening show only a few years later, the two of us were positively beset by cigar bars and bistros of all sorts in that same neighborhood, and Charlottean boulevardiers of many stripes tripped Mecklenburg's light fantastic and made a joyful, if at times less than intelligible, noise indeed.

Some nights soon after our show had come

down, I would be driving home 'round midnight, eastbound again on NC 49, past the little shop out in the woods beside the road east of Concord, the one that sold secondhand model railroad cars and equipment—as Christmas was approaching, I had bought an orange boxcar there for my ten-year-old son Hunter's American Flyer train set—and on east through the tiny towns of Davidson County and Stanly County and then once again up into the tall broad Uwharries, dark and undaunted, the ancient mountains.

For company I had the all-night Charlotte radio station spinning Bill Evans's "Waltz for Debby" and Miles Davis's "So What?" with Evans's piano in the mix and, too, songs from North Carolina's own musical greats Trane and Monk and Nina Simone of Tryon moaning "I Loves You, Porgy," a sweet, funky, soulful syncopated end to all those theatrical nights, majestic American music from other days, other times, dreamy dark-night jazz from the Queen City radio following me east down NC 49, then down even quieter lanes through Staley, Pleasant Hill, Snow Camp, Eli Whitney, to Clover Garden at last.

Don Dixon's way, the shortcut, the very best way home.

III
Jump-Up Country

Now he was in the world of mountain secrets, of lost ways and weasels.

JOHN EHLE, *THE LAND BREAKERS*

Hawksbill Mountain, Linville Gorge Wilderness

FONTANA FINDS
A FLATLANDS BOY

For many years now, when I have put my feet up, my bootheels have come to rest atop a little four-legged pine footstool. The legs peg through a piece of slabwood, and, though the pine bark has grayed over time and lost its deep, almost purple-brown cast, the stool is as sturdy now as it was one dusky summer evening sixty years ago, when it caught my eye in a Cherokee trading post and I paid out eight of my twenty-five dollars' traveling money to have something fine to bring home from the mountains for my mother.

This was my first trip to the jump-up country of the Carolina Smokies, my first sighting of the big blue hills, the Beaucatcher Tunnel, the cider shacks, and the fabled mountain cattle that we heard had shorter legs on their uphill sides and all that. I was only recently removed from the flatlands of Pasquotank and was barely used to the red-clay rise and fall of Chapel Hill and Orange County. The Blue Ridge and the Smokies beyond, to a boy from the black-water swamps, were simply grand.

It was a scout adventure, and we had the gear. I borrowed a big rucksack, a pear-shaped pre-Kelty pack that very neatly put a metal bar in the small of my back, and my mother and I paid a call on Sarge Keller, then Woollen Gym's quartermaster at the University of North Carolina, to see if he had any kneepads the college boys had worn out and that might be tossed my way. He did, and though I thought it an unnecessary motherly precaution at that moment, I blessed Mama and Sarge quite often over the many miles I spent on bended knee in our seatless canoe. There were two or three men and about sixteen boys on the Fontana expedition, so we had a flotilla of some eight or nine boats. Most of them were Grummans, one of yellow fiberglass and another, my favorite, an old-timey vessel of wood ribbing and black painted canvas.

When we had met as a troop in Chapel Hill and scrubbed and loaded the boats, we also went ahead and assigned them. I was one of the younger scouts on this mission and didn't expect to get my choice, but to my surprise and delight Gordon Kage, an Air Force colonel's boy, and I got the black canoe. We spent the first night at a scout camp near Bryson City, where after an enormous evening downpour we all lay in the bunks of our three-sided cabins and listened to the dripping woods and to a rising, rushing creek nearby. The next morning, we rode down to the boat dock west of Bryson City and put in there on the Tuckasegee River and began our westward trek to Fontana Dam, thirty miles away.

We were eagerly off, bound for a campsite at the mouth of Forney Creek about six miles distant. The Tuckasegee ran north for the first couple of miles, then made a sharp westward turn, and, as Gordon and I watched from a half mile back while all the other boats disappeared around that bend, there and then the gods of all small craft revealed to us why it was we had gotten our choice of canoes: it was heavy, nearly forty pounds heavier than any of the other boats, and it leaked, nothing titanic in nature, just a slow percolation that then puddled and sloshed about and licked at our packs and sleeping bags, that saturated Sarge's kneepads.

And we were barely out of Bryson City.

When we rounded that first big bend, our comrades up ahead spotted us, and they were not so far off that we could not hear their cheers, then their echoing laughter, and finally their crooning out the two words that were taunt and nickname all week long:

"Hey, *Ka-ro!*"

"Hey, *Mo-lasses!*"

Had I known more, I would have asked that they speak to us in Cherokee and call us *tsik-sitsi*, or *tuckasegee*, which meant *crawling terrapin*. But I was new to these hills, and all I really knew of Cherokee was the little pine footstool now stashed in the trunk of one of the cars. So we endured the slurs about our sluggishness, bailing away with

a mess-kit cup and digging at the lake for all we were worth, which Gordon and I assured each other must be precious little.

When we finally reached Forney Creek, twenty or thirty minutes after the rest, we found all the tents already pitched, everyone lounging around, and, though we cast the most covetous looks upon those Grummans as we pulled our black beauty out of the water and flipped it and trudged into camp, we knew much better than to ask any of our fellows to look mercifully upon us and swap.

Around the big fire that night there was talk of bear, and there was such keen interest and

respect and apprehension among us that I know we all half expected a bruin or two to stalk into camp once we were asleep and let us know whose country this really was.

We knew. And we knew well enough to duffel bag our food and hoist and hang this aromatic sack in a tree whose lowest limbs were at least twenty feet up. Next morning, after gallivanting around the falls and cascades just above Forney Creek's mouth into the lake, we packed some dehydrated chicken a la king for dinner and pancake mix for breakfast and then set out to conquer a mountain.

Hiking, walking, ambling, shambling,

stumbling, our troop made a varied but steady headway up the big hill—High Rocks Mountain—through beech and hickory and oak, on logging paths not oft traversed these days, at the top of which we intended to plant our flag and spend the night and gaze down on all creation as soon as the morning sun lit up the world.

Halfway up High Rocks' southeastern spine we ran out of water. Sixteen thirsty boys with empty pint-sized canteens and still 2,000 feet to climb. Clearly, the men had not counted on this, but if they were anxious, they masked it well. There would be water at the summit, at the abandoned fire tower and ranger station our maps showed awaiting us.

We were trudging now, midafternoon, four or five hours till dark. There was no shortage of joking about how much water different ones could drink once we found water again—a gallon, a bathtub, a swimming pool, Fontana Lake itself! But after a spell everyone was sucking on twigs, doggedly moving upward and accepting with resignation our presence in the high-slope realm of intermittent streams. We studied the maps, hearts leaping at the sight of each stream that lay ahead in our path, hearts sinking as we experienced each successive one in the dry period of its intermittence. None of us, I daresay, had ever been so parched before. At least one boy, overcome by the exertion and thirst, broke down and cried.

At dusky dark we reached the peak, where the angle-iron tower loomed over the vine-covered and padlocked cabin. Round and round the cabin we went, expecting a spigot, but there was none, and we were very low till one of the men cracked a cellar door and in the flashlight beam there before us lay the prize: a *full* 200-gallon cistern.

I stood at the top of the fire tower next morning, a solid mile above sea level, enchanted by the sight of Fontana far below, a silver-gold shifting and shimmering over the fingers of the lake as the sun came on and climbed.

Off the other way to the north was Clingmans Dome, and on up the spiny border between Tennessee and Carolina, just eight miles though we could not see it, was Mount Kephart, a 6,400-foot peak named for an American patron saint of *way out yonder where there ain't nobody never is.* Horace Kephart, a troubled soul who left his library directorship, wife, and six children in St. Louis for the outback of early 1900s western Carolina, published his extensive *Camping and Woodcraft* works five years ahead of the initial *Boy Scout Handbook* we carried in our packs. And although it would be years before I would learn of this man and his Appalachian portrait, *Our Southern Highlanders*, I would have thanked him that day—had I known—for his helping hand in getting the Great Smokies set aside as a park for the nation.

Years hence hereabouts, the inspired memoirist and fly-fisherman Harry Middleton would find himself drifting, in his words, on the spine of time, hearing mystical bagpipes on just-to-the-west Hazel Creek, airs played by a piper whom Middleton would never see. Tom Earnhardt would be renting a skiff when he could at the Almond Dock on the lake, motoring over and leaving it at the mouth of Hazel Creek and trout fishing for glory up Hazel himself. And another great future friend, David Perry, would one day be chasing trout higher up than Hazel on one of its tributaries, Bone Valley Creek, fishing late in the day till he came to Bone Valley's own tributaries—Defeat and Desolation Creeks—and in a pool there losing his leader. Out of the creek and starting down Bone Valley as the day faded, he mused about being in this place that he just knew no man had ever seen before, right up to the moment his boot kicked something in the leaf litter and he tripped over the remains of a wood stove. Perry had literally stumbled into the

Fishing on Hazel Creek, north side of Fontana Lake

remnants of an old high-mountain logging camp, where he would now find traces of a railroad grade and follow it on down the mountain.

That morning up on High Rocks, running through the dew that the night clouds had left us, we collected quart after quart of wild blueberries, mixed them up with the pancake batter, and then, in a real stroke, we made do for the cooking oil we did not have by greasing our pans with syrup. What we created atop that mountain was worthy of the state fair—we all got giddy off these sugar-imbued, crystalline-crusted flapjacks. We ate our fill of this sweet bait and started back for the

mouth of Forney Creek a considerably happier troop than had arrived the night before.

Even if we were not exactly Sherpas, we had endured a trial, slept uncovered under all God's stars, and climbed a real mountain that we could now come down in triumph. The black canoe was still the heaviest and slowest, but Gordon and I bent to our task with a vigor we had not had before High Rocks.

It rained, we bailed. And when one afternoon a high easterly blew down the lake, we rigged a big wind-grabbing sail out of our ponchos and paddles and for once caught up with and impressed the rest of the fleet.

On the fifth day we reached the Fontana Dam, the highest in eastern America. I remember staring goggle-eyed down the great swoop of cement at fishermen far below. We did not have time to wander into Fontana Village, the former construction camp rescued by tourists from the ghosts, but we learned that other Fontana villages—a lumber-company tent town, a mining camp with its own hotel and cornet band—lay far beneath the waters that had drawn us here.

Now we pulled hard for home, still Karo and Molasses, still trailing most all the time, but now openly enjoying our tenure with the toughest craft. One drizzly evening in camp, Gordon and I conspired to patch the boat's leak, which had grown steadily worse. We scraped resin from a pine, heated it, and effectively gummed up the little fissure and so brought ourselves back to Bryson City agreeably dry.

For most of us this was the longest time yet away from home and family and, too, the longest time between baths. When we bathed in the murky lake after loading the canoes but before lighting out for the foothills, everyone's soap immediately sank and disappeared, all but mine: a big cake of buoyant Ivory. I could not wait to get back to Chapel Hill and tell all about the trip, the floating soap, the pine-resin repair, the twenty thirsty mountain-climbing miles, the sixty more in our slow boat to Fontana Village and back—and to bring home the pine-bark trophy.

Upon my weary return to the Piedmont from this week of being a diminutive mountain man, explorer, and voyageur, I proudly presented my mother with the Cherokee footstool. I did not know then that I had really bought it for myself—I was only twelve. But she knew as soon as she saw the rustic little piece and quickly said that it would best fit my room, just beyond the bunk bed, where I loved to sit in an old easy chair with the 1956 Hammond *World Atlas* that I still have, forever studying the wilderness and, like

any rambler who has ever been pulled forth by the bend in the river and the curve in the road, forever roaming the world.

A FEW DAYS AT LOW GAP

Five years after that Fontana float, somewhere on the hill climb up NC 18 toward Doughton Park on the Blue Ridge Parkway, a place of green rolling highland meadows and deep steep hollows, our old Opel sedan lost its third gear, top of its shifting range. We four eighteen-year-olds soldiered on—nothing yet to be done about it. On climbs the car couldn't go out of second anyhow, and on any downhills it could simply coast. How we would ever return to the Piedmont from these high hills was a scary question that would have to wait.

At the small general store in Laurel Springs we sought help, and folks there directed us to a certain mechanic who *might could* help us. A mile or so outside of the village, we drove into his driveway, first crossing a creek and then coming around to his backyard, where the man himself stood in jeans, plaid shirt, and boots, beneath a broad maple, grilling steaks. As we got out of the Opel and approached, we all saw that he was moving the meat around the grill with a fork in his left hand while holding a 12-gauge shotgun almost straight up with his right, its butt on his hip. Before we got to him, without looking up from the grill he discharged it once into the evening sky.

I walked up to him very slowly and asked him if he knew anything about fixing third gears in Opels. He glanced over at the car, shook his head, and said that even if he *did* it would take two to three weeks to get foreign-car parts back up in here. He then allowed as *maybe* somebody could help us down at the 421 Speed Shop in Wilkesboro, the mountain town from which we had just come up into this higher country, the road to which ran up and down several lines of mountains and covered many miles.

We stood glumly for a few moments, as if, by our waiting, his pronouncements might change in our favor, till he suddenly blasted off another round from the shotgun.

From six feet away the roar was deafening. This time, he lifted his gaze from the grill to us, saying simply: "Bats."

In the morning, Sean Ripperton, the Opel owner, and I drove up and over the mountain ranges, winding out in second, coasting when we could, taking a couple of hours to go eighteen miles on roads the Wilkes County moonshine-and-champion-race-car-driver Junior Johnson could likely have handled in fifteen minutes—this was Junior's country, not ours, and as we struggled with the wounded little foreign car, I sorely felt our weakness on this vaunted road that Junior would have mortally torn up and, wishing we were in his Ford and he were behind the wheel, I thought, *Not for nothing had Tom Wolfe called Junior "the Last American Hero"!*

At the 421 Speed Shop, they reckoned dispassionately that no one this side of Winston-Salem would know *anything* about working on Opels. On the wall of the dingy office hung a calendar with a photo at the top of a scantily clad blond woman bestride an ottoman. Though she smiled (she was pitching Hurst shifters or some such), she did not seem as if she would take any interest in the likes of us, even if our Opel *were* in working order.

"Sorry, fellas," the man said. "You're kinda outa luck."

So back up to Doughton Park we drove, taking even longer going back up, with the added burden of knowing what a chore the ride home to Chapel Hill would be.

Once we eased onto the Blue Ridge Parkway, though, something quite wonderful happened.

We simply forgot about it.

We parked the Opel, caught back up with our two other fellow campers (George Penick and Dave Harrison) and walked the short distance to the Brinegar Cabin overlook, several hundred feet below which was a wooden-shingled outpost where one Martin Brinegar and his wife Caroline had once farmed and raised children. Without any discussion whatsoever, all four of us stepped over the guardrail and started down the sixty-degree grade, grabbing saplings to break our slides, leaning back, laughing at the ease of our descent, dropping in altitude 100 feet or more every couple of minutes, even through the dense low woods and brush.

In less than ten minutes we were at the bottom, which had looked like a clearing from way up above, but now, close in, turned out to be an area overgrown with pokeweed, poison ivy, broom sedge, and such. We stomped about this patch, stomped through the doorless frame, and toured the small, unadorned, ramshackle building, wondering in jocular fashion how a man and a woman and some children could live in this small place.

Some children? Four was the actual number, though one of them did not live past infancy. Small place? Indeed: just a one-room, south-facing cabin with a loft in a two-acre bottom, where the Brinegars had lived and farmed from the late 1800s till the middle of the Depression, when the parkway took it over. Martin had died a decade earlier, and Caroline at last deemed the roadbuilding noise and whining tires of parkway traffic high above to be way too obtrusive down in the bottom, and she took her loom and left her longtime home in the hollow to go live with her daughter a few ridges away.

What on earth did we young men think we could possibly *know*, or *divine*, from a brief mountain slide down to this remote spot, followed by a mere quarter hour's inspection?

What could we know of how hard it was to grow any damn thing, with a short growing season, one that might not top or even come close to 160 days, when the sun did not come over one

Stone Mountain, border of Allegheny and Wilkes Counties

ridge till midmorning and then was gone over the other before four? Which of us, who knew next to nothing of love, could say whether those several children were some real sign of true, lusty love between the Brinegars or only a blunt statistic of proximity for a man and woman living mostly in the dark just underneath the top of the world?

And what could we (I worked in my uncle's stationery store, Dave in his parents' camera store, George at the pharmacy) possibly comprehend of tough, endless subsistence-farming days in this clawed-out patch, five lives spent almost entirely this way?

Each of us would have little time to cipher on

such questions in the moment, as we hand-over-fist grabbled our ways back up the steep slope, holding and sometimes hooking elbows around the bottoms of tree trunks that would be now at eye level, next where we would put our feet, and push onward and upward. Magnificent exertions, till an hour later we found ourselves exhausted, again up top at the overlook.

Another day we would shimmy up the smooth granite monadnock of nearby Stone Mountain, which would become a state park three years later, and view the world from atop that cold curving rock, then slide slowly, trepidatiously back down. We would take on craggy, slanted, shrub-flecked, and aptly named Alligator Back, upon which one scrambled to gain any height, though in some step-by-step way this was better climbing than our slippery efforts on Stone Mountain had been. At one steep point I placed my hand high above me on a ledge and pulled up till I was almost even with it and then saw, less than a foot away, a very large snake. I went cold, but in a flash, just before I let go and tumbled down Lord knows how far, I realized that I was staring at the snake's abandoned *skin*.

Back at the Doughton Park campground, we met folks we might never have known had we not made this late-summer trek to the mountains, like the companionable long-haul trucker who strolled up to us at a cattail pond where we were fishing.

"Doing any good?" he said.

Not so much, we allowed, just as we were studying on how to get a bullfrog off a fishhook. "I been all over," he said and, learning we were students, he bragged:

"Delivered to *all* the colleges in North Carolina, I know I have, but I can't remember ever being in Chapel Hill . . ."

"Carolina," one of us said, and he lit right up. "*That's* the damn one!"

If the trucker could get from here to there and back, we began to feel that ultimately the wounded Opel was—somehow—not going to be such a trouble after all, not after what we had seen and come up against as we spent our days climbing about this stunningly rugged terrain. The laconic mechanic down in the valley, devoted only to American-made cars, enjoying himself grilling out and keeping the bats off his steaks with the occasional 12-gauge blast, made better sense to us now. So, even, did our intrepid fellow camper George's kneeling down and feeding potato chips to a visiting skunk that approached our campfire one evening, though the rest of us had backed carefully away.

And what could have made more sense to our eyes than the feast of a full sturgeon moon the night before we left, a blue moon at the end of August rising over the cushion of silver-lit valley clouds, sitting easy and proud and magical, held by the high-meadows country just for a spell? Maybe just for us who had walked down to watch it climb and light up the world through an opening the old-timers who lived there, way before even the Brinegars, had named simply: *Low Gap.*

HIGH COUNTRY

A common joke in the remainder of the state was that the only way to get to the Lost Province was to be born there.
Andrew Mason, head brewer,
Lost Province Brewing Company, Boone

Just west of the Blue Ridge, the two forks of the New River—the North, the South—drain Watauga, Ashe, and Allegheny Counties: the fabled, hard-to-reach "Lost Province." The headwaters of the New River here in our state are a remnant of the prehistoric Teays River, which drained much of eastern and north central America before the most recent Ice Age and prefigured the Ohio River system.

Only the Nile River in Egypt, some say, is older than the New River, and the only thing really *new* about this river was how it surprised its colonial discoverers, state-line surveyor Peter Jefferson in 1749 and Col. Abraham Wood of Virginia in 1654, the latter believing he was the first white man to see it and naming it for himself, though Jefferson may have been the one to change its name from Wood's River to New River. Of the discovery of the New, Governor Gabriel Johnston of North Carolina said: "No one had ever dreamt of it!"

Well, not exactly, Governor.

Native Americans—particularly the Cherokee—had been hunting, fishing, and traversing the basin of one of our country's few *major* northward-flowing rivers for 10,000 or

12,000 years. Even so, this northwestern North Carolina land was a lonely, uninhabited territory in colonial times. In December 1752, Moravian bishop August Spangenberg explored the upper reaches of the New River and complained in his detailed diary of his party's "bitter journey among the mountains … virtually lost … literally walled in on all sides … nothing but bleak mountains." He deemed the area unfit for his flock, and so the Moravians settled well east of here, in Bethabara, Bethania, and Salem.

Capt. Jonathan Cox, an early New River settler, recalled there being only two or three hunter's cabins in this part of the country in 1755. In the 1760s the great wilderness explorer Daniel Boone hunted the New River headwaters, staying in one of those cabins Captain Cox recalled, and led parties to the West through this part of the world in the fall of 1767 and in May of 1769.

Boone left his name behind on the Watauga County seat, while Ashe County seat Jefferson and its neighbor West Jefferson owed their names to surveyor Peter Jefferson's son, third president Thomas Jefferson.

One May day in 1986, about midafternoon, I met Frank Queen and his architect cousin Joe Sam Queen in West Jefferson, and we left one of our cars there in that idyllic little mountain town, where a small cheese manufactory sat on a side street and early-season tourists drifted lazily toward it through the cool highland air. We drove the other car a few miles out of town up a narrow valley to the Longhope Club, a plain, tucked-away trout-fishing outpost.

Tom Massengale, founding director of the North Carolina Nature Conservancy and our host, had invited a string band in for the evening, and though few of the dozen guests danced (one couple did whirling free-form pirouettes unrelated to the rhythm in the room but highly tied to one all their own, which Joe Sam and Frank, Haywood County heirs to their grandfather Sam Queen's historic smooth-dancing mountain traditions, laughingly called "a hippie dance"), the rest of us did listen closely to the excellent picking with real pleasure that night: "Little Birdie," "Uncle Pen," "Tom Dula" …

The next morning we were a few miles outside of West Jefferson, where the New River's two forks sit like a wishbone around a host of amphibolite peaks: Phoenix and Little Phoenix Mountains, Mount Jefferson, Three Top Mountain and Paddy Mountain, and one of North America's most treasured wonders of botanical diversity: Bluff Mountain.

Over 400 species of plants grew on spectacular Bluff, prized as the single most diverse spot for flora in the entire Southern Appalachians. Preserving Bluff Mountain by purchasing 701 acres of it from Ashe County's Edwards family was the successful goal of the first fundraising campaign mounted by Tom's then-fledgling North Carolina Nature Conservancy in the late 1970s. The conservancy would keep adding to the preserve in the years since, and it would grow to about 3,800 acres.

At a pipe gate at the foot of Bluff, the conservancy's live-in steward met us and hauled us in a small van up the steep-sided but almost flat-topped mountain, once on top showing us a rocky, marsh-grassed fen, through which most of the mountain's scant water flowed, then a dwarf Carolina hemlock forest on the east side.

These were aged trees, though not very tall, for they had grown in the face of strong, bitter winds and in almost no soil at all—their roots went way down into crevices for what little water and nutrients they could find, hemlocks growing out of the very rocks. Another dwarf forest nearby— red oaks and white oaks—showed equal hardiness under the harshest conditions, and like the hemlocks these gnarly trees were also portraits in survival.

The steward guided us to the border of this wood, to a sheer cliff hundreds of feet tall, off

Lookin' Off Place, Bluff Mountain, Ashe County

which, he said, a young camper, disoriented in the night, had walked to his doom not so many years earlier. The short woods had already struck me as eerie enough *before* I learned this chilling fact, and then afterward ...

There but for fortune, I thought, and we all backed away from this lip of oblivion. Atop Bluff Mountain seemed no place to be at night.

We walked on from the cliff around to a small, level, unfenced opening on the mountainside: the Lookin' Off Place, also hundreds of feet above the fields and forests of the North and South Fork

144

valleys below. In eons past, mountains taller than the Rockies stood right here, and the top of Bluff Mountain, this rare high wonder now, was *their* valley floor.

One could hardly help being awed by Bluff's loveliness. Not a place to let oneself be dizzied, though, by any living thing—the edges lay too near. We came down slowly, and slowly eased away and then went and climbed up another high spot Tom wanted to share with us that day, Bald Mountain near Todd, not far to the south.

On Bald Mountain's graceful surface we found nothing sheer, no dangerous drop-offs at all, just high, rolling, open hillsides with patches of wild flame azaleas in full bright-orange bloom. Our North Carolina west features a number of these open unforested spaces, like Roan Mountain and Max Patch, and author John Ehle spoke of them in *The Land Breakers*: "These balds were the footprints of a giant who had once walked through, some of the mountain people said."

"You like?" Tom asked me.

"Of course," I said. "This is fabulous."

And then I drifted away in space and time: What possibly was there *not* to like about this portion of Ashe County, this glorious almost-mile-high wide-open place, with waves of shorter blue-veiled hills going off forever? Looking out over this ocean of mountains, I could almost hear Sam Cooke and the Soul Stirrers singing "Nearer, My God, to Thee" in the top of my heart.

"Just imagine," Tom said, bringing it all back home, "being out here in these azaleas some moonlit night, with a lovely woman ..." His voice trailed off as he looked away, smiling, but his romantic vision at that moment in my life, clearly by no intention or awareness of his, struck at my heart.

"Yes," I said, suddenly melancholy. "Just imagine that."

Yet the time would indeed come when I no longer had to imagine, and prescient Tom was no small

part of it, for he and he alone introduced me to Ann Cary Kindell of Sea Level at the Nature Conservancy's southeast regional headquarters in Chapel Hill, where they both worked.

Thirty-odd years later, Ann and I at last made it to Bluff Mountain ourselves, just we two and June the Pomeranian one gorgeous August day, slowly switchbacking our way up it to glory in a rented four-wheel drive. No other place in the state was anything like this at all, for once up on top of it, one found Bluff as tabletop-flat as Edgecombe County down east, and that three-acre fen sprouted and sported all manner of wildflowers, coming up out of the fen's small wet rocks and pebbles, which let its water go slowly trickling through.

Small white flowers bloomed everywhere like dots of cotton.

One of the last things one might expect to find atop a mountain was this very rare creation, the *only* upland fen in all the great hills of the Southern Appalachians. The fen's stony soil was only nine inches deep, on average, almost always saturated, fed by groundwater percolating down from higher slopes on the mountaintop's west side. Up here the wind and cold was extreme—every month of the year felt freezing temperatures, and the shallow soil of the fen would freeze to the bedrock in wintertime. Yet records showed over 140 species of plants and mosses in this fen alone, one in every ten of them rare, if not endangered, in North Carolina.

Sun and shade alternated as big cumulus clouds went rolling over us in the blue sky above, and over the stunted oaks and the dwarf Carolina hemlocks, and barred owls kept sounding off: *Who cooks for you?* We walked the great oval trail that went all the way around the fen, flowers everywhere in the woods.

The land rose a bit on the west side, and I told Ann a tale from about 1830, of a stockman named Perkins who was on this mountaintop when a bad storm came up. He took shelter for the night

Wildflowers in the fen, Bluff Mountain: Virginia bunchflower (tall white),
obedient plant (pink), cottongrass (short white)

beneath a ledge, but before long, something so terrified him that he ran and leapt down the mountain, till he reached his home and collapsed. Perkins told his family and his neighbors he would reveal just what had happened up there on the ninth day afterward—but on the eighth day he died, so no one ever knew for sure what drove him down the mountainside during a storm in such terror.

The ledge where he hid has ever after been called Perkins Rock.

Along the oval trail, an old cabin lay in ruins, though its chimney stood tall. Not far from it stood another cabin, intact and with a small pond—what they now call the Gathering Spot.

Ann and I were filled with delight that we had finally *gathered* together up here and looked in as one on this enchanted mile-high Olympian sanctuary. Yet we were wary, too, as the sky clouded up to the west. None would ever wish for a wet road going down such a steep mountainside—no Perkins Rock event for us. So we slowly wound our way down the switchbacks, over the little swales in the road, down to the bottom of Bluff, and back on into town.

One July, Ann and I spent a week at a creekside cottage near the Todd Railroad Grade Road, leading from Fleetwood over to Todd. We got ourselves to the top of Mount Jefferson and for a long lazy time looked languorously off into thin air.

We toured the little cheese plant in West Jefferson below.

And we sought out Ben Long's celebrated frescoes in the chapels of Ashe County.

In a modern catacomb below one of them, Long's *Last Supper* at Holy Trinity Episcopal Church in Glendale Springs, we spied many an urn stored behind bars, the last remains of several dozen dead, conjuring yet again Dr. Browne's great seventeenth-century transits-of-the-dead meditation, *Urne-Buriall*. Among them stood a vessel holding the ashes of a fine history teacher at Carolina, Bill Geer, a highly affable man who asked big questions and made young people think; whenever the celebrated television journalist Charles Kuralt conferred with university president William Friday, he unfailingly inquired about his favorite former teacher: "And how *is* Bill Geer?"

Well, Bill Geer is now at rest and peace in Ashe County. And in that columbarium room, big white-bearded Professor Geer is also depicted as a patriarch in Jeffrey Mims's painting *The Departure of Christ*, for which Geer was a model.

At Saint Mary's Episcopal Church near Beaver Creek, we gazed upon Ben Long's powerful triune of frescoes: his *John the Baptist* (1976), his *Mystery of Faith* (1977), and his *Mary Great with Child* (1974), one of the world's relatively rare depictions of a gravid Mary, the idea for which had come from one Rev. Faulton Hodge, the priest at the very chapel at the time and whose expectant wife served as Long's model—a portrait so essentially natural, tender, and kind that one can still scarcely believe the eruptive scandal that accompanied its unveiling back in 1974. Seems that many of the faithful, well beyond this little mountain-town chapel, had bent their minds to the notion that a pregnant Mary embodied something obscene and that not only should such an image be foresworn, but it

should not even be *thought about*. Blessed Mary, mother of Jesus!

How very fitting that Ben Long, one of North Carolina's best and most revered contemporary artists, had in 1976 won—for his portrait *Mary*—the Leonardo da Vinci International Art Award.

Another day we rented a boat at Zaloo's Canoes outside Jefferson and floated the South Fork of New River for a spell, drifting at an easy pace for a few miles over riffles, around rocks. When I had been on the river in a kayak, a few miles below here the summer before, the river was so low in spots one had to walk the boat along at times, but not so now. One of the places I had floated on that earlier trek was at the confluence, where the South Fork came into the North Fork vividly and almost at a right angle. The eddies, whirls, and falloffs were an eyeful, and the cool clear waters revealed huge rock slabs set on end, their long narrow tips just barely above the surface, disappearing twelve, fifteen feet or more into these deep pools.

A few miles north of that confluence, toward Virginia, lay the Allegheny County component of the New River State Park, and Ann and I spent time there too. The park's main purpose here was a float-in access, and one had to go through Mouth of Wilson, Virginia, to get to it by road. Round House Road went up and over the last ridge before dropping down to the New River's floodplain, the way in curved and crooked in some of the tightest switchbacks I have ever seen, for one reason alone: the lane's reaches and the bends had long ago been chopped and worked out of the hillside to suit only the width and length of a horse—or mule or ox—and wagon, and this was still far more a cartway of old than a road.

Across the river from the New's lush green floodplain here, ravens soared above massive, sheer rock cliffs standing over 100 feet straight up out of the river itself. A flock of Canada geese went floating by on the far side of the river, then took rest and found shade among the sycamore trees. Those great granite bluffs stood patiently, implacably, mosses growing upon them, rusty orange veins across the rock face, the river itself rolling northward at a good clip.

Ten or twelve miles downriver from where we stood, along about 1910 my grandfather once approached the New River by night. He was returning to North Carolina from West Virginia, after fireproofing a courthouse in a county so rough that the day he arrived to start work, the high sheriff was in jail for killing the clerk of court.

When he reached Independence, Virginia, he rented a horse and buggy and lit out alone down the mountain toward the New River and, across and beyond it, Sparta, North Carolina. On the way down the grade, he felt the rear wheel of the buggy slip off the mountainside road, but the horse quickly pulled it back onto the road and carried on. The night was pitch black, Granddaddy told me, and when they reached the broad shallow river, by starlight alone he could scarcely make out the wall of forest beyond it. He said out loud, "Horse, you've got to find the road on the other side of this ford, because I don't know where it is, and I sure can't see it."

He loosely held the reins, and for many tense minutes there was only a slow clattering of hooves and buggy over the rocky river shallows on through the dark, till at last the horse, its fetlocks and the carriage wheels dripping wet, pulled up out of the river and right onto the road at the far side.

By midnight my grandfather was able to reach my grandmother, who eagerly awaited him at the hotel in Sparta. To the horse who forded the New River late that fateful night, my grandparents' descendants have always been grateful.

Granddaddy was but twenty-four then, Grandmama only a couple years older. We never knew the name, or age, of the horse.

Mindful of their travels, travails, and passions in this high lonesome territory over a century ago, Ann and I have carried this memory of them with us, walking the ancient hills day and night, floating the stream, keeping their moments in New River country close to our hearts.

Elk Shoals

Lanky, bearded Fred Hobson, one of the South's great scholar-critics (his *Mencken: A Life* is a classic), was not born in the Lost Province, but from his family's home in Yadkinville he got hauled up here as a young boy soon enough.

High above Elk Shoals, a big hairpin bend in the South Fork of the New River, Ann and I sat with Fred one evening, on the south-facing deck of a cabin his father had built in the early 1960s, a view an emperor would have loved. As the house's wooden exterior was one of wavy slabs, the old haunt seemed like it came from an even earlier era.

"River used to be higher," Fred said. "I remember many canoes back in the '80s—now it's all kayaks."

When he was twenty-five and working at the *Winston-Salem Journal* and *Sentinel*, Fred Hobson wrote about a third of the newspapers' editorials during the campaign to keep the New River from being dammed by the Appalachian Power Company, and he enjoyed sitting high above it on the open porch, smiling and remembering what he called "my small role in it all."

Of the eighty-mile shoreline the flooded New River would have created in Ashe and Allegheny Counties alone, Hobson wrote editorially at the time: "Thousands of acres of beautiful and productive land would be sacrificed to the reservoir, with only questionable recreational benefits in return." He noted too that one of the Ashe County streams to be done in forever by the APC's flooding carried a name with spiritual resonance, a revered source of restorative waters.

Healing Springs.

That power plan to dam the New fifty years

ago was beaten back by a broad, all-American coalition, the National Committee for the New River. North Carolina declared it a state scenic river, and then our state created the New River State Park on the South Fork, a park that today comprises 2,200 acres. The National Committee was so successful at building support that, just before Congress voted on the river's inclusion in the Wild and Scenic Rivers System, 231 newspapers across the country ran editorials in favor of it *on the same day.*

Later, Tom Earnhardt would recall for me a Capitol Hill hearing on the New River that he attended back then, as Governor Holshouser's assistant secretary for administration, in late summer 1974, during which four North Carolina congressional representatives stood in support of saving the New from the Appalachian Power Company's dam plan. First, Asheville congressman and conservationist Roy Taylor spoke eloquently "for preserving the best in North Carolina, preserving the best in the nation." Then U.S. senator Jesse Helms attacked the proposal as a governmental overreach, that is, the Federal Power Commission's possible full licensing of the APC dam, saying, "This appears to benefit another state—it won't benefit *us*—it's a bad idea, North Carolina doesn't need it." Third, U.S. senator Sam Ervin, vanquisher of President Nixon, gave what Tom remembered as a "lovely social history of the New River valley," referencing all the families uprooted and history lost due to Tennessee Valley Authority lakes and concluding, "This is a bad idea for the Appalachians."

Finally, Congressman Vinegar Bend Mizell, a strapping former major-league pitcher who now represented the New River valley, rose with typed-up note cards and read, "Most have given reasons I agree with; there's another reason: *if this dam is built, a vast array of Pleistocene flora and fauna will be lost.*" And as Mizell sat down, state senator Ham Horton of Forsyth, in the home state group with Tom, in an audible aside declared: "He said

what? He pronounced it correctly but doesn't know what he said—this is *brilliant!*"

From way up over Elk Shoals, Fred observed that, nowadays, lights in the distance were rare, "pretty much as it was in my boyhood." And he pointed out, far below us, an empty Methodist camp, set upon a modest hill at the north end of the peninsula the serpentine New River made at the shoals. "A great place for an escaped convict to hide out," Fred said.

"There's your novel, Fred," said I. (Ere long that camp would find new purpose, its 270 acres and three miles of river joining New River State Park for the use and glory of all.)

A wonderful colleague at Chapel Hill for many years, a fine editor there (*Southern Literary Journal*), and a witty and most thoughtful man overall, Fred Hobson from his lofty perch expressed, on this early fall day of 2016, a deep worry about current affairs, about the fate of the university—and of the state itself. Not wistfully but rather practically, he recalled and saluted such well-known, now-gone progressive heroes as UNC president Frank Porter Graham, Governor Terry Sanford, and UNC president William Friday. And then he slowly, quietly turned his attention back to the stunning view of Elk Shoals and the river flowing both a mile above them and a mile below, echoing Cowper.

"I like being something like the master of all I survey," Fred said, with a wry smile. "Even if I'm not."

Blowing Rock

After we turned in the hill-climbing rental four-wheel-drive Ford that had hauled us up Bluff Mountain's switchbacks in quiet stride, Ann and I headed south from Boone, home of the wonderful former North Carolina poet laureate Joseph Bathanti. We stopped shortly in dressy little Blowing Rock (a far cry now from the rustic Civil War–era outpost Stoneman's cavalry marched through at that conflict's close) to walk June

the Pomeranian and had been there only a few minutes when a car turned left onto Main from a side street, its driver honking and waving at us big-time.

"Friendly fellow," I said to Ann. As we strode on down that block, we saw a man at the corner of Main and Laurel, hand held high, waving.

"That looks like Tony Rand," I said.

"It *is* Tony Rand," said Ann.

As we walked to him, Tony smiling big as life came up and said, "That was me waving. Saw you and so glad to get a chance to catch up with you!"

The big, ready Fayettevillian, who as North Carolina Senate majority leader in an earlier time helped guide our state so well for so long in so many progressive ways (he was an alumnus and true champion of the university), said it was "just too damn hot down in Cumberland County" and that he had come up to enjoy the lofty coolness of Blowing Rock, where he had a place "in the old Mayview area." He was just coming home when he spied us—"We play bridge every Thursday till noon; we don't keep score, and we don't talk politics."

"Well," I said, laughing, "we're bound for Haywood County, where we certainly *will* talk politics!"

Tony grinned broadly. Down in Chapel Hill only a year or so earlier, he had suggested to me that the state's at-that-time regressive leadership needed "an ass-kicking of biblical proportions." But he was standing on this street corner in the High Country now, above it all, smiling.

"The real world," he said, "just doesn't intrude up here somehow."

GRAVITY: LINVILLE GORGE

And yet.

Thirty-odd miles south of Blowing Rock, past Moses Cone preserve and Julian Price Lake (two wonderful gifts to North Carolinians from those Greensboro philanthropists), reality in the form of *gravity* has often intervened.

On the last Sunday in June 2019, a thirty-one-year-old rock climber from Chicago started up Shortoff Mountain, one of the scores of steep slopes of the geologic phantasmagoria called Linville Gorge, an 11,000-acre canyon wilderness. His name was Austin Howell, one of America's most daring rockers, and he was free climbing without benefit of ropes or harness. In late morning either he lost his grip or a hold broke, and he then plummeted eighty feet down the mountainside.

"*No!*" Howell shouted as he fell.

Two other climbers heard him yell, then rappelled down to him and gave him CPR. They called Burke County rescuers at once; it took ninety minutes for them to rappel into the steep gully where Howell had fallen.

And the rescuers declared him dead on the spot.

The Cherokee have long called this incredible rock-ribbed declivity Eeseeoh, or River of Cliffs, though most of the world knows it by the last name of the hunter-explorers William and John Linville, whom Indians scalped at a riverside camp in the wilds between Shortoff Mountain

and Linville Falls in 1766. Guitarist and master acoustician Jerry Brown of the Shady Grove Band, who grew up in the nearby arts colony of Penland, once said to me that of all the dramatic landscapes of North Carolina, he thought Linville Gorge was the only one he had ever gazed upon that simply looked like it could not *possibly* belong here, that it was too literally outlandish and had no equal, no parallel in our land. Its stunning 1,500-foot walls, its river's 2,000-foot drop in a mere twelve miles between Linville Falls and Lake James, and its no-less-stunning panoramic vistas all add up to an unmatched level of remarkability that defies words, though it possesses points of focus with

telling names: Hawksbill, the Chimneys, Table Rock, Wiseman's View (perhaps as in a wise man will only *view* this and not dare enter and take it on).

In this intense world of jagged outcrops and rough crags, long ago carved and etched and left behind by the slender river far below, gravity has always held a merciless upper hand, and many souls have found their last ends slipping from heights, going over waterfalls. The Burke rescuers who attended to Howell reported that they annually answered fifty to 100 calls in the Shortoff area alone, not all of them about falls but also calls from the lost, the disoriented. The

153

astonishing attraction of these breathtaking looks out upon all creation has also, in the shadows, long been a puzzle of magnets and lures to the other side: *l'appel du vide*, the French call it, *the call of the void*.

Did not Percy Bysshe Shelley become similarly entranced and enthralled by Mont Blanc, penning the passionate homage to it in his poem of that same name? Lovely as we might find the gorge on a cool sunny September day, had Shelley ever looked upon some of Linville's rugged slopes, might he have said of them something resonant with what he wrote of Mont Blanc?

… how hideously
Its shapes are heap'd around! rude, bare, and
  high,
Ghastly, and scarr'd, and riven.—Is this the
  scene
Where the old Earthquake-daemon taught her
  young
Ruin?

Austin Howell declared that what he was about as he took on whole mountainsides was nothing less than "my lonely dance with gravity." Well, now: gravity belongs to the family of some of our

most serious words—*gravitas*, *gravid*, *grave*—and very rare is the dance without a misstep.

UNC professor Elisha Mitchell fell to his death from our Black Mountain heights while trying to advance scientific knowledge and human understanding of North Carolina's superlative natural features. Austin Howell fell to his in the gorge while employing his prodigious skills at moving precisely and almost impossibly up and over some of the most difficult surfaces on earth, stone faces leaning back *against* him, as he used and, indeed, *dedicated* this pursuit trying to calm what he called "my tumultuous mind." Because

this was rock, he depended upon it to stay put, every single time he laid his hand and then put his weight upon it, because just one ice-fractured piece the size of his lower arm that could not bear his weight would be all it took to send him on into the other world.

More than a little of the Tree of Knowledge lay before one, and beneath one, in such a place. If God made the river that made this mighty canyon, He also made gravity and made Linville Gorge a grand ballroom for gravity, the great unsympathetic force that holds us down and can bring us down for good. Anyone partaking of this vast sacred space—dancing here, so to speak—should only do so with full, true-hearted, and most gracious respect. For in such a valley, in an instant in broad daylight, the shadow of death may fall.

Vaya con Dios—go with God—or go not at all.

My great friend Tom Earnhardt has made many treks into Linville Gorge, mortally loves the place, and has rarely passed within range of the gorge without stopping for an hour or two just to worship there. Early one morning in the fall of 2019, he stopped by Wiseman's View and looked out and down upon a great sea of fog and mist—knowing it would burn off and clear, he stayed and waited it out, till all the grandeur of the gorge lay there before him once again. A passionate and expert fisherman who has taught and shared his skills all over the world—in Russia, China, and here on the North Carolina coast with the likes of President George H. W. Bush and actor-director Paul Newman—he recalled his first time going down into the gorge with vivid clarity and great awe.

"Those were passionate fishing summers—I tied my own flies, made my own rods, wanted to fish all the great waters of western North Carolina. I'd been with my father and friends to Davidson River, Hazel and Wilson Creeks, snuck into private waters like Cane River—I was a *poacher* and I was proud of it!" he said. He called Linville Gorge the holy grail for real fishermen and said people were impressing upon him "This isn't Linville *Falls*—you're going into the *gorge*."

He had to make that first trip on a Wednesday, his day off from lifeguarding at Chestnut Hill Pool in Gerton. "I drove to Morganton, up 181, Jonas Ridge, that's the easiest way, people said. I went down near Table Rock, there's a big notch on the gorge, ran between Hawksbill on the north and Table Rock. You had to use your hands, a lot of rhododendron. From the rim of Linville Gorge,

it's 1,500 feet down to the river. Eight thirty or so time I started going down, kept thinking I was going to break my rod—it was a trail, but a very *rough* trail, rough as a cob.

"Down toward the bottom, some enormous hemlocks—this was never logged, no road down the valley—absolutely giants, 300, 400 years old. ... Then I got to the bottom and got out in middle of the river, jumped on a few rocks, looked up both sides of the gorge, 1,500 feet straight up—nobody else there, I was absolutely awestruck, dumbfounded by the sheer scale of Linville Gorge from the bottom!

"I was there to fish, there to catch a trout, the biggest trout in the world. I got to work quickly. It had taken me one and a half hours to get down. Midmorning, fairly low water, absolutely spectacular—caught a few small brown trout, nine to eleven inches ... but I saw a couple that were ... *submarines*! My little box of flies was not enough to attract these big brown trout.... I was *undertackled*!"

He started back about five thirty, having marked his way down, now going exactly the same way back up, and he made it to the top of the rim about six thirty.

"The Linville River was spectacular," Tom said, "and back in 1962, Linville Gorge was the wildest place on the planet. And it's still being created.

"It's a work in progress."

THE FRENCH BROAD VALLEY
Court House Falls

This is a grand place to start a river, I thought, gazing at Court House Falls in Transylvania County, high upon a south slope of the Blue Ridge below a ragged black rock called the Devil's Court House.

Within the mountainside, though, the waterfall sat low down, spilling away into an elongated oval granite bowl it had long ago made for itself. No one but our party—the Queens: lawyer Frank and his little girl Grace Ellen and architect Joe

Sam and his boy Charlie; rangy Carolina student Christopher Holt; and my wife, Ann, daughter Cary, and I—was there for a spell that late May Saturday noontide.

Presently more pilgrims wandered in, drawn as we were to this charmed font. A light mist was in the air from all the creek's commotion. The water's veil spread from a little over a foot, where it started its fifty-foot fall, to a broad white band of eight feet where it hit its deep pool, and the steady pouring, splashing noise of the onrushing waters of Court House Falls and Creek filled the long bowl.

Below the pool was a small gravel wash on the far bank, and an emerald moss lay smoothly upon the wall of rock rising above as if it had been painted there. The noon sun fell like a shaft down into this deep basin, lighting up the pool, the great rock walls, the small lavender moths that were flitting about. Hemlock sentinels towered above the falls, lofty but with what seemed scant purchase at the edgy tops of the high walls. Rhododendrons flowered above us, and littering the stream and its narrow banks were scores of small blossoms like bits of waxy linen.

From here the waters of Court House Creek flew into a fluted chute and fell away, racing over the boulder field of former falls, on down the mountain to the North Fork, which meets the West Fork at the tiny town of Rosman. A mile below and east of Rosman the Middle and East Forks join in. The big stream gentles along a broad farm valley until it is through Asheville and starts racing again, on down through a majestic gorge, and passes Paint Rock into the state of Tennessee.

The Cherokee called it *Long Man, the River*, and all the streams he pulled in—among them the Davidson and the Mills and the Swannanoa and the Nolichucky and the Pigeon Rivers, before meeting the Holston and the two becoming one as the Tennessee—were his *Chattering Children*. This is the bona fide French Broad River, the first of the wide "broads" the old-time huntsmen met that flowed away from the ocean they or their parents had crossed and ran instead north and west into what was then French territory, on to the mighty Mississippi, where the waters of the Long Man at last met venerable Old Man River himself.

So let it start then, at least in part, at a place called Court House Falls, where the real sweet honey in the rock is water, and at this source—emblem, even—of a mountain river let a judgment be entered in favor of its purity, its vitality, its force.

Upriver Float

At the confluence of the French Broad North and West Forks sat the hut and rainbow-colored yard of Headwaters Outfitters. A bit downriver, the outfitters' boat-filled trailer was pulled into Rosman's Champion Park, a half acre of easy, sloping lawn by the water with some sycamore shade off to the side. Fifteen people were getting onto the French Broad in kayaks; with our two green canoes and one white, we added half that again.

It was a hot afternoon and seemed busy in Rosman, the little upriver town with gigantic school-spirit tiger-paw tracks down its main street. A good day to spend living on river time. After a couple of light rapids and riffles, we glided along at a lazy pace for quite a ways before the next batch of tumbles.

Ann and I had the two little girls in the white canoe with us, and we enjoyed these occasional

jogs in the river. Along the riverbanks were cascades of pink roses, blackberry blossoms, now and again a fallen-over willow. Cary named one bankside feature—her favorite of the day— "the Elephant Log," for it lay in the water with an empty knothole for a pachyderm's eye and a branch for a trunk aiming up at the big blue Transylvania County mountain-valley sky.

While we were seeing an elephant, Joe Sam and Charlie Queen were watching red-winged blackbirds, catbirds, swallows in the riverbanks, a little green heron. Rounding one bend, they came upon a groundhog just standing there staring back at them. In deeper pools we spotted wary fish swimming quickly, clearing out of our way. The upper French Broad has been trying for years to come back as a celebrated muskie fishery, and trout anglers toasted such cold-water tributaries as the Davidson River, which came down off the Pisgah Ridge into the French Broad.

We passed the outfitters' party of boaters, already landed, and where we pulled over to take out farther downstream, a man and woman were fishing from the bridge above. Just as Ann and Cary and I were stepping from the white canoe the fisherwoman shrieked, "I got one, I got one!" and the man helped her reel it in, the both of them quite surprised, their catch on the shortening line glistening and shining in the summer sun.

One Autumn at Flat Rock

Robroy Farquhar, a British actor who led the self-styled Vagabond Players, in 1940 settled his troupe in a 150-year-old gristmill here and, soon after World War II, developed the Flat Rock Playhouse at the Flat Rock itself, and his illustrative image (a walking man with all worldly goods tucked into a cloth at the end of an over-the-shoulder stick) appears on its low-slung building and all attendant materials. In 1961 he had gotten the powers in Raleigh to proclaim his stage "the state theatre of North Carolina," a long tall claim indeed here in our powerfully thespianic province. Yet whatever Flat Rock's precise ranking was in the scheme of things, we were pleased indeed to be invited to run *King Mackerel* there in October 1995, under the auspices of Robroy's son, Robin Farquhar.

That fall was mostly sunny and dry and golden, and as I ran back and forth between Chapel Hill and the Flat Rock theatre, I decided to make one leg of those many treks be through the woods: that is, from Old Fort (the village at the eastern foot of the grand Black Mountain range, the eastern continental divide, with the enormous sculpted arrowhead on a pedestal next to its now-ceremonial old train depot) up the switchback hills on Bat Cave Road to Bat Cave itself on the Broad River at the bottom of Hickory Nut Gorge. From Bat Cave, to the northwest lay Hickory Nut Gap Farm, the McClure-Clarke family's pioneering, long-running contribution to healthy sustainable farming: "Building community through agriculture," as they say; to the southeast, Lake Lure and Chimney Rock. I would head southwest, on up US 64 past Edneyville (where I bought onions and cabbages and apples at the roadside produce shop and where one of my best writing students, Brooke Calton of Fletcher, had gone to school, a building I gazed at wistfully on her behalf till I later heard her call it "that old wreck") and on into well-heeled Hendersonville and Flat Rock itself.

We opened *King Mackerel* on the same night Hurricane Opal chose to come up from Atlanta and take on the Carolina mountains, Don Dixon and Jim Wann and I striding out upon scenic designer (and our old Carolina classmate) Dennis Maulden's fine-looking set, with its coastal shanty upstage left and its fishing pier upstage right, life preservers and oars all about, here and there a saltine can, a big fish, the ghost lantern.

At the show's finale came a hurricane party and full-out storm sequence, replete with archival film from North Carolina's longtime benchmark 1954 blowout Hurricane Hazel and subsequent high-wind humdingers (the 1955 Carolina hurricane triune of Connie, Diane, and Ione), and in what few quiet moments there were onstage, one could hardly fail to hear the tree clatter and fierce whine of rising winds outside.

Once the show came down, Robin Farquhar threw an intimate cast party for us backstage, just a half a dozen Flat Rockers and the three of us Coastal Cohorts. An autumnal chill had filled the theatre, and as I drifted the few yards down from the loading dock to our billets to fetch a jacket, the tree crowns were smacking each other in a steady, rackety, noisy rhythm, and the whine had now become a howl.

During first light, the peak of the storm passed over us, blew a window out of Don's room behind the theatre, and went on, over the Pisgah Ridge, to blow down most of the locust trees in the Carolina mountains.

Stiff breezes indeed, which none had expected at all, and yet the show must go on and did.

One Saturday, when Ann and then-three-year-old Cary had come up to visit, we strolled down the slope and over the road to Connemara, the mountain home of Confederate treasurer Christopher Memminger and, later, poet, Lincoln biographer, balladeer, and goatherd Carl Sandburg and his wife. We strode lightly through his rooms and gazed upon his goats (rather, their descendants), and I remembered that my great friend and top-tier Buncombe County poet Michael McFee had drafted a poem reimagining his uncle Homer's actual pilgrimage to Connemara to see Sandburg, his hero, and Homer's eager hike across a pasture till here came Sandburg himself, waving his arms and shouting in greeting, or so Homer thought till he drew close enough to hear Sandburg more clearly, screaming at him: "Get away! Get away! Get away from my goddamn goats!"

We left Flat Rock and its noted playhouse

not much worse for wear, though Opal had laid a mighty storm upon us, and headed home to Clover Garden on my forty-seventh birthday, stopping only once for a cake lunch—Ann and Cary and I—at the shady Friends Meeting's Memorial Spring in the rolling dairy land just west of the Alamance County crossroads of Eli Whitney.

For us vagabonds, the days lay golden in our paths.

Brevard (2001)

We came to Brevard, this small important campus where experiential education has long been the order of the day, to read and meet students just a few years after our time on Flat Rock's stage, and we stayed in a lovely visitors' cottage there, which had upon its windows not a single set of blinds or drapes. What interlopers' mischief the school's administrators anticipated or feared, we never knew, and we were in the main quite bemused.

Our daughter Cary, then nine, was enchanted at once by the colorful display of coat-of-arms flags hung all about the dining room, and she there and then determined that she would attend Brevard when she was just a bit older. After breakfast, while Ann went to meet a photography class and before I met with the estimable naturalist and author Jennifer Frick-Ruppert and her class, Cary and I walked out into the crisp October mountain morning in what would be an unrequited search for even a solitary member of the school's famed crop of white squirrels—descendants of overturned-carnival-truck escapees, so the town says. Our stroll led us to the outer reaches of the campus, and though the fall morning was now quickly warming, a coat of frost still lay upon the grass.

Cary held my hand tightly and led me forward, off the walk and onto the white carpet, studying each of our shadowy footprints as we made them, our marks of being, as one might at the tide line of a seabeach. Though she would find

herself in college elsewhere, at the family school in a scant ten years, in this moment of her show of delight at the dining-room décor and her enthusiastic march across the frost, I found it not only possible but also immensely pleasing to think of her up here among the staunch environmentalists, reading the seasonal flora at different altitudes of the Pisgah peaks and watching the mystical blue-ghost fireflies of May there, playing in the deep woods around Sliding Rock and Looking Glass Falls, joining the Voice of the Rivers students as they beheld and traversed southern streams summer by summer. I fancied I could see all that.

Yet what I *did* see and recall so well were the slant lines of early-morning sunlight striking the silhouette prints from our feet in the frost and enlarging them evenly, impressively keeping the integrity of their shapes, so that on this one and only one October morn at 2,200 feet above sea level, this father and this daughter for a few moments happily walking the Brevard mountain earth seemed to be much, much larger globe striders than we really were.

Such a memory is not only a recollection; it is a grace.

APPROACHING ASHEVILLE
Old Fort

Approaching Asheville on the big highway Frank Queen calls "the superslab," the switchbacks curve and slalom majestically up the mountain above Old Fort, the bottomland village below the great range at the headwaters of the Catawba, and if the upward climb seems like one of forty-five degrees rather than a mere six or eight, the pilot may be pardoned for thinking it so. And pardoned, too, for invoking Southey's poetic prayer:

O God, have mercy on the mariner.

From the prospects atop that great hill, near the Black Mountain range, I can see a long imaginary way.

Even in a waking dream I can see the old

nineteenth-century driver John Pence and his six-in-hand team of horses picking up passengers at Henry, till 1879 the end of the rail line just west of Old Fort, Pence then pulling his stout nine-passenger stagecoach the *Hattie Butner* up, over, along, and beside the cliffs and precipices of Swannanoa Gap, a couple miles north of where the interstate runs, as he brought travelers from Old Fort over to the Eagle Hotel in Asheville's East End—with nary an accident for the twenty-five years that Pence showed the way. So well thought of was Pence that the novelist Christian Reid, who gave the Ashevillean world its nickname by titling her 1875 book *Land of the Sky*, wrote him into an early cameo role in that fictional text, without even changing his name. John Ehle gave his stagecoach driver a choice moment of wonder during the railroad-building of his barely fictional novel *The Road*, when an eastbound coach met and could not get around the railroad's engine, which was being dragged up the mountain by convicts and oxen: "The morning stage was waiting, anxious for a chance to get by, but the driver was more curious than angry about this delay. 'I've had everything else happen at least once, except this. I've had sick horses and sick passengers; I've had women bear babies; I've broke wheels; I've had runaways; I've had one tornado, a fellow said it was. But this is the first time I've had a locomotive.'"

What I cannot see are the scores of graves of the African American prisoners, maybe 139, maybe 400, most of them from eastern North Carolina, who were given over by the state to the Western North Carolina Railroad to build the climbing Old Fort Loops up Mill Creek, up the Swannanoa Grade to tunnel through this mountain between 1877 and 1879, to make Asheville reachable by train, and coincidentally to put driver Pence and the stage lines out of business, and to die in cave-ins and to disease and to awful, unaccustomed cold.

No one can see their graves—for they were unmarked from the start alongside the train line, the building of which killed them. A new effort, the Railroad and Incarcerated Laborer Memorial Project, seeks for the first time to find those graves and to honor those men, those who died and those who lived on, with a plaque at Andrews Geyser just west of Old Fort.

Noted by folklorist Cecil Sharp in 1916, collected and recorded several times by banjoist Bascom Lamar Lunsford, and sung authoritatively in 1939 for folklorist Frank C. Brown as the real hammer song it was by African American Will "Shorty" Love, the prisoners' tragic work song "Swannanoa Tunnel" must also always stand for them, for their immutable and grievous loss, and in memory of those who really built the Western North Carolina Railroad:

Asheville junction, Swannanoa Tunnel
All caved in, baby, all caved in
I'm going back to that Swannanoa Tunnel
That's my home, baby, that's my home
When you hear my watchdog howling
Somebody around, baby, somebody around
When you hear that hoot owl squalling
Somebody dying, baby, somebody dying

Grandfather Mountain viewed from a high spot off Old Johns River Road, Blowing Rock

Black Mountain

"Mount the mountains!" Albert Einstein is supposed to have said when he visited Black Mountain College, and well he might have. Mount Mitchell is only eight miles distant and a challenging 4,000 feet higher than the small, charmed Swannanoa River valley town and its famed liberal-arts campus.

Elisha Mitchell, the nineteenth-century scientific polymath professor (first of mathematics and natural philosophy, later of geology, mineralogy, and chemistry) at UNC Chapel Hill, who designed and directed the building of what he termed "New England rock fences" all over our campus there (and which we call our "old stone walls," as if they are and always were somehow a *southern* thing), has long lain in a stone cairn right at the mountain's peak.

Professor Mitchell made the climb with his barometers in 1835, believing that the tallest of North Carolina's high hills lay in the Black Mountain range and establishing one of them as the peak of peaks. Yet in the 1850s, when his former student Thomas Clingman, then a congressman and later a Confederate general, challenged the accuracy of Mitchell's particular claim (and not without some reason, as scholar Tim Silver tells it, given potential confusions involving instruments, weather, guides, memories, and the range's proximate peaks having very similar altitudes), the aging professor dragged himself back up onto the high, rugged Black Mountains to re-prove himself, his claim, his highest hill.

At 8:19 P.M., June 27, 1857, as recorded by the pocket watch he carried, Mitchell slipped in a

thunderstorm's gloaming on high rocks, plunging down a waterfall—now Mitchell Falls—to his death in its pool forty feet below. The hunting guide Big Tom Wilson, for whose cabin Mitchell was bound the night he fell, led the ensuing search party and discovered the professor dead in that cold pool on the eighth of July.

After resting just shy of a year in the First Presbyterian Church cemetery in Asheville, Professor Mitchell's remains were exhumed and reinterred on June 16, 1858, atop the summit of the 6,684-foot mountain that was already coming to bear his name and which in time would become North Carolina's very first state park. The Right Reverend Bishop James H. Otey of Tennessee and UNC president David L. Swain both spoke at the reburial, Swain saluting Professor Mitchell's "indomitable perseverance, untiring industry and unflinching courage" and, too, his "kindness of heart."

At the College

We Red Clay Ramblers often performed at the Black Mountain Festival and the Lake Eden Arts Festival when they were held at what had been Black Mountain College—the former each May, the latter each October, both joyous soirees.

One warm Saturday in May, we had just finished a late-morning set beneath the great central tent. My son, Hunter, aged ten, and I then stood listening to the remarkable, sunny musician and storyteller David Holt holding several hundred children and their astonished parents in thrall with his gnarly-voices-and-all rendition of the grisly "Taily Bone." We drifted through the festival's bazaar of leather belts, sarongs, lapis jewelry, and candle stands along the eight-acre lake. Walking around Lake Eden with Hunter, we suddenly were talking about bygone days, mythic days he had only heard of. Seeing all the young, spotless tie-dye wearers, he exclaimed, "The *sixties*!"

A great wave from a past before that past

Hunter was invoking hit me with a good hard passion. For here we were on the old hillside campus, its stone buildings originally intended as an amusement park, where the radical artists, writers, and theorists of Black Mountain College had held forth and pushed the limits of imagination for twenty-four years, from 1933 to 1957. "America's Bauhaus"—after the renowned German design school whose modernist standard it picked up and carried—was the nickname for Black Mountain, this progressive, holistic, art-for-art's-sake school that urged students to "leap before you look" and that gained an international reputation due to the comingling of students with poet Jonathan Williams, architect Buckminster Fuller, writer-dancer-potter M. C. Richards, composer John Cage, dancer Merce Cunningham, painters Elaine and Willem de Kooning, and many others. No grades, no tests, no metrics, and in the judgment of one maintenance man from back in that day, "Nothing to do but moonshine and sex."

On this day, with children and youths cavorting in and around Lake Eden, dizzily hopping and kicking hacky sacks about, zip-lining joyously down the looming mountain into the lake waters, the place looked a good deal more like Walt

Disney's world than Henry Miller's—or that of Bucky Fuller, who built his first geodesic dome here on this spot.

"Hey, fellow, give it a try," called a stout barker from a food trailer, as he pushed the trigger on a keg tap and filled a clear plastic cup with foaming amber liquid.

"What've you got?" I asked.

"Highland Gaelic—it's a new Asheville microbrew. Fifty cents a pint."

"Man, you're giving it away."

"Finest kind. Come on!"

It was a bright, sunny, balmy mountain spring day, just now noon. We would not take the stage again for another eight hours.

"All right, I'm game," I said.

"You won't get a better deal—pretty good, huh?"

I daresay. The full, rich, mellow ale was a hit with me from the first. When I returned to the foothills, I would ask the folks at Weaver Street Market in Carrboro to load up on Highland Gaelic—"Get it here as fast as you can and you'll be racing to keep it in stock!"

"That good?" they asked.

"That good," I said.

But for now, nothing to do but deeply savor the amber brew and this midday moment at the venerable school grounds. This was 1995, the first year of Highland Gaelic's operation, years before Asheville became Beer City and before a wild gaggle of fine microbreweries started operating there and, indeed, all over North Carolina.

Hunter, whose musical taste at ten ran more to Tom Petty than string bands, nonetheless really took to the Black Mountain folk scene. He liked the big hills, and he was finding himself enamored of the tie-dyed couture turned out here in such explicit and almost regimental flair.

"Still having fun?" I asked him.

"Yeah, Dad," he said. "This *is* just like the sixties, right?"

I gazed over at the bright, rainbow-shirted throngs on the lakeside path and over the water, remembering way back to the grubby hirsute men and the proud braless women who led if not loved them, the casual couplings and intermittent commitments (Jake Mills once described 1960s and early '70s weddings as "the bride and groom briefly exchange a host of weak vows"), the stunning Kerouacian peripatetics and the options-kept-open freewheeling-ness of it all, all of it a *long* generation away from where we now stood.

"Well," I said, "similar."

He looked a little confused and tried bolstering his own opinion by saying again, "Just like the sixties!"

"This," I ventured at last, "is a whole lot cleaner."

Asheville

On down the Swannanoa Valley, many times now I have followed the slender river that carved it, little more than a creek in sycamore shade most all the way to where it joins the French Broad, just below the Biltmore château. Pulling off before that confluence, going to the northwest, crossing the Swannanoa, passing through the sliced-apart Beaucatcher Mountain, its summit once the much-ballyhooed height of nineteenth-century hilltop romance, and once through it, I have found the wondrous city laid out before me, the red terra-cotta tops of First Baptist Church and city hall and Pack Square up yonder on the midtown hill where Zeb Vance's obelisk long stood.

Asheville stands as Capital of the West, most of which towers over the little city, though it holds more people than the nine western counties combined (excepting Henderson County, rich with retirees). In *Look Homeward, Angel* Thomas Wolfe called Asheville Altamont, Latin for *high mountain*, though the real city nestles along several miles of the great river running from high-mountain valley into abject gorge, held in place by the Black Mountains, the Blue Ridge, and the Pisgah Ridge. Even up on the broad, west-facing porch of the Grove Park Inn, with its fortress

Dancers on a wall, Black Mountain

walls of brown fieldstones and its own terra-cotta roof hanging over it all like a vast cowling, even at Wolfe's Riverside Cemetery knoll-top grave, where late the robin sang, one feels the town at sunset lying low in the long shadows of the big rangy endless blue hills beyond.

Wolfe gave his fictional mother the surname Pentland, showing us how he saw his hometown and its setting, both real and spiritual: *pent land*.

Pent, penned, held in—and perhaps it is.

Yet this is also a land so finely recorded and awarded, even, an astonishing collage of literary remembrance and artistic grace. John Ehle wrote of the railroad's climbing and tunneling through Old Fort Mountain in *The Road*, over the gap to territory that his *Land Breakers* had already helped open, and Wilma Dykeman assayed the French Broad from Transylvania County to Tennessee. In Robert Morgan's poem "Real and Ethereal," the steamboat *Mountain Lily* still floats the river upstream of Asheville, from Fletcher to Brevard. Fred Chappell's "that puts me in mind of" storytelling uncle from *I Am One of You Forever* is still abroad in the land, and Gail Godwin's "mother and two daughters" are just around a corner in Asheville. Charles Frazier's *Cold Mountain* looms nearby, his "thirteen

moons" shine over all these western counties, and Wayne Caldwell's *Cataloochee* and its valley sit abidingly high back up in the Smokies, awaiting us. Ron Rash's *Hard Times* world is still far too easy to find here, which Keith Flynn's and Charter Weeks's *Prosperity Gospel* proves out. John Standingdeer Jr. has written a method to give learning, speaking, and *saving* his native Cherokee language a better chance; and Cherokee author Annette Saunooke Clapsaddle, in *Even As We Breathe*, tells of young Cherokees in difficult times during World War II in Asheville. Mountain boy and future author Gary Carden sent out message-filled "mason jars in the flood" of 1940, seeking friendship, and Tommy Hays with *What I Came to Tell You* shows us another boy trying to weave his life together in an Ashevillean bamboo grove.

Elizabeth Engelhardt sees deeper tales than most in *A Mess of Greens*, and Darin Waters reveals the importance of African American life here through "The Appalachian Urban Folk Photography of Isaiah Rice," featuring the work of his grandfather. Poet Michael McFee stepped out of Buncombe's forest of Arden and elegiacally reminded us of his Scotch Irish forebears, with hillbilly fatalism, no less, declaring with conviction that "we were once here." Kay Byer's *Wildwood Flower* blooms forever, as the pink beds of Pisgah bear witness, and the clawhammering balladeer and memoirist of the nearby Kingdom of Madison, Sheila Kay Adams of Eskey's Ridge, invites us with a tenderness that is also an elixir and a balm to "come go home with me" and wakes mornings and looks out over it all.

If Wolfe was right, and these hills *are* indeed pent land, his literary successors have made sure, through a righteous outpouring of true and heartrending and inspiring words, millions of them, that they are rather unpent as well.

Our first time together in Asheville, in the early summer of 1988, Ann took me well out the

Grove Arcade, with Battery Park Hotel beyond, Asheville

north side of town to show me where she had lived during her year there a decade earlier: in a one-story log cabin up Merrimon Avenue near Beaverdam Creek and Beaver Lake. The cabin was so fogbound every morning, she recalled, that she never knew till almost noon what the weather of the day *really* was. We were staying at the Bridle Path Inn, tucked away just north of hillside UNC Asheville, and after black coffees and tall orange juices on its long, wickered-up porch the next morning, she drove us downtown and we toured the big ivory art deco Grove Arcade with its long glass ceiling, where she had worked for the U.S. Fish and Wildlife Service as a photographer and writer back in 1978 and '79.

The venerable downtown building—now full

of upscale artisans' shops—had been nearly empty then, she recalled, with only Fish and Wildlife and the National Weather Records Center renting rooms there. "That's where we developed all our photographs in their astounding, amazing photo lab," she said. "They had this huge camera on a long track that they used, I'm pretty sure, to print satellite photos, actually printing them on paper, big photographs. And they gave us a corner of their lab to develop our Fish and Wildlife pictures in."

Puddles from rainwater leaking in had stood here and there on the arcade's light terrazzo floors, and Ann's lone footfalls as she dodged those little pools echoed eerily about, those hollow reflecting steps and the Grove's gargoyles staring down on her from above, lending a frightening noir air to her workplace as she came and went during that single long-gone year.

Our first visit came only a dozen years or so after native Perry Deane Young made a classic you-can't-go-home-again trek and penned for *Harper's* his didactic lament, "Goodbye, Asheville" (1975), in which he mourned the tearing down of or sitting-in-ruins state of many of the city landmarks of his youth, buildings that a half century earlier Thomas Wolfe had decried going up in the first place (key among them the Battery Park Hotel, which E. W. Grove tore down a floral hillside to site, and where several of Wolfe's mourners would gather and drink to him and eat big steaks in his memory after his September 1938 interment in Riverside Cemetery). Writer Young, who grew up in a Woodfin market-gardening family, would also find his heart sinking over that process of cultural sweeping aside and population removal, strangely named *urban renewal*, which had knocked down the significant, long-standing African American neighborhoods of Hill Street, Southside, Burton Street, and East End.

Yet much remained, and ironically, no small part of Asheville's turn-of-the-twenty-first-century rejuvenating boom depended on the architectural appeal and attractiveness of the now old-time town. And saving and protecting what was still left of the early twentieth-century skyline and architectural landscape, which so many felt had made this one of North Carolina's most interesting cities, fell to a campaign in the streets, in the government halls, and at the ballot box in the early 1980s—Save Downtown Asheville, chaired and led by author-designer and longtime Ashevillean Wayne Caldwell, with great help from his sister-in-law Kathryn Long, Save Downtown Asheville treasurer Jan Schochet, and a thousand other comrades-in-arms.

Caldwell (of the Cataloochee Caldwells)

helped inspire a forceful local crowd intent on holding on to Asheville's old boomtown buildings, which to all post-Depression Buncombe-ites was mainly what the city *was*. Even thirty-five years after that 1980s fight and the 1981 two-to-one *Nay!* referendum that put an end to a mall-development plan to level eleven acres in northwestern downtown Asheville (and to propose paying odd homage to all that destruction in the form of grotesquely pasting the facades of ruined buildings on the sides of a massive parking garage, to remind the populace of what had once been), Caldwell still seemed amazed at the crassness and lack of thought he and his allies had felt honor-bound to go up against, and how much work and time had gone into saving the heart of his hometown, now so beloved by those of the progressive, grassroots-arts, crafts, and farm-to-table boom that has followed.

"That took up a bunch of years," Caldwell once said to me.

From Seely's Castle high on Sunset Mountain to Biltmore way across town (a "strange, colossal heart-breaking house," Henry James said of its chilliness and overblown size, where one would "sit in alternate Gothic and Palladian cathedrals"), Asheville holds no shortage of architectural wonders, and I am not just speaking for Buncombe in saying so. Some of the best of the former frontier town may be some of the simplest, such as the Queen Annes and colonial revivals in the Chestnut Hill neighborhood on Asheville's near north side, which Wayne Caldwell once slowly strolled me through.

Caldwell, who lived with his wife Mary out in Enka-Candler, the "twin cities," remarked upon all these fine, well-over-a-century-old houses created by the George Vanderbilt–sponsored Richard Sharp Smith, a British-born New York architect who served as the site superintendent for Biltmore and who met and married a

Scottish Biltmore staffer (one Isabella Cameron) and stayed on to thrive in the Land of the Sky. Caldwell, then in the interior design business with his sister-in-law, had reason to take note of such things. He told me he used to be on the historic commission back "when it had teeth" and added: "Yeah, I got called a communist for voting to deny somebody in this district a chain link fence."

Through music I would come to see this whole town anew, in the early and mid-1990s playing piano with The Red Clay Ramblers at Be Here Now, a lovely hall on Biltmore Avenue, bright lacquered wood everywhere, a sprung floor for contra dances and Irish sessions mixed in among the touring musicians' shows. It was a "listening room," in the parlance of the day, and a no-smoking one at that (*except* for the night that bluesman Clarence "Gatemouth" Brown played and got a pass on the use of tobacco), just a few storefronts down Biltmore Avenue off the Pack Square hilltop, a 200-and-some-seat place named for Ram Dass in-the-momentism.

Pack Square and thereabouts had few features back then—the Noodle Shop up top, yes, Market Place around the corner, but not the great yet-to-come music halls Orange Peel and Jack of the Wood (where the Sons of Ralph Featuring Ralph would in time hold forth—the eminent Lewis family bluegrass trio, Ralph who logged many miles touring with Bill Monroe and sons Marty and Don, who picked a mandolin Monroe himself had given him, blistering the walls of that taut little club). Down below the River Arts District, the old Harley-Davidson shop would be rechristened the Grey Eagle, which we heated up one December night when ice had sheathed the city. Not yet, then, the polyrhythmic drum circle and the oh-so-zany purple bus that would tour visitors around increasingly artsy Asheville.

With Frank Queen leading us on, Ann and I have often over the years scoured the old town, dropped in on Tops for Shoes with its cheerful

black-and-white-striped, red-ovaled bags; had dinner in an arcade once where one white blade of an overhead fan simply exempted itself from further whirring and sailed off its hub and with a smack landed at our feet; put on shows for Best of Our State gatherings at E. W. Grove's huge hillside rock pile, the Grove Park Inn, Coastal Cohorts singing with full faith about the wind and the water still abiding and about king mackerel and the blues a-running at the ocean end of the state and Red Clay Ramblers bearing string band witness to the two things that Ramblers love most: *home … and away from home.*

And doubtless we would have even gone up Sunset Mountain and crawled through the old fortress Seely's Castle, named for Grove's son-in-law who built it, one peak up from the Grove Park—where President Warren Harding had brought his entire cabinet to hide out when they were all on the run from the Teapot Dome oil scandal and where UNC Asheville spent a dozen years on its way to its current home—had it only been open for us.

We hoofed about the low ground of Biltmore Village and its tall, red, drooping-roofed All Souls Episcopal Church. We got black coffee and the best of bread at City Bakery on Biltmore. We stared at architect Douglas Ellington's art deco

First Baptist Church, domed art deco design by architect Douglas Ellington, Asheville

wonders down the Pack Square slope to the east: the city hall and the First Baptist Church, where my great friends Michael McFee and David Perry (his father the longtime music director there) once sang their heads off and their young choirboy hearts out both in service of the Lord and in teenaged praise of whatever choirgirls they may have also sought to meet.

Other voices, other musics, have moved the air here, too.

In Asheville during 1919, composer Charles Ives, diabetic and heart-diseased, recuperated from a breakdown for a couple of months while getting his sonata *Concord* ready for print.

Modernist composer and European folk-song celebrant Béla Bartók spent several of his last twenty-four months in Asheville, living at the Albemarle Inn on the north side during World War II when this was a soldiers' town, famously hearing the hillside songbirds and incorporating them into his Third Piano Concerto, finished at the Albemarle's room 8 and sometimes called the *Asheville Concerto*. And Robert Moog, the internationally recognized champion of electronic music and inventor of the Moog synthesizer, moved here and set up shop in the 1970s.

One summer morning years ago, my Bingham Township neighbor Cyril Lance, an accomplished bluesman and engineer, invited me to his shop in

a small garage in the woods about a mile from my home.

"You want to see the Moog II?" he asked.

Intrigued, I dashed over, heard the classic round bubbling sounds of a Moog and rapped on the door, which Cyril, grinning ear to ear, threw open, saying, "You want to *play* it?"

Wires, a rainbow of them, and all manner of electronics, tubes, testers. Of course I wanted to lay my piano-playing hands on the prototype of the second edition of one of the world's most revolutionary musical instruments, sitting out here on a workbench in the woods. In the exuberant, bearded, soft-spoken Cyril Lance and his crowded shop, I saw one of the Wright brothers.

Cyril had become senior engineer with Robert

Moog's synthesizer company in Asheville just a few months before Moog's death in 2005, and to Cyril's astonishment, it fell to him to organize Moog's memorial service. He commuted between Clover Garden and downtown Asheville for fifteen years, and one evening not too long ago on our lane, he came forth in all his good humor with a tale from the Moog factory.

A mountain fellow had shown up with a very old theremin, an *original* Leon Theremin instrument. "There were only three originals known in the *world*, and *this* was the *fourth*!" Cyril said, reminding us that Bob Moog "had a direct line to Leon Theremin." The man asked, "Can you all fix this?" and Cyril, knowing at once what he was looking at, said outright, "Don't even turn it on!"

He brought the instrument back here to Clover Garden and got it fired up and running in his living room, and his son Kai after a fashion played it, "flapping his arms around near it," Cyril said, smiling.

Cyril thought it possible that the instrument may have made its way to North Carolina back when composer John Cage was in residence at Black Mountain College in the late 1940s and early 1950s. Perhaps.

"Where did you *get* this?" Cyril had asked the old theremin's new owner.

"Bought it at an auction in Swannanoa, for $700," the man replied. "They said it'd been stored forever out there in somebody's henhouse."

The New in the Old

From that Swannanoa henhouse to America's biggest house and the many smaller manses and castles around town, sprung forth for healers and health seekers once the Western Carolina Railroad opened Asheville up 140 years ago, the truly new life in and around the town's old bones seems to be what now distinguishes contemporary Asheville and its thinkers, scholars, artisans, and environmental and civic leaders and sets them well apart from the Grove- and Vanderbilt-driven "boomtown" that Wolfe ridiculed a century ago.

UNC Asheville has made the old new by bringing the healing theme forward into the twenty-first century with its North Carolina Center for Health and Wellness, which opened in 2007. "In past generations, seeking the salubrious Asheville air was a way to cure tuberculosis and other ills," said our friend Anne Ponder, chancellor of UNC Asheville from 2005 to 2014. "Building on these unique healing and creative properties, with all their attendant academic power and import, was a perfect role for Asheville's university. Being an Asheville native, whose entire family is from western North Carolina, I knew personally as a young girl most of the people our buildings were named after; this helped to assure that our history

was always part of the dynamic future we were building.

"For example," she added, "making sure that UNC Asheville could acquire property adjacent to the campus that once housed a sanitorium/hospital in the last century was not only a strategic decision for our future but an intentional embrace of Asheville's rich history of health and rejuvenation."

That old National Weather Records Center, no longer in the leaky run-down Grove Arcade where Ann had known it, has morphed and moved onto Patton Avenue as the National Oceanic and Atmospheric Administration's National Centers for Environmental Information, which also hosts the North Carolina Institute for Climate Studies (NCICS). The impressive NCICS recently and importantly forecast, apparently without fear of political repercussions, in its *North Carolina Climate Science Report* of March 2020 just what a future of hotter days, more frequent three-inches-plus rainstorms, and coastal flooding our state is in for, looking out across this century.

One proud to have had a hand in that report was Jenny Parmar Dissen, NCICS's engagement officer, a Waynesville-raised, NC State–trained environmental engineer who worked for consulting firm Accenture in developing its climate change and sustainability practice before going to Vietnam for the Clinton Foundation—"the only enterprise I could find that was addressing climate change from a solutions point of view." Asheville's Market Place restaurateur William Dissen in time asked Jenny Parmar to come home from Vietnam to the North Carolina mountains, where the two married and where she found the spot she could thrive, the North Carolina Institute for Climate Studies.

Jenny Dissen praised her colleagues as "solution providers" and added, "Being part of the institute has allowed me to push forward." Recalling a series of executive forums on business and climate that she developed and staged during her decade at NCICS, she spoke forthrightly of the "value chain of climate data to the decision context."

"We sell climate risk for free," she said. And she asked eagerly, "How do we deal with the next thirty years? We *have* to adapt." Whatever the problem and corrective policy under review might be, the essential need, she stressed, was "to embed the environment into the value of it."

Jenny Dissen dated her powerful environmental motivation to a hazy moment during a family trip in the Smokies, a stop for a view she loved on the way to Clingmans Dome, from which "you could see 250 miles. One day, tenth grade or so, I couldn't see *my view*, and it stuck with me that nature and the environment were being polluted." She felt the development and destruction of nature right up against her bedrock belief: "I *knew* there was a way we could live in harmony with nature."

An innovative interdisciplinary thinker, Jenny Dissen observed that the Carolina mountain nexus of the National Centers for Environmental Information and NCICS on Patton Avenue comprises one of the up-and-coming science and environmental centers of the United States, and she declared with a deep and energetic conviction: "The work we do is extraordinary—we're at the crossroads of so many things."

Whatever one's reasons for being in the Capital of the West nowadays, the gustatory rewards were all about. Down-home gourmands have enjoyed the hip spots of West Asheville: breakfast at the old gas station Sunny Point, with its herb-filled kitchen garden where one whiles away the requisite wait time, and dinner at the low-slung southern nouvelle bistro the Admiral, featuring Texas caviar (black-eyed peas and pickled red onions). Or dinner back over near Pack Square at William Dissen's vaunted farm-to-fork exemplar, the long-running Market Place, with its wood-grilled chicken skewers and Brasstown strip steaks.

Or dinner on the Block, where the spirit and the recipes (collard purloo, Farm and Sparrow succotash) of celebrated Southside Kitchen's Hanan Shabazz inform the African American traditions of Benne on Eagle and its chef de cuisine Ashleigh Shanti, or down the fine arts–overflowing hillside of galleries, studios, and craft beer (care for a Burial Innertube Lager?) of the River Arts District, where the holy smoke swirls and the sauce flies and the true 'cue ribs of 12 Bones have even drawn Barack and Michelle Obama to come souge down among its patient, lunch-only bunch, just a few steps away from the north-flowing French Broad River.

The River

"Who killed the French Broad?" river chronicler Wilma Dykeman asked in her 1955 Rivers of America landmark book, *The French Broad*. It was a powerfully good question back when people said of the degraded river such things as "You can smell it way before you can see it." They derisively termed it "too thick to drink, too thin to plow."

Such disdain may well have also come from the French Broad's long-remembered legacy of death and destruction, the great flood of 1916, of which Thomas Wolfe wrote direly: "There was a flood in Altamont. It swept down in a converging width from the hills, filling the little river, and foaming beyond its banks.... It looted the bottomlands of the river; it floated iron and wooden bridges from their piers as it might float a leaf; it brought ruin to the railway flats and all who dwelt therein. The town was cut off from every communication with the world."

A slow cure came, in part, with the preserving of the Great Smoky Mountains National Park and the Nantahala and Pisgah National Forests—over 1.5 million acres in all—and the healing regrowth over decades of the mountainside forests, which had been shorn rapaciously by big timber interests in the late nineteenth and early twentieth centuries, causing that ruinous, rapid, valley-wide runoff in 1916, what Wolfe had called "liquid avalanche" and "foaming welter."

Fifteen years after Dykeman's indicting query, the federal Clean Water Act of 1970 passed, also helping enormously in the restoration of the French Broad. A concerted joint effort began in the late 1970s by the Land-of-Sky Regional Council and the Tennessee Valley Authority to establish river access points. So, too, had a coming together—over many years, since before the American bicentennial—of legions of representatives from a wide variety of Asheville's and Buncombe County's civil, nonprofit, and academic institutions (such as the Land-of-Sky Regional Council, the City of Asheville, Biltmore Estate, Tennessee Valley Authority, UNC Asheville, and Warren Wilson College) as well as from area businesses. Working through the French Broad Riverfront Planning Committee and its successor, RiverLink, their purpose was nothing less than a commonwealth vision: making "French Broad revitalization a documented goal of all Asheville citizens." The Riverfront Plan, a detailed and intriguing design scheme for a French Broad makeover, appeared in the spring of 1989 with a profusion of illustrations for gateways, greenways, waterways, parkways, and bikeways—a proud statement indeed.

Central to the regional revamping effort a generation ago was Becky Rideout of the Land-of-Sky Regional Council. Concern for the watershed had brought her home from South Carolina, and she coordinated clean-water efforts throughout the valley.

"There's still room for improvement," she told me back then, strongly supporting streamside buffers and the control of storm-water runoff. "The area's developing very quickly, so there's a strong need to take protective measures to restore the river."

And she paused a moment, reflecting upon her family and an icon from her youth.

"My grandmother was born on the French Broad, in Alexander. She always had a copy of Wilma Dykeman's *The French Broad* on a table by her easy chair. As I grew up, it's something that I always noticed there, and it really came to mean something to me when I got the opportunity to move home to western North Carolina and to work on the French Broad River.

"Coming back as I drove across it, I said, 'That's gonna be *my* river.'"

For making good on French Broad River Park—which arrived in the 1990s well stocked with a picnic pavilion, enhanced wetlands, observation decks, a restroom, native wildflower beds, picnic tables, benches and grills, and more than half a mile of paved greenway trails—RiverLink won a Gold Award in 1997 from the American Rivers National Urban Hometown River Program. The award's citation stated: "Today the river is viewed as a community healer that unites the community as a place where people can live, work and play."

For thirty years, leading the RiverLink charge was Karen Cragnolin, an attorney who had moved to Asheville in the 1980s and gone to the chamber of commerce looking to get involved with her new community.

Years ago, she recalled for me: "They said, 'We're trying to do something with our river,' and I said, 'I didn't know you had one.' I drove down Patton Avenue and spent the rest of the day trying to get off the bridge to the river. With a hotel coming on the Biltmore Estate, we see more and more people seeing this river," she said. "We put junkyards and landfills on the river before, but we're not doing that anymore—we're saying this is a place where people really want to be."

RiverLink staged dozens of events every year to raise money and French Broad consciousness, among them sunset cruises, a day at the races, an anything-that-floats parade, and a tour of artists' studios in the River Arts District that drew 10,000 people. Even a mythical French Broad

River Yacht Club came into being, its membership open to anyone who has ever floated a boat on the river. Even with allies and believers, skeptics and detractors still told Cragnolin that the river was too far from downtown, too hard to find, that West Asheville would always be "Worst Asheville" and so on.

Yet now the waters coming down from Court House Falls, through Rosman and past Brevard and Flat Rock and Hendersonville, pulling in the Davidson and the Mills Rivers, all find a greener bend below Biltmore.

The lovely narrow Swannanoa flows down its valley to its confluence with the French Broad at this bend just upstream of the New Deal–era Amboy Road bridge. When the French Broad Yacht Club floats its boats thereabouts from time to time, these craft will surely pass a new riverside place of honor: Karen Cragnolin Park.

A Toast from Brendan Gill

If imagination floats lightly as a ghost on the evening air here, so be it.

I imagine I can see the inimitable New York theatre critic Brendan Gill, way back in the late 1930s, just twenty-five, dapper and bow-tied, when his bride-to-be was being feted at Biltmore and he found himself in Asheville, seeking (no less than a Wolfe or a Fitzgerald, or a Byer or an Adams) to get above *everything* in the French Broad valley town and its river for a few moments on a Saturday night, driving up to a quiet place where a man might sit, sipping his moonshine in peace in a roadhouse high upon tunneled but not yet cut and breached Beaucatcher Mountain.

"Those were the days," Gill wrote much later. "And these are the days too."

The Gorge

Below Asheville, the French Broad tumbles down a broad-shouldered, rocky-bluffed gorge—past the towns of Alexander, Marshall, Barnard, and Hot Springs—for forty-three miles to Paint Rock at the Tennessee line. Over that course, it falls more than 700 feet.

Tahkeyostee, the Cherokee named the Long Man's rapids here: *here they race.*

This was a stretch of river wild enough for whitewatering to have become central to the economy of Madison County, with five boating and rafting enterprises between Marshall and Hot Springs. And gorge coursers who have come into this territory more recently than the Cherokee have also left a cascade of names for the river rocks and forms they found along the way: the Maze, with its myriad openings and its many dead ends; the Big Pillow; the Ledges; Rebar Rapid, with its iron-bar relics of the dam that once powered Stackhouse but that the great French Broad flood of 1916 knocked out; Needle Rock; and the Frank Bell Rapids, named in honor of a legendary camp leader and river runner. Asheville's RiverLink in the late 1990s built Ledges Whitewater Park, a canoe-and-kayak practice course funded by the state Division of Water Resources; there were nine rapids to be dealt with in the eight-mile section of river—the French Broad's steepest—between Barnard and Hot Springs.

In the now-distant past, most of the French Broad's traffic was not so much on it as alongside it, bound upriver instead of down.

By the 1830s and 1840s a rolling, roiling stream of livestock was boiling up out of the grasslands and pasturelands of the lower French Broad in Tennessee. The drovers were using the river and its gorge as the best way to reach South Carolina, slaughterhouses in Spartanburg and markets in Charleston. Every autumn, pork and beef moved up the river on the hoof, mules, too, turkeys in flocks of 500—even a drove of 400 ducks caught the eye of an 1857 Warm Springs visitor. Tennessee hogs were shuffling up the gorge at a rate of 150,000 a year and more. Institutions called "stands"—nineteenth-century inn-and-stockyard hostelries—grew up at points along the river, and the biggest of these was the one in north Buncombe run by James Mitchell Alexander. Today the place is known as the town of Alexander, but then, according to Wilma Dykeman, Alexander's stand was "known from Cincinnati to Charleston as a summer resort, [and] it came into its own during the fall drives when ten or a dozen droves might be stopped there for a single night." That might mean as many as 100 men and 10,000 hogs.

Two generations later—long after the coming of the railroad ended the livestock tides—moonshine culture came to the French Broad valley, and perhaps Dykeman captured the spirit of Prohibition and Civil War legacy as well when she interviewed a lawman ironically named Jesse James Bailey, sheriff of Madison County from 1920 to 1922. "Bloody Madison, you know," Sheriff Bailey said, alluding to the infamous Shelton Laurel massacre of early 1863, Confederate executions of supposed Union sympathizers there: thirteen men and boys.

Of county seat Marshall, the sheriff added, "Folks say it's the town that's a block wide, a mile high and hell deep." One plumbing those depths in the modern moment, in his well-received debut *A Land More Kind Than Home*, was novelist Wiley Cash.

The drovers, the Civil War soldiers, the moonshiners, and their times were faded and storied now, and just below the Buncombe-Madison line, on a summertime afternoon at Walnut Island Park, I once watched families picnic, boys toss rocks in the river, girls slip and slide down a small chute the river had worn through a gray-and-white granite reef, a man and his son walk across the wide shallows to the far shore and then back again, and dogs run free.

There was charcoal smoke and Spanish in the air, no shortage of either, for tens of thousands of Hispanic residents now made western Carolina home. Downriver, just a few miles above Marshall, upon a long rocky island in the middle of the French Broad sat a porcelain commode, flanked by North Carolina and American flags flapping in the breeze. Something surreal here, I thought. And newly real as well—the new coin of the realm hereabouts was neither hogs on the hoof nor popskull but was measured rather in gaily colored rafts and kayaks scooting, careening, and slip-sliding merrily down a French Broad River considerably cleaner than it had been at any time since those hog drovers and bootleggers left the mountain stage.

La vida es sueño, they say: *Life is a dream*. And here the dream about a revivified French Broad seemed to be coming true.

Es verdad.

Hot Springs

If you stood upon the US 25 bridge over the French Broad at Hot Springs and looked south, you could take in a good deal. Upriver there to your left on the east bank was craggy Lover's Leap Mountain, and the river itself would be coming vigorously at you in about the last of its rapid fall and run. Your perch would give you a major mountain perspective, for here the Appalachian Trail bridged the French Broad, and here in this little corner of Carolina, paddle culture met and crossed the boot world in spades.

Hot Springs had only been hot for a little over a century and a quarter. Before that, the waters and town were called Warm Springs and were widely reputed to be restorative enough, as much for their mineral qualities as their heat. What warmth there was depended not on geothermal activity but friction. Some low streams of the French Broad, apparently siphoned off upriver, pushed briskly through narrow subterranean fissures and heated themselves—if mildly—during their clandestine transits. When the village's grand resort hotel burned in the mid-1880s, the building of its successor occasioned an upward reappraisal of the springs' temperature as well as a felicitous commercial appeal of a name change, and Warm Springs became Hot Springs.

"For several decades before the Civil War," Wolfe wrote about Asheville, "it had enjoyed the summer patronage of fashionable people from Charleston and the plantations of the hot South." They came to Flat Rock in Henderson County, "the little Charleston in the Mountains"; to Asheville with all its proclaimed curative and recuperative values; and they came downriver to Hot Springs.

In Hot Springs yet, there were still a few footprints from those old spa-and-springs days. Though the great Mountain Park Hotel that Col. J. H. Rumbough built in the 1880s fell to fire in the 1920s, the colonel's mansard-towered home Sunnybank, at the corner of Walnut and Bridge, not only stood but glistened, put back to right as—what else?—a bed-and-breakfast, "inspired by the ancient hospitality traditions of Taoist and Zen mountain inns," so its keeper stated simply.

Once longtime home of the Dorland-Bell mission school, a precursor of Warren Wilson College, and briefly, as Terry Roberts dramatized so well in his celebrated novel *A Short Time to Stay Here*, site of a huge World War I internment camp, "the German village"—Hot Springs just about closed up in the late 1900s. But by the early twenty-first century the little river town was again on the rise, and the crossroads of sport was why.

One summer day Ann, daughter Cary, and I stood on Bridge Street, the main avenue through town, outside Bluff Mountain Outfitters, a trail shop literally right *on* the Appalachian Trail itself, looking on as hikers passed by with their staves—some striding, some staggering—as string band music came clawhammering boisterously out of the store.

A civilian cavalry of two dozen horses ambled by, clip-clopping through town.

Out on the US 25 bridge that day, a slight young woman and a bearded man were heading south, both grimly determined. Then came a long-haired twenty-five-year-old man, shirtless, holding hands with his blond girlfriend, both of them loping along easily in the heat. Across from the open grounds of the Hot Springs Spa were more young hikers in the shade, one man in an olive-drab slouch hat, another in a khaki foreign-legion lid. Boys with red-and-blue bedrolls lay out like overheated hounds, lucky to have escaped to the shade.

In the French Broad River itself, people were swimming upstream of the bridge, a few with a big old inner tube, one bunch with a pink float.

Wilma Dykeman, the author who helped save the river, lived long enough to be aware and glad that the stream she described as having been "killed" in the mid-1950s not only had come back to life but by the 2000s was also getting more than a little of that good and magic quotient she once called *respect*.

DANCING OVER THE MOUNTAINS
Meeting

The first time I ever laid eyes on Frank Graham Queen of Haywood County was in Chapel Hill, right after a performance of our saloon musical *Diamond Studs* came down in the old Ranch House in October 1974. He was at the back of the Moulin Rouge red–wallpapered hall, shifting side to side, hopped up, it seemed, by the excitement of the show's big finale, and he said at once:

"Great show! I can do the *Alabama Jubilee*!"

And then Frank started scat singing, almost yodeling, that hot old number and smooth dancing, sliding off right and left, circling round a time or two, and finally stopping with a flourish to shake hands.

In that moment I could hardly have known I was meeting one of the best friends I would ever have or that we would go together on jaunts to the new-plays festival in Louisville,

Kentucky; to Tootsie's Orchid Lounge and the Opry in Nashville; to the New Orleans World's Fair and Cajun country and Whiskey Bay and a huge hidden lake full of thousands of ibises in the Atchafalaya River basin; to the Democratic convention of 1980 in New York City; to the politically rambunctious Hawk and Dove bistro on Capitol Hill in Washington; up and down the Caledonian Canal in Scotland; but mainly all over North Carolina high and low ... and who would show me the mountains in ways that he made sure would be comprehensible yet still full of mystery to this flatlander—around and about the peaks and coves of Haywood County, to Bethel and Mauney Cove, Crabtree and J-Creek, Cataloochee, the Pigeon River Gorge, the Newfound Gap, Max Patch, and simply, consummately, all throughout the wide wild ranges of the Carolina west.

Patriarch: Sam Love Queen

Sam Love Queen, Frank's grandfather, was born and reared on a farm maybe ten miles below Soco Gap in the Blue Ridge and in the shadow of the peak Ad Tate Knob, named so for the desperate young woman who had abandoned her infant to the mountaintop elements sixty years before Sam first saw the late nineteenth-century light of day. Small-family farming was a scratching-it-out business, yet Sam soon figured that whatever farmers grew or did, whatever the weather gave them or imposed upon them, they all needed stock—they all needed horses and mules.

And so he became a stockman. In league with another man, Black Charlie, an African American friend with an equally astute eye for horseflesh, he began to make twice yearly traverses to Tennessee, up over the great blue jump-up country of the Smokies to buy animals and drive them back to North Carolina. Over on foot, back riding. As drovers, the two men could handle several dozen horses and mules, and they liked mules: smarter than horses, surefooted mules never foundered and stopped when they had reached their limits,

hence the British Army proverb "One never sees a dead mule."

Once back at Queen's Farm, on the Maggie-and-Dellwood Road near Junaluska, Sam and Black Charlie could set up shop, sell their stock at their price, and stack up money at a time when there was nearly none. And because Sam had cash on hand, he found a second profession that would keep him out of dirt farming for the rest of his life: Bail bonding.

When a man needed somebody on his bond, including Cherokee men on the Qualla Boundary just over Soco Gap from the Queens, he would call on Sam Queen and Sam would pay his bail. Over the years, Sam paid so many bonds among them, and did so much for them and their families, that many a Cherokee woman chose to name a son for him.

And yet.

Most knew him not for livestock or bail bonds but for dancing—as the Square Dancing King. He took smooth dancing and put couples in figures and put on a show. He took up dancing when he was hoe-handle high, and he said dancing was the only way in the world you would ever get to hug every woman in the room. Along with banjo picker Bascom Lamar Lunsford, the song-writing and song-catching Squire of Turkey Creek who handled the musicians, Sam Queen staged the Soco Gap Dance Team and Band. They called him the Square Dancing King all over America, and people turned out to see these mountain dancers all over the big hills and way beyond, across the long years of the Depression that had started a decade earlier for farmers than it had for anybody else, turned out to see them and paid a quarter at a time when nobody had a dime.

Eleanor Roosevelt caught the Soco Gap Dance Team up in Virginia, the festival at White Top Mountain, and straightaway she booked them into the White House, and suddenly there they were, performing on Pennsylvania Avenue for FDR and his friends, who that night just happened to include the King and Queen of England.

"Did you talk to 'em, Sam?" folks asked him when he got back home.

"Well, course I did," Sam said.

"What'd you say?"

"I asked the queen if she'd like to dance," Sam said. "Mama always said I needed to be sure and find the least attractive girl in the room and ask her to dance, so she wouldn't set there like a wallflower."

"Damn! Well, what'd *she* say."

"She said *no!*"

One of his sons, Richard Queen (Frank's father, who had worked in Washington for U.S. senator Frank Porter Graham and who would come out for Kennedy early on in 1960, when most of the South was still touting Johnson), became one of the lead dancers for the Soco Gap bunch, till he went off to war in the early 1940s. A captain who had seen him dance now saw him in the mess hall up at Camp Butner and called out, "Richard Queen, what the hell are you doing with a potato peeler?" and yanked him out of kitchen service and got him headed off to officer candidate school and on to the Pacific as a "ground officer" (in his words) in the Fifth Army Air Corps in New Guinea.

Sam Queen left home one January Saturday, went downtown, and bailed Johnson Locust out of jail—Locust, once out, asked Sam if he might borrow a car, but Sam refused. Sam drove home and that night went on to bed with his wife Glee,

but then he got up, worried that Locust might just be lurking around outside the house. While Sam was out back, Locust entered the house, found his way to the bedroom hall and shouted out for Sam. Glee quickly arose and told Locust through the door that Sam was gone. When Locust started to open the bedroom door, he lowered his .22 rifle barrel into the gap and Glee grabbed it and tried to jerk it away. Just then Sam, Owl Head .32 pistol drawn, came down the hall behind Locust, and in the wrestling that ensued, Locust turned Sam's pistol hand around and shot Sam in the eye. The authorities soon caught Johnson Locust in Sam's stolen car, and Sam died later that same night. They said the bullets had been in the pistol so long, and the gun had gone so long without being fired, that the shell casings had tarnish and mold upon them.

When the Queens mourned and buried Sam at Maple Grove United Methodist Church, up the hill toward Waynesville away from Queen's Farm, 5,000 people came.

And a great many of them were Cherokee.

Waynesville

Years later, Frank showed me where his grandfather was buried.

He showed me the Waynesville alley beside Onionhead Stovall's store, where a local man lured a policeman who was notorious for beating suspects and yelled from the darkness, "Oh, no, don't beat me again!" and then fired his pistol, killing the lawman but getting off on self-defense.

He told me about fishing at Turkey George Place in the Smokies for three days, he and his brother Sam and Charlie Mills, a Cherokee-trained guide, ahead of Terry Sanford's campaign visit in 1960, so to have a Queen family fish fry and rally for the future governor.

He told me about Jack, the man who constantly walked back and forth between Waynesville and somewhere in northern Virginia, who had a hundred ideas for small businesses and wrote them up and mailed them in, asking Frank and another great friend, lawyer and later judge Richie Holt, to get his plans (which all came to naught), as he put it, *certified*.

He told me about the fellow who showed up at Richie Holt's law office wanting to know if Richie was up on his *Bible law*?

"What part of it exactly?" Richie asked.

"Well," said the man, "the part about no one supposed to alter the monuments of the ancestors."

"How does that apply to you?" asked Richie.

"Well, my neighbor's gone out and moved the pile of stones that marks my northwest corner, moved 'em more towards me so he can claim some of my land—my granddaddy put them stones there and that's a monument of my ancestor— I got Bible law on my side and I want to *law him*!"

Frank spoke of the town inebriate who mistakenly received a large payroll tax bill meant for a factory owner of the same name and who brought the bill around to Frank to get him out of trouble. When Frank assured him there had been a mistake and that he would get it all straightened out, the man wandered off, relieved, but in his subsequent relief celebration he imbibed overmuch and came to believe that he really *did* own a big manufacturing facility and that the workers were asking way too much of him. Fogbound and overamped, he then came *back* to Frank, shouting that his workers were killing him—"They're eating me alive!"—and that he might just have to shut the plant down and fire them all and put an end to it!

He let me in on the story of a local fireman and his gold medal upon retirement, and how that all turned to ashes when a rumor went around holding that this same fireman had from time to time siphoned gas out of the fire trucks for his own personal use. In came the fireman and his furious wife, to a meeting of the town board—he said not a word, but she said aplenty, closing with her slamming the retirement totem down on the table before the board and saying, "Here's your damn medal back!" then grabbing her husband and the both of them stomping out as she proudly said, over her shoulder: "We ride on *bought gas* or we don't ride at all!"

Once Frank and I were having breakfast in a little diner at Mauney Cove, near Queen's Farm, when J. Lynn Noland, another attorney and a keen student of mountain ways, joined us and before long asked, "Frank, did I ever tell you about that old man and Bunches Creek?"

"Don't believe so," Frank said.

Lynn went quickly on, quoting the old-timer and warbling his voice upward of its natural register to approximate age:

It was along about nineteen ought eight. I was up in the high hills, fishing on Bunches Creek, and it was late afternoon, mists already starting to form, and I could hear the last log train of the day coming down the mountain, approaching the high trestle bridge there.

And the sun was just setting, right up over the notch beyond the trestle, I tell you, it was just so pretty, everything . . .

And here come the train, coming on down, every flatcar loaded up with logs, you know, heavy, and it was really something to see, the mists, the sunset behind it as the Suncrest Lumber Company train and all its cars pulled out across that high trestle and just then it gave way and that train collapsed it, every bit of it, and fell on down through it all the way to the bottom and settled, steaming away, that whole train wrecked right there in front of my eyes in Bunches Creek.

One of the most beautiful things I ever saw in my life.

Frank made sure I was there the night before cousin Joe Sam and Dr. Kate got married, out at

Queen's Farm for the dance on the patio, Joe Sam calling ("Ocean Wave!" and more), first spreading corn meal all over the flagstones so everyone's feet would move smoothly in keeping with the family's Soco Gap style of dancing, soon as Quay Smathers and his Dutch Cove String Band cut loose.

And he made sure that I would see a different kind of mountain night, years later, when fellow Rambler Chris Frank and I were stopping over on our way to Memphis to stage *Life on the Mississippi* in a park high above that great river. Frank, Joe Sam, Chris, and I drove up to Soco Gap just to stand alongside the parkway awhile and watch the waning strawberry moon lay its shimmering light onto all the clouds hanging in the hollows of the Plott Balsams just below us, moonlight moving and ever shifting over the mists as if they were slow-spreading surf in the waves of an ocean.

At Sam and Mary's on Hillview

For a spell after Frank came back to Waynesville from Washington, D.C., he lived at his cousin Joe Sam's house on Hillview, near the cemetery. Or rather, Joe Sam's *parents'* home, Frank's uncle Sam and aunt Mary's place—like all Queens, Sam and Mary were the greatest of hosts, and I often stayed there too when I came to visit.

They were both schoolteachers, smart, wise, well spoken, and witty, and a dynamic life revolved around their kitchen and the large unscreened porch of the old Queen Anne house, and the aphorisms flew. While school was out in the summertime, Sam ran a burley tobacco and stake-tomato farm over in Bethel, a valley village just south of Waynesville on US 276 as it ran up toward the Pisgah Ridge and over to Hendersonville and Brevard. Frank and Joe Sam had worked the tomato farm when they were young men, spraying fertilizer and picking hornworms off the plants. One August morning I was sitting on the porch about 8 A.M., drinking

coffee and writing, when Sam got back from checking on his tomatoes. He stopped abruptly when he saw me and then pronounced: "If a man gets his day started at six, he'll have everything he needs to do done by ten—but if he doesn't start till ten, he'll still be putting up hay against the rain at six."

And then he walked off into the house. I thought this was a clever-sounding but vague, even silly, saying—right up until the day I became the father of twins and started living by it.

At other times, he delivered such commentary as: "A man can eat all the vegetables he wants and never gain any weight."

"A man's got to eat by the clock if he wants to keep his weight up."

"A fat chicken don't show it in the face."

Sam was a large man.

He and Mary loved fish, and I recall that in warm weather there was most always a two-and-a-half-gallon pickle jar full of brown trout filets from Sam's fishing trips up to the creek at Soco Gap.

Sam always kept up a remarkable good humor. Frank said he and Sam got into the habit of watching the North Carolina shows on public television together on Thursday nights, and one evening they were drawn into a Roy Underhill *Woodwright's Shop* wherein Roy intended to show the *entire* process of how to make a cabinet with wood milled from a tree he would cut down. Frank said Roy's chopping commenced and kept on going and going with little progress till they thought he intended to do the whole chop-down in real time, and, at one out-of-breath point, Roy looked into the camera and said, "You realize that to get the wood I'm having to *kill this tree!*" and, given the slow pace of things, Sam responded: "Well, I don't know about *that*, Roy, but you sure are aggravating it a right smart!"

One August evening, Frank and I rode with Sam over to Hendersonville, home of the tomato cooperative where Sam had sold his crop, so he could settle up. On the way there Frank pointed out some stunningly steep territory to the north of the highway, property he was dealing with in an estate and saying he did not know why the heirs were fighting over it so—"It's not good for anything except to hold up the sky!"

To which Sam said, of the folks who would inherit it, "They'll sell it, Frank, and whatever they get for it, why, they're *Fergusons*, they're *Scottish*—they'll hold on to those nickels just as long as they can!"

Not overly concerned with money himself, Sam just shrugged in Hendersonville when he learned he had hardly come out on that year's tomatoes.

"Well," he mused on the drive back, "they say them shrouds don't have no pockets."

Max Patch

Among the many Great Smokies spots Frank carried us to was the grassy high-mountain bald where Haywood and Madison Counties come together with Tennessee: a top-of-the-world corner called Max Patch.

"It's remote," he said, as we climbed into his golden Buick ("You always want to have a car that's the color of some form of currency," he steadfastly maintained) to head out of Waynesville. "Hope you don't mind *re-mote*!"

Not at all.

Nor was he leaning on the word in jest. Max Patch was not all that far away as the crow flies, and yet the crow does not *drive*: you drove north on NC 209 up past Crabtree, past the dairy farm where no-till farming decades ago first found favor in America, then peeling off of this highway beloved of motorcyclists, with all its quick switchbacks and its valley floor straightaways, the Luck-Trust-and-Bluff route, and then headed up Max Patch Road and onto one of the many spines in the Smokies, Buckeye Ridge in extreme western Madison County.

There was plenty of time for talk as we ascended, for it took us over an hour, and in the last going we were on unpaved lanes in the Pisgah National Forest, switchbacking over and over again, the lengths of the road sections shortening as we climbed. Frank, hailing as he did from a highly political family, had near-endless stories of elections wherein ballot boxes in far-off precincts (and some in town too) got hit and stuffed where they sat between the vote-count reports and the morning after polling, whereupon various village worthies innocent as guinea hens suddenly called for recounts in certain specified precincts and— surprise—whole outcomes changed.

On this ascent, though, Frank also told a darker tale. A young man pulled by a state trooper in the nearby Pigeon River Gorge had simply eased off on the roadside (steep, rocky laurel cliffs to the east, the river way down below to the west), rolled down his window as if to respond fairly, and shot the trooper dead. Then he drove west to the next exit, turned off, and abandoned the car and took flight into the wilderness, near a place the press endlessly called during the ensuing manhunt "*remote* Harmon Den," always emphasizing the adjective. The slayer eluded his 1,000 pursuers for three days, when he finally came back down from whatever laurel hell he had been hiding in and thirstily found the river.

And when he did, he was spotted almost immediately, and the forces of the hunt converged, every one of them armed, all those firearms trained on the slayer when the posse's leader raised a bullhorn and told him to hold up where he was, put his hands over his head, and not move.

"He knew they had him, and he did just what they told him," Frank said, as we neared the sky. "But I'm telling you there was a lot of 'em up top by the road had him in their sights, and that trooper, everybody really liked him, felt for him and his family, and they were really wishing that

View from Max Patch Mountain, Madison County

fellow standing down in the river would just go on and make a run for it, or maybe even just flinch a little bit."

Quite near the peak, we parked and then walked the narrow trail for a quarter mile or so to the 4,629-foot summit of bald, grassy Max Patch. With a 360-degree view, we looked down upon a rim of hills all around us and rolling blue hills beyond us in all directions, at crags and haze and clouds already in valleys near and far below, this midafternoon of a summer's day. And we looked off toward Tennessee, not just Tennessee in general but an infamous portion of it where

chicken fights were still popular. "There's no law in Cocke County, Tennessee," Frank said. "Not a place you want to break down."

Just us. Cool and quiet up here.

Thinking back on stuffed ballot boxes, on a highwayside murder, on a Haywood sheriff who had once stormed into a snake-handling Pentecostal revival and yanked a hefty rattlesnake out of the preacher's hand as he (the sheriff) denounced "snake chunking" and then got bitten and like to died, thinking of such a myriad of Frank Queen tales as these, way up here I could not hold on to them all.

The stories eased away and lost themselves in

JUMP-UP COUNTRY

182

the hazes, as part and parcel of a contentious, bellicose territory below, unable to keep their multiforms of meanness, unable to hold their shapes, unable to upend us latter-day pilgrims who for a couple of peaceable-kingdom hours really did have most everything all set and settled from this bright lofty perch, sun starting to fall away to the west and still only the lightest of breezes stirring and sounding the old grass harp up here at the top of the world.

Many years later, we returned to Max Patch on a chilly October afternoon, Ann, Frank, his friend Charmaine, and I, to see if we could hear that old harp one more time.

But this time a transient village had formed aloft: forty or fifty people, some of them tent camping beneath the vault of sky, one man flying a large white radio-controlled glider, skillfully so,

yet one wondered why, for the act that might have been done anywhere had become more or less the main event of this rare gorgeous spot on this day, distracting most everyone who had pushed on and gotten to the top of the bald. Wisps of breeze in the forest below might have been nice up here, as they were that long-ago summer afternoon, but the real wind whipping across Max Patch this day had formed up north somewhere, or over in Tennessee perhaps, and had swarmed unfettered across the ocean of mountains beside and below us, with great long fetch, nothing to stop it.

And suddenly Max Patch presented itself as a mountaintop in January, and a flurry of snow blew through fiercely all at once, and we soon descended.

At the forest service road by the woods below the bald, a white-bearded man was sitting quietly on the porch of a very small camper-cabin

perched upon his pickup's bed, his wood stove going inside, hardwood smoke pouring forth out of a small silver stovepipe, and he just waiting patiently for that Lilliputian aircraft to land for the last time, for the crowd to leave, so in the early evening he could take his unobstructed turn at summiting Max Patch alone.

Bear Pen Gap

And Frank also made sure I saw the highest point on the Blue Ridge Parkway.

Down in the Pigeon River valley a warm summer day advanced, yet at the 6,053-foot point, the Haywood-Jackson county line, on the last day of May, cold damp clammy mists flowed over the road like water, and water itself both dripped and fell in thin sheets from the nearly bare rock walls beside the parkway.

On a clear day, he assured me, you could see most of forever to the west, but not this day, just these vivid mists and the fogs they were swiftly building in the hollows below.

"How about a little walk in the woods?" Frank said, and in a few minutes we were hiking along an old line-drive narrow-gauge railroad grade toward Bear Pen Gap, a trail of even altitude following the ridgetop at 5,400 feet for a couple of miles to the west. The path through the woods held up nicely, damp though not slick, and this was just fine by us, as our third companion that day was June, our small snow-white Pomeranian, raised as a woods dog back home at Clover Garden in southwest Orange County. Her ancestors, tradition held, were Icelandic sled dogs brought to England by Queen Charlotte and, later, bred down in size and shown by Queen Victoria, and June took well to her current wilderness assignment—curious and, like her forebears, sure of foot.

We crossed a couple of small, slow-flowing rills coming out of nearby springs, and June, thirsty, stopped and partook as we got farther and farther from the parkway, the green enveloping the three

of us. Until suddenly we burst out of the woods and stood at the edge of an eight-acre bald, the outer point of the ridge, and June took off on a run in the grass. When she held up midbald, I kept the calls coming till she turned and started back our way. This was no place to lose anything, and you knew full well that up here you would lose a dog only once.

"Land falls off a right smart just past the tree line there," said Frank, gesturing toward the curtain of bright and solid white just beyond the bald, enclosing everything in deepest cloud, so thick I was surprised we had such a good look at the bald.

Then he spoke vigorously about how the Clean Smokestacks Act had caused the clearing of the high-elevation air and the opening up of the view.

"Before, you'd come out to a place like this, nothing but haze, murky mountains. Nowadays," Frank said, "if it's not all misty like this . . .

"You can see clear out to Tennessee."

Yet again, Frank was right as rain: clean air in the Carolina mountains is indeed one of our best stories.

Several summers after our Bear Pen walk, I awaited Governor Roy Cooper in a sitting room off the executive mansion's main hall, a den with a green couch, large card table, and fireplace. Tucker Hayes set up his lights and camera for an *Exploring North Carolina* interview, and director Tom Earnhardt placed the chairs where he wanted them. Bearing witness as key grips for *Exploring North Carolina* that day, former environmental secretary Bill Ross and I took our places at the card table, rising when Governor Cooper entered the room and went straight to Tom, shaking his hand and saying genuinely, "Welcome to *your* house—this is such an important story and I'm so glad you're telling it."

Once the camera started rolling, here came more of the tale Frank had been telling out at that bald at the end of the ridge.

For Roy Cooper, too, recalled the old days' mountain haze when, as he said, it was "hard to see ten miles." As attorney general, using North Carolina's Clean Smokestacks Act of 2002, he had moved in 2006 against the Tennessee Valley Authority, whose power plants created the smoke that then blew east over the high Carolina hills and lay over them like a pall.

"The TVA lawyers were *so arrogant*," Bill Ross recalled.

"We were laughed at, at first," agreed Governor Cooper.

The Bush-era Environmental Protection Agency, they both remembered, had not shown much interest in this effort, yet things had changed with the Obama EPA. Judge Lacy Thornburg (himself a former North Carolina attorney general) had found for the State of North Carolina, and by the time, years later, the case against the TVA was heading for the U.S. Supreme Court, the power authority's lawyers were no longer laughing.

In 2011, North Carolina and the TVA settled.

In 2012, owing to all the air-quality improvements the Clean Smokestacks Act had brought, researchers estimated that about 1,700 premature deaths were prevented.

Governor Cooper recalled how a ranger at Mount Mitchell had gestured to First Lady Kristin Cooper about the mountainside's trees all around, telling her, "This has all come back!" And of talk then current in 2019 about rolling back emissions and particulate standards at the federal level, the governor said at the close of the interview: "We *can't* go back. We can't go *backward*."

HIGHLANDS

Ann and I were coming up a long slow climb, rolling eastward late one October morning from Franklin, moving up the Cullasaja River gorge toward the top of the big broad Highlands Plateau, the bright, deep, late-morning light saturating and backlighting the red and yellow tree leaves in the gorge, and the natural, painted canvas through which we were rising, entering, had a phenomenal visual effect. Cullasaja country, the Cherokee's *honey locust place*, had drama to burn: its deep ravines, its glades, rises, sudden drops, the almost-midday light shining pure gold through the yellow leaves on the trees and upon those falling in waves of wind, and more sunlight glancing like silver off long patches of hillside laurel.

With pure delight, Ann exclaimed: "This is like being in a jewel box."

Walker Percy, a UNC–Chapel Hill chemistry graduate from Greenville, Mississippi, who crafted some of the finest post-Faulkner fiction of the American South, sought escape from the Lake Pontchartrain heat and found solace here on Mirror Lake in Highlands. And because he did, Carolina writers and artists sought him out. Pulitzer-winning cartoonist Doug Marlette once called upon Percy, bringing his fiancée Melinda Hartley from Dilworth in Charlotte up to Highlands and obtaining marital advice when, after lunch, Percy walked Marlette down to the water's edge and told him simply, "She's a keeper."

The elegant poet and critic Dannye Romine Powell of the *Charlotte Observer* met up with the then-sixty-three-year-old Percy here when his novel *The Second Coming* appeared, and she reported his telling her: "I'll walk out to the highway and meet you down at the bottom of the driveway," in a last-gentleman voice. "I'm a guy who's wearing yellow pants, and there ain't many other guys up here wearing yellow pants."

Of *The Second Coming*, Powell later remarked that though it was fictionally "set in Linwood, NC … much of the landscape here is pure Highlands."

One particular corner of Highlands landscape had drawn us here, several buildings with an artful and crafty rusticity set on a hillside of pines and cedars, the campus of the small, significant

Highlands Biological Station, a marked and cloistered contrast to the tony watering hole and village of *shoppes* through which we had just driven. The station, in continuous operation here in this lush, temperate rain-forest world since 1931, comprised laboratories, bunkhouses, a nature center, a small amphitheater, a woods walk, and ten-acre Lindenwood Lake. The whole place seemed quite simply of a piece and thoroughly in keeping with the high, wide Carolina-mountain world that has so long been the object of its studies.

This station and the town lay at the crossing of two great trading routes: the coffee-and-beignet route from New Orleans to New York, and the rice-and-straw-hat way from Savannah to Chicago. At least that was the odd belief of a pair of nineteenth-century land developers who drew those two straight lines and plotted a commercial capital for their intersection: right here. But the men's grasp of the true lay of the land was clearly slim to none, for the idea of ascending this substantial North Carolina mesa and crossing it with freight, only to descend on its steep other side, appealed to no traders at all, and the notion lives on today only as Highlands' creation myth.

The vision to put a substantial biological study and record-keeping center here came from Clark Foreman, grandson of the *Atlanta Constitution*'s founder, and one of its early directors was the celebrated UNC botanist W. C. Coker, the professor who back in Chapel Hill had overseen the conversion of a boggy six-acre sheep's meadow into the stunning native-plants arboretum and who ran Highlands late in his life and career, from 1935 to 1944. North Carolina native Julia Sprunt Grumbles started coming up to Highlands in the 1970s, when she was working in Atlanta's media world, finding Transylvania County's high-mesa hideaway "a special place" whose rain-forest features fostered a community in love with the natural world here, its streams, its waterfalls,

its weather. When she got involved with the Highlands Biological Station, she felt it was "the best-kept secret in town" and soon helped raise funds for it and sang its praises, as Highlands Biological Foundation president celebrating and elevating the profile of this near-century-old outpost of scientific training and exploration.

And natural beauty: a hillside botanical garden above the lake.

On our October day here, Ann and I strolled with Highlands' genial director and Western Carolina University biologist James Costa up one of the paths, and there in a shady grove he showed us something truly special, a patch of ground cover rescued from the Jocassee Valley by volunteers in station wagons, back in the 1960s before Duke Power flooded the bottoms. As Ann and I stared appreciatively at these modest plants, we were also looking far beyond them—deep into wild mountain time and into a grand botanical mystery story, the long-running nineteenth-century search for the ancestors of the plants over which we stood: *Oconee bells*.

Their tale of provenance was this: Celebrated French botanist André Michaux, encamped in December 1788 beside a Cherokee homestead (eight Cherokee and their six dogs, he noted), came upon the little plant while scouting around near the headwaters of the Keowee River, took a specimen home with him, and stashed it in a cabinet in his Paris herbarium.

Fifty years later, botanist Asa Gray sailed for Europe on the packet *Philadelphia*, disembarking in Liverpool and studying his herbal way across England, then France, where he laid hands upon Michaux's dried specimen, fell in love with it, and pored over his predecessor's few notes, which simply said it could be found in the *hautes montagnes*, the "high mountains" of western North Carolina. If only the Frenchman had been just a tad more specific—yet his was the phrase that launched a thousand trips.

For Dr. Gray came home to America, promptly

named the rare little plant in honor of the elder botanic scholar Charles Wilkins Short— *Shortia galacifolia*—and there things stood. Everyone heard of it, but no one since Michaux had reported actually *seeing it* in the wild. So popular and well known in the far-flung world of herborists was the drive to rediscover it, in flower, that the joshing byword among them across much of the 1800s came to be: "Found *Shortia* yet?"

Finally, the herbalist Hyamses, father and son, of Statesville did come across it—in 1877 on the banks of the Catawba River in McDowell County, about seventy straight-line miles from where

Michaux had originally laid eyes and hands upon it. Asa Gray et al. had simply been searching in the wrong times, wrong places, and wrong altitudes for *Shortia*.

Some call it by its nicknames: little colt's foot, or Oconee bells, or "brave acony bell" when the sublime songwriter Gillian Welch sang of it as "the fairest bloom the mountain knows."

We walked on past *Shortia*, ducking low-hanging branches over the footpath around Lindenwood Lake, till we crossed the lower lake road and climbed a steep ravine, along one of the lake's tributaries, to regard some giant dead hemlocks, another devastated stand giving mute testimony to the awful success of the small, white woolly adelgid's attack upon western Carolina's hemlocks, so many thousands of which have perished. This ravine should have been dark at three o'clock in the afternoon, yet it was bright and wide open to sunlight, with only these big ruined skeletal trees against the sky.

And yet, I thought, just as tiny clover will grow beneath a fallen sequoia out in California, here the modest little *Shortia* grew nearby, and we had been given the gift of seeing it, which so many who once sought it had not.

The way back to Waynesville and Frank's home led us past the 750-foot-tall, sheer cliff of Whiteside Mountain, a longtime tourist attraction and fairly recently the reintroduction site of peregrine falcons, and then on down through Cashiers, Cullowhee, and Sylva, home of the cupolaed Jackson County Courthouse up on the hill and its cascading 107 steps. We two had done just exactly what the odd nineteenth-century land developers had envisioned: we had hauled our freight up, over, and on down off the Highlands Plateau.

And we were by far the richer for it.

JOYCE KILMER AND THE CHEROHALA

One early August morning, the cedar and spruce woods out from Frank's hillside house in Waynesville lay in a deep, heavy morning mist, and most all the trees were lost in those mists, all but a few nearby cedars and pines. Yet how quickly the mists lifted, suddenly treetop high and just above them, with a gorgeous array of blue sky and white cumulus clouds, a morning buttermilk sky high above them sliding slowly toward the east. And then just as quickly the spectral vapors sat and settled back down again, to where only the near-ridge neighborhood was visible a scant 300 yards across Frank's little

valley. By midmorning, though, the day had warmed up with a sky of blue.

That evening, we sat out on Frank's high deck, gazing out across the small valley below and up toward the far ridge over Camp Branch. The rain started up and got steadily heavier over the next hour, as a beautiful storm came into the valley and closed it all down with mists, till at the height of it the far side was scarcely as visible as it had been that morning, and the far ridges loomed behind a great gray *obscura*.

We spoke of the next day, when we planned to get out to the far west, to the Cherohala Skyway and to the Joyce Kilmer Forest, where, in Conrad's words, "the big trees were kings."

A bright sunny day opened over the mountain world, and, on the way, Frank gave Ann and me his analysis of Fontana Lake—"Summertime recreation," he said, as we passed Almond Dock and big flocks of pontoon boats, "and a culture of 'go to the lake.' Till Labor Day, then they draw the lake down for power."

When I reminded him about my week-long Fontana paddle and the little pine footstool I had bought so long ago at Cherokee ostensibly for my mother, he laughed and said, "It'll probably end up on *Antiques Roadshow*," and commented further on how its value might grow, citing Gene Ferguson back in Haywood County, whose motto was: "I buy junk and sell antiques."

Soon we were in Robbinsville, the seat of Graham County, at lunchtime drifting into Lynn's café ("All roads lead to Lynn's") across from the county courthouse. On the wall was a lit-up map: the Tail of the Dragon, a torturous route on nearby US 29 starting at Deals Gap, beloved by bikers and sports-car enthusiasts for its 318 sharp curves in only eleven miles. Those who drove it knighted and called themselves *Dragonslayers*.

Lynn set us up all right with cheeseburgers big as hubcaps, which we ate while sitting on concrete benches in front of the courthouse, where scenes

Hemlock, Joyce Kilmer Memorial Forest,
Graham County

from the 1994 Jodie Foster film *Nell*, about an isolated and unusual young mountain woman, had been shot.

An extra, a parolee, was in one morning's courtroom filming but failed to show up for the afternoon, breaking the film's continuity and holding up the shoot. When his parole officer quickly found him by telephone, the man said moviemaking was boring and he was *on strike* till he got more money. The officer said you get down here inside of thirty minutes or we revoke your parole.

The man appeared at once.

And the filming of *Nell* proceeded.

Up in the big Poplar Cove of Joyce Kilmer Memorial Forest fifteen miles west of town, few

besides us three walked the midafternoon woods. A couple of young families passed us, they coming down and trying to keep their small children from slipping on the sleek damp clay of the steep path. We had crossed the bridge over Little Santeetlah Creek and were rising swiftly on wood-block steps and a worn path. A half a mile up we reached the Kilmer Memorial, a bronze tablet laid upon a huge rock—dedicated July 30, 1936, eighteen years to the day that Kilmer, author of the short, eternal poem "Trees," died by sniper's bullet in a forest near Seringes-et-Nesles in northern France, just a few months before the end of World War I.

In the continuing hillside above his memorial ran a three-quarter-mile loop around a high portion of the cove, filled with magnificent old-growth, five- and six-foot-diameter poplars, some standing 120 feet tall. Their crowns spread and met, and what very little understory grew below obscured nothing.

If men and women and children may still be awed, they would be so in this place. The psalmist sings, "The heavens declare the glory of God; and the firmament sheweth his handywork," and that these majestic poplars are the handiwork and fine art of the creative power of the Universe, there can be no dispute. Fortunate were we to walk beneath them and say *hallelujah*.

For it might not have been so. Logging equipment was standing at the ready back in the 1930s, ready to take down these last mountain giants, when the Roosevelt government moved in and saved the place, paying twenty-eight dollars an acre when an acre of mountain timberland was going for little more a tenth of that price. On dedication day, someone read Franklin Roosevelt's letter about the immense, ongoing value of the Kilmer Forest, about saving "this most beautiful, unmarred and natural setting," though not before Civilian Conservation Corps tractors had dragged celebrants' cars up the mire that torrential rains had made of the road to Poplar Cove.

On the way back down the cove's trails leading

Little Santeetlah Creek, Kilmer Forest

out of this spectacular cathedral, June the Pomeranian, dwarfed by the immensity of it all, kept stopping to sip water from tiny puddles in the merest dimples of flatter rocks along the way, thereby keeping communion with all the rest of us small and grateful creatures.

At last we rolled on up the Cherohala Skyway from Santeetlah Gap (2,660 feet) to Hooper Bald, most of the last distance from the Kilmer Forest out to Tennessee.

At the Hooper Bald Trailhead (5,290 feet), the holes of two rifle shots in a sign stared back at us like strange and empty spectral eyes. Of such a spot, you hear wild tales: of the horseback riders and accompanying wagon train coming through the forests and up over top of these mountains every year since 1958, lobbying for the skyway; and a generation before that, of Cotton McGuire's hog hunt gone bad, with a dozen hounds torn up and done in and hunters hiding in trees, all while 400-pound Russian boars penned for hunting parties now rampaged through split-rail fences and escaped into the arms of the wilderness,

where they have now been breeding nearly unchecked for 100 years.

A motorcyclist when not holding forth in court (he rode for a right long spell with the Choir Boys), Frank spoke as we were coming down the mountain about "the steady, even radii of curves built using parkway-style construction, which is what the Cherohala Skyway has." Good riding, he felt, and a huge contrast with the Tail of the Dragon, which he dismissed briskly: "Sharp turns, poor sight lines, and dangerous as hell!"

No houses up in here, and few signs of any sort met us as we dropped down eastward on a 9 percent grade, just the seemingly limitless forests extending and stretching out forever, the vast impressive vistas of mountains rolling forth upon mountains.

"Really something," I said, "to look out on all this territory and know there probably aren't even four or five people moving about in it."

"That's just about right," Frank said. He lifted his left hand from the wheel, gesturing broadly at the great deserted hills, and, with a sense of honor, judging: "This is one *empty* place."

IV

Epilogue

A MOMENT ON HOOPER LANE

How We See, How We Are Seen

Waters of the Haw (left) meet waters of the New Hope (right), confluence above the Jordan Lake Dam, Moncure

I

The first of March nine years ago warmed to an unseasonably high seventy-eight degrees in Chapel Hill, an overcast day with wind out of the west, gusting to thirty.

I stood out upon a front porch at the east end of Hooper Lane and spoke for half an hour with one of my father's University of North Carolina law school friends from the vaunted Class of 1948 about the future and nothing but the future. He was one of the state's greatest elders, and though he had only a few months left to live, his vision was as clear, strong, and far reaching as it had been all his life, during which he had helped lead the post–World War II wave of progressive thought and deed that had made North Carolina the best-regarded and in many ways most favored state in the American South.

His name was William Clyde Friday, our former university president for thirty years, the best of the best of North Carolina.

Mr. Friday had called and asked me how he might obtain copies of some waterways programs I had made for *Our State* on UNC public television. What he sought, I had right at hand, and I told him I would gladly bring them by the next afternoon.

We met out front of his Hooper Lane home that early spring day. Mr. Friday was putting together a foundation proposal about taking a hard, detailed look at our state's water supplies. He was extremely concerned that we might soon fall short—"I'm wondering if we might have to raise the heights, the levels, of our reservoirs," he said.

Well might he have been worried, given that the great nearby impoundments of the upper Cape Fear and the upper Neuse watersheds (Jordan Lake and Falls of the Neuse Lake) were under increasing pressure from pollution *and* population. Stringent watershed protection rules for the areas above Jordan and Falls Lakes, state

policy as of 2009, were still not in place when Mr. Friday and I spoke.

Nor are they now.

Land trusts such as the Conservation Trust for North Carolina, the Conservation Fund, and the Triangle Land Conservancy are at work today to protect the watersheds of these lakes, with a generous quarter-million-dollar grant from the Caterpillar Foundation in late 2020, all to do what the State of North Carolina should have done over a decade ago, and thank heaven for their help.

President Friday's twin concerns about water that day in March 2012 were its availability in sufficient volume for our citizens from Manteo to Murphy, from Wilmington to Watauga, and its cleanliness.

He was well acquainted with such an exemplary watershed project as Asheville's 22,000-acre district, with its stringent protections, though he would not see the state legislature attempt to take it away from the city, a battle that led to the state supreme court and the court's decision to leave the water district in the hands of the city that had spent a century putting it together. He was well aware of such environmental challenges as the pollution of public-trust waters by hog-farm runoff, spills and vapors in the east, and the potential dangers that hydraulic fracturing for natural gas in the Piedmont (which the majority of North Carolinians opposed and for which no sensible wastewater solutions had, or have yet, ever been determined) could pose to surface and groundwaters and to our aquifers.

That we might somehow have water enough and yet find such a sufficiency simply unfit and unusable was a cruel and untenable irony that Mr. Friday would neither have accepted nor brooked.

Why would we as a state wish to be seen as militantly unwilling (in practical effect, *unable*) to tackle the hard problems of keeping water clean and protecting clean water?

What possible positive message could come

Falls, Mitchell County

from such actions as the attempted Asheville watershed seizure or such inactions as the failure to implement the Jordan Lake watershed-protection rules?

With over 3,000 miles of our rivers and streams qualified as *impaired* and an astonishing half a million acres—*one-quarter*—of our state's 2 million acres of shellfish waters *permanently closed*, how do we see that? And how are we seen by those who live beyond our borders?

When every demographic trend howls at us to protect every drop of water in every river and stream in this province, and yet still we do not, how *should* we be seen? What possible positive message have we sent?

None.

What Mr. Friday saw—and *fore*saw—was instead a message of carelessness, recklessness, negligence, and even defiance of common sense, and this was what had so clearly driven his

EPILOGUE

198

concerns about water during the last months of his life.

As the Jordan Lake rules languished, in 2014 the state legislature would launch a doomed experiment to clean up the lake with whirring aerators called SolarBees. This puerile ploy would have been comical had it not revealed such a deeply cynical irreverence and disregard both for clean water and for the science that would keep it so—what it did accomplish, though, was further significant *delay* in the Jordan Lake rules' implementation.

Following the absurd SolarBees debacle, a new law, passed by the state legislature in the summer of 2017, directed our Division of Water Resources to move into outright poisoning of the lake's algae. Yet the U.S. Army Corps of Engineers, which built the lake and controls its waters, in November 2017 refused the North Carolina state legislature and disallowed the law's intent from taking effect. A news report stated that, in the corps' judgment, such poisoning would render the lake waters affected to be unfit for human consumption.

One initially promising early 2018 development—unanimous passage by the state House of a bill funding equipment and staff to investigate the hazardous per- and polyfluoroalkyl substances (PFAS), including forever-chemical GenX and its effects on the people and environment of the Cape Fear River valley— lay untouched by a state senate that simply adjourned, having given the bill no consideration, as if blind to it.

But by summer 2020, the North Carolina Department of Environmental Quality, led by Secretary Michael Regan (soon to be President Biden's choice to head the federal Environmental Protection Agency), in various actions had ordered Bladen and Cumberland County PFAS polluters DuPont and Chemours to cease, desist, and clean up their Cape Fear desecrations. And then the hand of environmental champion Josh

Stein, our attorney general, came down upon DuPont and Chemours et al. with a lawsuit in October 2020, holding the defendants "accountable for their actions that have severely contaminated North Carolina's environment, causing extensive harm to our State's natural resources and creating significant risks for the people of the State."

II

Mr. Friday deeply loved the Carolina coast, and he more than once reminisced with me about going out from Roanoke Island fishing with his father when he was just fourteen, Moon Tillett their guide, and hearing the word *sunburn* for the first time when Tillett piloted the skiff back to the docks and shirtless Bill Friday was cooked.

He remembered, too, when Republican governor James Holshouser, Democratic legislative leaders Willis Whichard and Bill Staton, and Institute of Government legal craftsman Milton Heath joined forces many years ago to create and gain passage of the triumphantly visionary Coastal Area Management Act of 1974, a forward-looking framework for governance, guidance, and regulation in the outer coastal plain and sound country that this big, wide, wet, highly dynamic territory truly needed. For over four decades, though, opponents of this justly celebrated act of public policy have tried to diminish its vision and trim its effect.

Top-tier geologist Stan Riggs of East Carolina University, one of North Carolina's premier coastal thinkers, has long been showing photographs of Hatteras Island beachfront cottages and their all-too-easily exposed septic tanks storm after storm and saying trenchantly, "Is *this* the message we want to send to the world? Is *this* how we want to be seen?"

When by law the state legislature denied our coastal planners and emergency managers the ability to use in their important work the current knowledge of exponential sea-level rise predicted

Snow geese filling the sky, Pocosin Lakes National Wildlife Refuge

across the twenty-first century, we earned the mockery of the world. Why should anyone have been surprised when Dr. Riggs gave up on the Coastal Resources Commission's science panel and, citing the increasing political pressure to allow "unlimited growth and development" of the North Carolina coast, resigned from it?

III

Mr. Friday had been very generous, saying yes when I asked him if he would be an honorary cochair, along with Greensboro conservationist and now legislator Pricey Harrison, for the North Carolina Coastal Federation's 2005–8 capital campaign. The morning I called him to let him know of the campaign's broad support and successful $3 million conclusion, he said sagely, ever encouraging: "That's just wonderful—you know, you'll never get to where you really want to be, but if you set a reasonable goal in that direction, you can get on down the road towards it a pretty good ways."

One great positive message, one I dearly wish Mr. Friday had lived to see, was a long-term, broad-based citizens' movement led by the Coastal Federation, which succeeded in standing down the astonishing air-and-water insult Titan Cement would have brought to southeastern North Carolina, an effort ultimately so strong that the Greece-based corporation bowed out in March 2016—just five days before the Obama administration withdrew its massively opposed plans to open our coast for oil and gas drilling.

Even the subsequent federal administration's policy reversal could not undo the message of unending opposition to assaulting our coastal waters and its creatures, and our coastal tourism, in this way. "Not off our coast!" said our sitting governor, Roy Cooper, and he was joined by the multitude. In early February 2018, Governor Cooper sought from U.S. Interior secretary Ryan Zinke the same offshore-drilling exemption for North Carolina that Zinke had earlier granted to

Florida, stating that if this were not forthcoming, our state would sue to make it so.

As to how we are seen: nothing says *faith in the future* to the world as powerfully as a people's abiding protection of the clean air, clean earth, and clean water in its domain. Inasmuch as the health of the water is the same as the health of the people, this is precisely what President Friday was getting at during that long moment on Hooper Lane. And his good sense not only was practical and personal—it was *constitutional*: the prime document of the State of North Carolina in its last article *requires* the state and its people to "protect its lands and waters for the benefit of all its citizenry" and "to control and limit the pollution of our air and water."

Recent, unconstitutionally gerrymandered legislative majorities may not have grasped article 14, section 5, but the rest of us North Carolinians, having a near-spiritual relationship with our great land and our many waters, certainly do.

IV

Perhaps Mr. Friday did not see the worst of the decade: the challenging of women's right to privacy; the continuing denial of a federal insurance program—Medicaid expansion—that would provide health care to half a million of our

Snow ponies, Rachel Carson Reserve, Town Marsh, Beaufort

brothers and sisters and bring $2 billion a year of federal taxes we have already paid *back* into our state's health-care economy; the suppression of both the vote and the effectiveness of certain voters; the notorious bathroom bill that cost us further loss of respect for our state, as well as half a billion dollars; and the tax giveaways that took $3 billion a year of the people's revenues and put it into the pockets of corporations and high-end earners, even as public school teachers and public schools went wanting—*Education Week* in 2020 declared us thirty-third in education in the nation, and we should be ashamed. And he did not see the pandemic that has painted the awful inequities in the health of our people as plain as day.

Yet Mr. Friday foresaw back in 2012 what was coming, all right. He felt it: that the Old North State's noble motto—*To Be, Rather Than to Seem*—was for quite some time going to be shamelessly and abjectly reversed.

As our Hooper Lane conversation about water carried on, we turned to the population growth that state demographers had predicted, advising us all that we should expect a North Carolina of 12 million people by the year 2030.

"We *really* need to be prepared for it," Mr. Friday said, as he grew increasingly animated. "And it's not just water—it'll affect *everything*. Our schools, roads, agriculture, health care, environment, you name it!" After he spoke about each of these areas and more, the clouds gliding by above as the wind rose, at last he looked past me (he was facing east) and shook his index finger vigorously toward Raleigh, saying, "How are we *ever* going to provide for the 12 million in the future when we are not even taking care of the 9 million we have today? Where is the vision?"

Taylor's Creek, Beaufort

We must leave those lost years, that lost decade, behind, lest (even worse) our state suffers *two* lost decades in a row. We must answer President Friday's questions — spoken over nine years ago, yet as germane today as they were then — in ways we know from his great life he would have us answer them.

This is hard work and, in the political arena, it is contentious work. But it is good and necessary work, and we must do it. The vision to do so is all across North Carolina, if only we can once again apply it toward a progressive public life for *all* North Carolinians, the ones here now, and the ones yet to come.

Would that we could greet each and every one of these millions of newcomers, whether they are born here or come from away, like the original Native Americans, the first peoples

twelve millennia ago. Would that we could give them each a few grains of sand from a seabeach or a pinch of pocosin peat, a bit of red clay from a Piedmont field, or a rounded stone from some Blue Ridge stream, so they might all touch and be touched by "the goodliest land." And then tell the stories of our gains, our losses, our many identities and our big, deep culture so compellingly that everyone — newcomers and old-timers alike — truly understands what it means to say, with great feeling and pride: "I am a North Carolinian."

That afternoon with Mr. Friday at his Hooper Lane home would be my last moment with him, and then and there I heard my marching orders reaffirmed and elevated in such a way that they will carry me, as upon a cresting wave, for the rest of my life.

Acknowledgments

Order of the Long Leaf Pine awardee David Perry, former longtime editor in chief at the University of North Carolina Press, proposed that I write of North Carolina from mountains to sea; for his purposeful persistence and for David's and his wife Heidi Perov's lifelong friendship, Ann and I are deeply grateful. I am equally grateful to the wonderful historian and my comrade David Cecelski—we two have floated many North Carolina waters together—and to two other great friends, writers David Zucchino and Katherine Proctor, who read and commented on the book in manuscript. At UNC Press, Mark Simpson-Vos, Mary Caviness, Kim Bryant, Rich Hendel, Jamison Cockerham, Dominique Moore, Cate Hodorowicz, Dino Battista, and Alison Shay have helped edit, develop, design, produce, and publicize this work, for which much thanks. Also, our appreciation to Carolyn Sakowski for her most thoughtful commentary and to Heidi Hannoush of UNC for her excellent photo editing.

Several of the pieces herein, in slightly different form, have previously appeared in *Wildlife in North Carolina*, the *Independent Weekly*, *Our State*, and the *North Carolina Literary Review*; I am thankful to these publications and their editors, and to Malinda Maynor Lowery, who graciously gave me permission to use Willie French Lowery's chorus from his anthem "Proud to Be a Lumbee."

To our families, starting with our children, Cary, Susannah, and Hunter; to my fellow musicians in The Red Clay Ramblers (Clay Buckner, Ed Butler, Chris Frank, Rick Good, Jack Herrick, Rob Ladd, Don Lewis, and Mark Roberts) and the Coastal Cohorts (Don Dixon and Jim Wann); to the Queen family of Haywood County; to our wonderful friends in the North Caroliniana Society, the North Carolina Humanities Council, the North Carolina Collection at UNC's Wilson Library, the Owls of Minerva and the Tindall Table, the UNC Creative Writing Program and the Department of English and Comparative Literature, North Carolina Land of Water, the North Carolina Nature Conservancy, the North Carolina Coastal Federation, the North Carolina Coastal Land Trust, Sea Grant, the North Carolina Botanical Garden, the North Carolina Native Plant Society, the Core Sound Waterfowl Museum and Heritage Center, the North Carolina Maritime Museum, the Museum of the Albemarle, the North Carolina Department of Natural and Cultural Resources, Audubon North Carolina, The Conservation Fund, the Conservation Trust for North Carolina, and the Southern Environmental Law Center; to the UNC–Chapel Hill Herbarium's director, Alan S. Weakley, and curator Carol Ann McCormick; to our old friends Belinda and Michael McFee, Jane Oliver and Jim Byrum, Homer (Homah) Foil, John Shelton Reed, the Order of the Persimmon (Ted Teague, Kevin Cherry, and Patrick Wooten of Pender), Emily and Greg Gangi, Lew and Dannye Romine Powell, Jack and Martha Betts, Tom Rankin and Jill McCorkle, Bryan and Kristi Giemza, Jim Seay, Lee Smith and Hal Crowther, Penny Leary-Smith and George Ramsey, Jan and Jeff Smith DeBlieu, Susan and Fred Irons, Kristina and Clyde Edgerton, David Robert, Daryl Walker, Capt. Jim Rumfelt and Anechy Padron, Patti and Tipper Davis, Mike and Corliss Bradley, David and Allison Dubuisson, Alison and Jim Vernon, Deborah and Charles Llewellyn, Candy Rogers and Elton Ellis, Carolyn and the late Bob Meadows, A. C. and Mary Bushnell, John L. Haber, Mister Rick Nichols, the late Loyd Little,

Bill Parsons and the late Donna Davis, John Foley, Michael Sheehan, Jan Davidson, Barbara and Wilson Snowden, Dennis and Robin Chadwick, Bryan Blake and Barbara Garrity-Blake, Lida Pigott and David Burney, Bill Stokes and Chilton Rogers, Daniel and Beverly Patterson, Rachel V. Mills and the late Jerry Leath Mills, George and Blair Jackson, Feather and Willy Phillips, Kelley Shinn and Scott Bradley, and the late David Stick; and to our friends and neighbors, on both a Bingham Township, Orange County, hillside and at the coast, fellow skiff builder Bill Garlick and his wife Isa Cheren: we are so thankful you have all been with us in so many ways sharing so many places over so long a time. Two devoted friends and colleagues, UNC–Chapel Hill Department of English and Comparative Literature chair Mary Floyd-Wilson and Creative Writing Program director Daniel Wallace, granted me a fall 2020 leave in order to complete this book.

Our dear friends and photographer-collaborators Scott Taylor of Beaufort and Tom Earnhardt of Raleigh have helped us to broaden greatly its pictorial range, and their wonderful mates, Lenore Meadows and Dana Jennings, respectively, have encouraged us all the way.

To all those who speak through these pages, Ann and I offer our immense gratitude, to all the living and the dead.

MBS III & ACS

Selected Sources

The watery outdoorsman's world my father often entered is well illustrated in Neal Conoley's *Waterfowl Heritage: North Carolina Decoys and Gunning Lore* (1982), in Travis Morris's *Duck Hunting on Currituck Sound: Tales from a Native Gunner* (2006), and at the Core Sound Waterfowl Museum and Heritage Center on Harkers Island.

Rachel Carson names "the sound country" early in *Under the Sea-Wind* (1941), her first book; she reports beautifully on an early coastal chain of national wildlife refuges in her U.S. Fish and Wildlife pamphlet *Mattamuskeet* (1947), with comment on Swan Quarter and Pea Island as well; and she describes Beaufort's Town Marsh and Bird Shoal in *The Edge of the Sea* (1955). Jack Spruill of Roper told me the Top of the Mark tale one evening at the Southeastern Center for Contemporary Art in Winston-Salem thirty-odd years ago. Thomas Butchko's *On the Shores of the Pasquotank* (1989) has been a fine, informative friend over many years, as I have sought to learn ever more about my childhood home. A slender book my father left to me, with his signature upon it, is Catherine Albertson's fanciful *In Ancient Albemarle* (1914).

Kevin Cherry and LeRae Umfleet of the North Carolina Department of Natural and Cultural Resources sponsored and set up the May 2018 "Around the Albemarle" cruise on the *Belle of Washington*. One account of the loss of HMS *Bounty* is the National Transportation Safety Board's report *Marine Accident Brief: Sinking of Tall Ship* Bounty (accident number DCA-13-LM-003); another report of its harrowing end and coast guard rescue efforts is that of Kathryn Miles, "Sunk: The Incredible Truth about a Ship That Never Should Have Sailed" in *Outside Online* (February 11, 2013). I wrote of the heroic Capt.

Moses Grandy in *Two Captains from Carolina* (2012). Ben McGrath told of Dickie Conant's exploits afloat in a pair of *New Yorker* pieces: "Southbound" (September 22, 2014) and "Dick Conant, the Missing Boater" (December 14, 2015). John Hudson's piece "Satellite Images of the CIA's Secret Bin Laden Training Facility" appeared in the *Atlantic* (October 9, 2012). Catherine Bishir and Michael Southern discuss Edenton's Cupola House, Courthouse Green, and the J. N. Leary Building, as well as Somerset Place, in their notable work *A Guide to the Historic Architecture of Eastern North Carolina* (1996). Judge Boyle's 2005 decision in the outlying field case is at www.courtlistener.com/opinion/2330385/washington-county-nc-v-us-dept-of-navy.

Will Rimer of University of North Carolina (UNC) communications created an informative, one-minute-twenty-second film of Professor Brent McKee's and my UNC Changing Coasts course (see www.unc.edu/discover/exploring-the-changing-coasts-of-carolina).

Dr. Tony Rodriguez and Jeff Plumlee of UNC's Institute of Marine Sciences brought two skiffs to the Plymouth waterfront for our class's lower Roanoke River exploration; Windsor mayor Jimmy Hoggard provided kayaks and lunch for us on the Cashie River; and former longtime Windsor fire chief Billy Smithwick gave us a tour of the Cashie tree houses, his innovative ecotourism idea for Windsor and Bertie. North Carolina Nature Conservancy's Merrill Lynch told me long ago about the abandoned locomotive on Bull Run Island.

More about the HMT *Bedfordshire* memorial on Ocracoke Island may be found at https://docsouth.unc.edu/commland/monument/249. The Fish Meal Company in Beaufort is profiled at http://beaufortartist.blogspot.com/2016/02/harvey-ward-smith-and-fish-meal-company.html, and more about Bonehenge appears at https://bonehenge.org.

Jake Mills's tale about the fishing lure caught in his head first appeared in our show *King Mackerel & The Blues Are Running* (1985).

The December 1943 double train wreck near Panther Branch was widely covered by the press, including the *New York Times* report "WARNED TOO LATE, ENGINEER ASSERTS" (December 19, 1943). More on Warwick Mill Bay and its environmental importance appears at https://nc.audubon.org/news/warwick-mill-bay-forever-protected-wildlife-preservation.

The 1979 *Sea Crust* case appeal document may be found at https://law.resource.org/pub/us/case/reporter/F2/604/604.F2d.304.78-5115.78-5114.78-5112.html; the July 1982 Beaufort Inlet bust and where it led is covered in Doug McCullough and Les Pendleton's *Sea of Greed* (2014). For more on Minnie Evans and *Airlie Oak*, please see https://americanart.si.edu/artwork/airlie-oak-113102. Our film *Rich Inlet and Figure 8 Island: A Natural Partnership* is posted at www.youtube.com/watch?v=reke2oPT1K4.

David Stahle's remarkable recent discovery in the Black River's Three Sisters is discussed at https://ncseagrant.ncsu.edu/coastwatch/current-issue/autumn-2019/river-of-time and www.charlotteobserver.com/news/state/north-carolina/article230191724.html. Elizabeth "Lee" Graham Jacobs is profiled in *North Carolina Folklore Journal* 44, nos. 1–2 (1997). John Bartram recorded his July 29, 1765, Lake Waccamaw visit in his *Diary of a Journey through the Carolinas, Georgia, and Florida*, and A. J. O'Leary's Changing Coasts class essay "Harry Foley Walking on Water" (Fall 2019) brought the Waccamaw endemic species and more about that great lake to my attention. My wonderful UNC colleague Brent McKee showed me the Toxic Gumbo map locating far too many toxins and

hazards lying in the flood-prone coastal plain, from "Florence's Floodwaters Breach Coal Ash Pond and Imperil Other Toxic Sites" by Kendra Pierre-Louis, Nadja Popovich, and Hiroko Tabuchi (as updated in the *New York Times*, September 24, 2018).

Leading the organic farming movement in North Carolina was the late, remarkable Bill Dow, whose work *What I Stand On: Practical Advice and Cantankerous Musings from a Pioneering Organic Farmer* was published posthumously in 2015, with great help from his equally remarkable partner, our dear friend Daryl Walker.

We learned a great deal about Milton and its extraordinary artisan Thomas Day and saw a number of his pieces displayed in the Museum of Milton/Milton Renaissance Foundation, through which director Angela Daniel-Upchurch and her husband Jim Upchurch graciously toured us on Labor Day 2020; the Milton Presbyterian Church, of which Day and his wife Aquilla were members, still uses pews that he made. Friend, neighbor, and former UNC Department of Geological Studies chair and professor emeritus Paul Fullagar kindly shared with me his essay "Economic Geology at and near Gold Mine Property near NC-54 and Gold Mine Road, Orange County, NC." My longtime colleague Charles G. "Terry" Zug III wrote the book on North Carolina potters and pottery: *Turners and Burners* (1986). Janet Lembke's redbud comments appear in her book *From Grass to Gardens* (2006).

In "Pumpkin Delights" (*Our State*, October 2005), D. G. Martin writes of Chicken Bridge, the pumpkins upon it, and the Halloween tradition's ultimate move to the Haw River bridge at Bynum. More about historic Lindley Mills is at www.lindleymills.com/about-lindley-mills/history.html, and Lawrence Earley wrote of our emblematic tree in *Looking for Longleaf* (2005). Moore County's literary and life-afield traditions are well represented by authors Stephen Smith (*Complete Bushnell Hamp Poems*, 1991) and

Audrey Moriarty (*Pinehurst*, 2005). The Maco Light is one of North Carolina's most popular ghost stories (see www.ncpedia.org/maco-light). The remarkable saxophonist John Coltrane's work on Miles Davis's *Kind of Blue* is signal, as is his lengthy interpretation of "My Favorite Things."

Writer Julia Ridley Smith has described to me the extraordinary immigrant city Greensboro has become, as evidenced by the fortune of different languages children have brought into the public schools in recent decades and as reported by UNC Greensboro's Center for New North Carolinians (see https://cnnc.uncg.edu/immigrant-demo graphics-of-guilford-county). Colin Quashie's mural *Service* hangs in Knapp-Sanders Hall, home of UNC's School of Government, which commissioned it. Kendra Pierre-Louis covered Reverend Barber's and Vice President Gore's Belews Creek and Greensboro events: "A Leader in the War on Poverty Opens a New Front: Pollution" (*New York Times*, August 24, 2018). North Carolina's major coal-ash settlement with Duke Energy is addressed at https://deq.nc.gov /news/press-releases/2020/01/02/deq-secures -nation%E2%80%99s-largest-coal-ash-excava tion-nearly-80-million. Of adult puppet theater and its coming into being in Greensboro, see http://jabberboxpuppettheater.com.

A modest paperback picked up in a US 64 gas station long ago led me into the great central Carolina range and its lore: *An Afternoon Hike into the Past: Roving in the Uwharrie Mountains; Maps, Trail Lore, the Way Settlers Lived, Old Herb Remedies, Ghost Stories and Much More* (1975) by Joseph T. Moffitt. Reflection Studio is profiled in Courtney Devores's *Charlotte Observer* piece "End of an Era: Charlotte's Reflection Sound Studios to Close" (May 20, 2014) and in "The Song Is Over: Reflection Sound Studios" by Greg Lacour in *Charlotte Magazine* (September 24, 2014).

My great lifelong friend Dave Harrison reviewed the events of our Doughton Park, August 1966 venture with me, and Tom Wolfe created the portrait of the North Carolina mountain driver none of us would ever be in "The Last American Hero Is Junior Johnson. Yes!" (*Esquire*, March 1965).

The North Carolina Nature Conservancy has graciously allowed us several trips to the top of the Bluff Mountain Preserve (see www.nature.org/en -us/get-involved/how-to-help/places-we-protect /bluff-mountain-preserve). More on the estimable artist Ben Long IV is at www.benlongfineart.com. My friend Sarah Geer shared details of her father, much-loved longtime UNC history teacher Bill Geer, and his story in Ashe County. Fred Hobson generously gave me copies of some of his New River editorials from the early 1970s campaign to save the river. More on Austin Howell and his final climb is in "Broken Holds and Lost Lives: How Loose Rock and Free Soloing Ended Two Climbers' Lives" by Zoe Leibovitch (Climbing. com, July 23, 2019). Wilma Dykeman's signal *The French Broad* (1955) is essential reading toward gaining a social, historical, and hydrological grasp of the river and its valley. Michael McFee's poem "Uncle Homer Meets Carl Sandburg" first appeared in *Carolina Quarterly* 39, no. 3 (Spring 1987).

The stagecoach *Hattie Butner* may be seen at www.digitalforsyth.org/photos/9622 and www .clemmons.org/237/History. A dramatic 1890 photo of prisoners who labored on the Western North Carolina Railroad is at www.ncpedia. org/media/convict-labor-working; more on the Railroad and Incarcerated Laborer Memorial Project to honor these exploited imprisoned men is at https://therailproject.org. "Somebody Died, Babe," an important discussion of the song "Swannanoa Tunnel" by Kevin Kehrberg and Jeffrey A. Keith (*Bitter Southerner*, August 4, 2020), is at https://bittersoutherner.com/2020 /somebody-died-babe-a-musical-coverup-of -racism-violence-and-greed. Timothy Silver gives a fine, gripping rendition of Elisha Mitchell's explorations in the Black Mountains and the bitter contention with Thomas Clingman in his *Mount Mitchell and the Black Mountains* (2003), and David L. Swain's reinterment remarks come from "An Address, Delivered 16th June, 1858, by Hon. David L. Swain, LL.D., President of the University of NC," in *A Memoir of the Rev. Elisha Mitchell, D.D.* (Chapel Hill: J. M. Henderson, 1858). An overview of Black Mountain College appears at www.ncpedia.org/black-mountain -college.

Perry Deane Young's lament "Goodbye, Asheville" ran in the March 1975 issue of *Harper's*, and the Asheville downtown battle of the early 1980s is recorded in Marla Hardee Milling's *Only in Asheville* (2015). Of Henry James at Biltmore (in February 1905), please see Sarah Luria's "The Architecture of Manners: Henry James, Edith Wharton and the Mount" (*American Quarterly* 49, no. 2 [June 1997]). Of Béla Bartók at the Albemarle (1943–44), please see Carl Leafstedt's "Asheville, Winter of 1943–44: Béla Bartók and North Carolina" in *Musical Quarterly* 87, no. 2 (Summer 2004). Cyril Lance, Paul Gaetna, and Zach Briggs made us very welcome at the Moog shop in Asheville. The North Carolina Institute for Climate Studies 2020 climate report is available via https://ncics.org/programs/nccsr. Brendan Gill recalled his moonshine moments on Beaucatcher Mountain at the close of his *New Yorker* (January 27, 1975) notice of our show *Diamond Studs*.

One indication of the massive twentieth-century scope of the Suncrest Lumber Company, suggesting the potential for antipathy in the native population, may be seen in a map (and notes) of its 33,055-acre Cataloochee Tract 200 (see https://wcudigitalcollection.contentdm.oclc .org/digital/collection/p16232coll10/id/7930). The Clean Smokestacks preventable-deaths figure appears in "Health and Air Quality Benefits of Policies to Reduce Coal-Fired Power Plant Emissions: A Case Study in North Carolina" by Ya-Ru Li and Jacqueline MacDonald Gibson in *Environmental Science and Technology* 48, no. 17 (September 2014).

More on Highlands Biological Station, UNC's W. C. Coker, and *Shortia galacifolia* is at https:// highlandsbiological.org; www.ncpedia.org/bio graphy/coker-william-chambers; and https:// plants.ncwildflower.org/plant_galleries/details /shortia-galacifolia. I first read the botanical-sleuthing story surrounding the Oconee bells in John Harden's "The Plant That Was Lost for a Hundred Years" in *The Devil's Tramping Ground and Other North Carolina Mysteries* (1949). FDR's letter about the Joyce Kilmer Memorial Forest is quoted at www.go-north-carolina.com/Indian -Lakes-Scenic-Byway. The Hooper Bald hunting tale comes from a short North Carolina Wildlife Resources report by Perry Jones, *The European Wild Boar in North Carolina* (1959), distilled by Bryson City writer and naturalist George Ellison, with further personal observations, in his most informative *Mountain Passages* (2005).

Word of the work of the Triangle watershed alliance is in "Private Investment in Watershed Protection Advances Triangle Conservation Efforts" (November 30, 2020, https://ctnc.org /caterpillar). UNC School of Law's Boyd Tinsley Distinguished Professor Gene Nichol took a trenchant look at the state's legislative landscape during the 2010s in his book *Indecent Assembly* (2020). The suit that North Carolina attorney general Josh Stein brought against DuPont, Chemours, et al. over PFAS pollution in October 2020 may be seen at https://ncdoj.gov/wp-con tent/uploads/2020/10/Signed-Final-Complaint .pdf. And Lisa Sorg, writing about water-quality issues in the Cape Fear River basin (*NC Policy Watch*, December 7, 2020), asked the question that so concerned President Friday, one that we all must take as a call to action: "What happens when there's no clean water left to drink?"

Photograph Credits

Index

Page numbers in italics refer to illustrative matter.